CHILD ABUSE — BETRAYING A TRUST

INFORMATION PLUS®
WYLIE, TEXAS 75098-7006
© 1981, 1983, 1985, 1987, 1989, 1991, 1993, 1995, 1997, 1999
ALL RIGHTS RESERVED

EDITORS:
MEI LING REIN, B.S.
NANCY R. JACOBS, M.A.
JACQUELYN F. QUIRAM, B.A.

CHAPTER I

CHILD ABUSE — A HISTORY

OVERVIEW

Recognizing child abuse in its several forms (neglect and physical, emotional, and sexual abuse) is a twentieth-century phenomenon. Child abuse is also more likely to be recognized in economically developed countries than in developing countries. Children have been beaten and abandoned for many thousands of years, based primarily on the belief that children are the property of their parents.

Early civilizations regularly abandoned deformed or unwanted children, and the ritual sacrifice of children to appease the gods took place in the Egyptian, Carthaginian, Roman, Greek, and Aztec societies. In Roman society, the father had complete control over the family to the extent that he could kill his children for disobedience. In both Greek and Roman societies, sexual abuse of children was common. Children were sold as prostitutes. Women were just as likely as men to participate in abuse. Petronius, a Roman writer, recorded the rape of a seven-year-old girl witnessed by a line of clapping women.

In the Middle Ages, the Roman Catholic Church contributed to infanticide when it declared that deformed infants were omens of evil and the product of relations between women and demons or animals. Unwanted children were apprenticed to work or offered to convents and monasteries. In the seventh century, the Archbishop of Canterbury ruled that a man could not sell his son into slavery after the age of seven.

In thirteenth-century England, the law read, "If one beats a child until it bleeds, it will remember, but if one beats it to death, the law applies." By the child's fourth year, harsh discipline played a major role in his or her socialization. Children were taught that beatings were in their best interests. A mother taught her daughter to take a "smart rod" and beat her children until they cried for mercy. "Dear child by this lore/they will love thee ever more."

Children were beaten not only by their parents but also by their teachers. In a poem from about 1500, a schoolboy wrote that he would gladly become a clerk, but learning was such strange work because the birch twigs used for beating were so sharp. The children at an Oxford school must have felt justice was served when their schoolmaster, out early one morning to cut willow twigs for a switch to beat them, slipped and fell into the river and drowned.

The late Middle Ages and the Renaissance were marked by ambivalence towards children. Neil Postman, in *The Disappearance of Childhood* (Delacorte Press, New York, 1982), theorized that the idea that children were small adults started to change. Among the upper classes, children began to receive a long, formal education, where they were increasingly separated from adults and kept with their peers. It eventually became apparent that children were not so similar to adults after all. Children were then regarded as mounds of clay to be molded.

In sixteenth- and seventeenth-century Europe, fathers commonly placed their children in apprenticeships to provide inexpensive labor. The apprentice system was the major job-training method of pre-industrial Western society. The apprentice who trained with a master frequently worked under conditions that, by today's standards, would be considered severely abusive.

The practice of paternal control was brought to the American colonies, and the father ruled his wife and children. A child was little more than the property of the parents. At the same time, the child was an asset that could be used to perform work on the farm.

Parental discipline was typically severe, and parents, teachers, and ministers found support for stern discipline in the Bible — "Spare the rod and spoil the child" was cited as justification for beating children. It should be noted that the biblical rod referred to was a shepherd's rod used to guide the sheep in the right direction, not to beat the sheep. Church elders taught that children were born corrupted by original sin, and the only path to salvation was "to beat the Devil out of the child." Some colonial legislatures even passed "stubborn children laws," giving parents the legal right to actually kill unruly children.

By their teens, many children were living with other families, bound out as indentured servants or apprentices. It was common for heads of households and masters to brutalize these children without fear of reprisal, except in cases involving excessive beatings, massive injury, or death.

Holding a Child Abuser Accountable

The earliest recorded trial for child abuse involved a master and his apprentice. In 1639, in Salem, Massachusetts, Marmaduke Perry was charged in the death of his apprentice. The evidence showed the boy had been ill-treated and subjected to "unreasonable correction." However, the boy's allegation that the master had been responsible for his fractured skull (which ultimately killed him) was called into question by testimony that he had told someone else the injury resulted from falling from a tree. Marmaduke Perry was acquitted.

In 1643, a master was executed for killing his servant boy. In 1655, in Plymouth, Massachusetts, a master found guilty of slaying a servant boy was punished by having his hand burned and all his property taken away. Other early records show brutal masters being warned for abusing young servants, and in some cases, the children were freed because of the harsh treatment. In 1700, Virginia passed laws protecting servants against mistreatment.

Most of the early recorded cases of child abuse were specifically related to offenses committed by masters upon servants and did not involve protecting children from parental abuse. Society generally tolerated the abuse of family members as a personal matter while condemning the abuse of strangers.

The few recorded cases involving family matters were limited to the removal of children from "unsuitable" home environments, which usually meant parents were not giving their children a good religious upbringing or were refusing to instill work ethics. In two Massachusetts cases in 1675 and 1678, children were removed from such "unsuitable" homes. In the first case, the children were taken from the home because the father refused to send them out to apprentice or work. In the second case, the same offense as the first was compounded by the father's refusal to attend church services. Physical abuse was not an issue in either case.

With the coming of industrialization in Europe and America, this implied right of abuse was transferred to the factory, where orphaned or abandoned children as young as five years old worked 16 hours a day. In many cases, irons riveted around their ankles bound the children to the machines, while overseers with whips ensured productivity. In England, the Factory Act of 1802 stopped this pauper-apprentice work system, but the law did not apply to children with parents. Those youngsters worked in the mills for 12 hours a day at the mercy of often tyrannical supervisors.

Nor did nonworking hours offer relief to poor orphaned or abandoned children. Dependent children were put into deplorable public poorhouses with adult beggars, thieves, and paupers. Not until the beginning of the nineteenth century did the public recognize the terrible abuses that occurred in the almshouses, and major efforts were made to provide separate housing for children.

In the nineteenth century, middle-class families began to see their children as representative of the family's status and, for many families, education for the child rather than labor became the goal. Many of the labor abuses gradually ended. Eventually, child labor laws were passed to limit the kinds of jobs underage children could do and the number of hours they could work (see below).

The New York Society for the Prevention of Cruelty to Children

In 1840, a Tennessee parent was prosecuted for excessive punishment of a child. According to the testimony, the mother had hit her daughter with her fists, pushed her head against the wall, whipped her, and tied her to a bedpost. A lower court convicted the abusive parent, but a higher court reversed the conviction.

The first case of child abuse that caught public attention in the United States occurred in 1874. Neighbors of Mary Ellen Connolly, a nine-year-old child in New York City, contacted a church social worker when they heard disturbances from the little girl's apartment.

Upon investigating the child's home, the social worker found her suffering from malnutrition, serious physical abuse, and neglect. Mary Ellen was living with Mary and Francis Connolly. The girl, who was the out-of-wedlock daughter of Mrs. Connolly's first husband, was apprenticed to the couple.

At that time, the laws protected animals, but no local, state, or federal laws protected children. Consequently, the charity worker turned to the American Society for the Prevention of Cruelty to Animals (ASPCA) for help. The case was presented to the court on the theory that the child was a member of the animal kingdom and, therefore, entitled to the same protection the law gave to animals. The court agreed, and the child, because she was considered an animal, was taken from her brutal foster mother.

In court, Mary Ellen related how her "mamma" beat her daily with a leather whip and how she was cut on her face with scissors (Figure 1.1). She was not allowed to play with other children and was locked in the bedroom whenever her "mamma" left the house. The court placed her in an orphanage. Mary Ellen was later adopted by the family of the social worker.

Mary Ellen's mother, Mary Connolly, was found guilty of assault and battery for felonious assault with scissors and for beatings that took place during 1873 and 1874. She was sentenced to one year of hard labor in a penitentiary.

Mary Ellen Connolly's case led to the founding of the New York Society for the Prevention of Cruelty to Children. Similar societies were soon organized in other American cities. By 1922, 57 societies for the prevention of cruelty to children and 307 other humane societies had been established to tend to the welfare of children. With the beginning of government intervention into child welfare, the number of these societies declined.

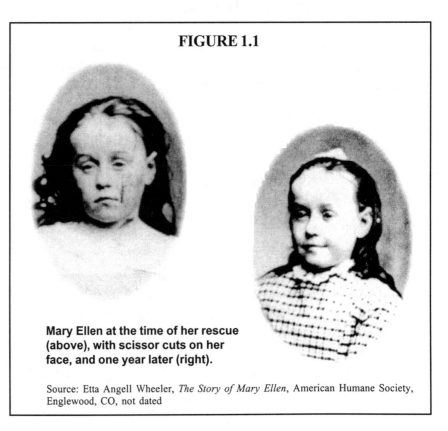

FIGURE 1.1

Mary Ellen at the time of her rescue (above), with scissor cuts on her face, and one year later (right).

Source: Etta Angell Wheeler, *The Story of Mary Ellen*, American Humane Society, Englewood, CO, not dated

GOVERNMENT INTEREST

The first White House Conference on Children took place in 1909. It recommended the creation of the Children's Bureau (under the U.S. Department of Health, Education, and Welfare) to research and provide information about children, a recommendation President William Howard Taft signed into law in 1912. The Children's Bureau promoted the passage of the Keating-Owen Act (39 Stat 675) in 1916, which limited the exploitation of children in factories and mines, although it did not cover youngsters employed in agriculture, domestic work, and sweatshops (small manufacturing plants with long hours, low wages, and poor working conditions). The Bureau also advocated improved prenatal care, especially among the poor, and was a major supporter of the Sheppard-Towner Act of 1921 (42 Stat 224), which promoted prenatal care for mothers.

Government Intervention in Child Welfare

The federal government first provided child welfare services with the passage of the Social Security Act of 1935 (49 Stat 620). Under Title IV-B of the act, or the Child Welfare Services Program, the

---

TABLE 1.1
The Primary Federal Programs That Support Child Protection

Program	Federal Support of Total	1995 Funding (in millions of dollars)
Title IV-E (Foster Care Program)		$3,050
Foster care assistance payments	Open-ended federal match at Medicaid rate	
Placement services and administrative costs	Open-ended federal match of 50%[a]	
Training expenses	Open-ended federal match of 75%	
Title IV-E (Adoption Assistance Program)		411
Adoption assistance payments	Open-ended federal match at Medicaid rate	
Nonrecurring adoption expenses	Open-ended federal match of 50%[b]	
Placement services and administrative costs	Open-ended federal match of 50%	
Training expenses	Open-ended federal match of 75%	
Title IV-E (Independent Living Program)	100% federal funding, with a funding ceiling[c]	70
Title IV-B (Child Welfare Services Program)		
Child welfare services	Federal match of 75%, capped at state allotment	292
Family preservation and family support (subpart 2)	Federal match of 75%, with a funding ceiling[d]	150
Child Abuse Prevention and Treatment Act	100% federal funding for some programs and variable state or local match for others	78
Title XX (Social Services Block Grant)	100% federal funding, with a funding ceiling	2,800

[a] A 75% match is available from Fiscal Year 1994 through Fiscal Year 1996 for certain costs related to data collection.

[b] The federal government reimburses 50% of up to $2,000 of expenditures for any one placement.

[c] Beginning in Fiscal Year 1991, states are required to provide a 50% match for any federal funding claimed that exceeds $45 million.

[d] Program authorized through Fiscal Year 1998.

U.S. House of Representatives, Ways and Means Committee. *1996 green book: Background material and data on programs within the jurisdiction of the Committee on Ways and Means.* Washington, DC: U.S. Government Printing Office, 1996, Tables 12-1 and 12-2, pp. 694–95; and Collins, Gail. Child Welfare Specialist. National Center on Child Abuse and Neglect, personal communication, January 13, 1997.

Source: Mark E. Courtney, "The Costs of Child Protection in the Context of Welfare Reform" (from *The Future of Children*, Spring 1998, Volume 8, No. 1). Reprinted with permission of The David and Lucile Packard Foundation.

TABLE 1.2

CHILD ABUSE PREVENTION AND TREATMENT ACT

Legislative Authority: Child Abuse Prevention and Treatment Act, as amended

U.S. Code Citation: 42 USC 5101 et seq; 42 USC 5116 et seq

ACF Regulations: 45 CFR 1340

Summary of Legislative History:

The Child Abuse Prevention and Treatment Act (CAPTA) was originally enacted in P.L. 93-247. The law was completely rewritten in the Child Abuse Prevention, Adoption and Family Services Act of 1988 (P.L. 100-294, 4/25/88). It was further amended by the Child Abuse Prevention Challenge Grants Reauthorization Act of 1989 (P.L. 101-126, 10/25/89) and the Drug Free School Amendments of 1989 (P.L. 101-226, 12/12/89).

The Community-Based Child Abuse and Neglect Prevention Grants program was originally authorized by sections 402 through 409 of the Continuing Appropriations Act for FY 1985 (P.L. 98-473, 10/12/84). The Child Abuse Prevention Challenge Grants Reauthorization Act of 1989 (P.L. 101-126) transferred this program to the Child Abuse Prevention and Treatment Act, as amended.

A new title III, Certain Preventive Services Regarding Children of Homeless Families or Families at Risk of Homelessness, was added to the Child Abuse and Neglect Prevention and Treatment Act by the Stewart B. McKinney Homeless Assistance Act Amendments of 1990 (P.L. 101-645, 11/29/90).

The Child Abuse Prevention and Treatment Act was amended and reauthorized by the Child Abuse, Domestic Violence, Adoption, and Family Services Act of 1992 (P.L. 102-295, 5/28/92) and amended by the Juvenile Justice and Delinquency Prevention Act Amendments of 1992 (P.L. 102-586, 11/4/92).

The Act was amended by the Older American Act Technical Amendments of 1993 (P.L. 103-171, 12/2/93) and the Human Services Amendments of 1994 (P.L. 103-252, 5/19/94).

CAPTA was further amended by the Child Abuse Prevention and Treatment Act Amendments of 1996 (P.L. 104-235, 10/3/96), which amended Title I, replaced the Title II Community-Based Family Resource Centers program with a new Community-Based Family Resource and Support Program and repealed Title III, Certain Preventive Services Regarding Children of Homeless Families or Families at Risk of Homelessness.

Source: *Child Abuse Prevention and Treatment Act, as Amended, October 3, 1996*, National Center on Child Abuse and Neglect, U.S. Department of Health and Human Services, Washington, DC, no date

In 1962, the Social Security Amendments (PL 87-543) were enacted following the federal government's finding that states were using the Title IV-B grants to pay for the foster care of children but not to help children in "unfit" homes. Subsequently, each state was required by law to make child welfare services available to all children. Funding was initially provided under Title IV-A of the act, also known as the Aid to Families with Dependent Children (AFDC) program. The law also revised the definition of "child welfare services" to include the prevention and remedy of child abuse. (In 1996, under the new welfare-reform law, the AFDC was replaced with the Temporary Assistance to Needy Families, or TANF.) For more information on social welfare, see *Social Welfare — Help or Hindrance?*, Information Plus, Wylie, Texas, 1998.

In 1980, Congress moved federal funding for foster care from Title IV-A and created a separate Foster Care Program, or Title IV-E of the Social Security Act. In 1981, the Social Services Block Grant (Title IV-A, renamed Title XX) was amended. Previously, Title XX mainly granted funding to provide services for welfare families. Since 1981, it has given states more options as to the types of social services to fund. Moreover, child abuse prevention and treatment services remained an eligible category of service. Table 1.1 illustrates the primary federal programs that supported child protection in 1995.

The "Battered Child Syndrome"

One of the reasons for the lack of prosecution in child abuse cases has been the difficulty in determining whether the physical injury was a case of deliberate assault or an accident. In recent years, however, doctors in the area of pediatric radi-

Children's Bureau received funding for grants to states for "the protection and care of homeless, dependent, and neglected children and children in danger of becoming delinquent."

ology have been able to determine the incidence of repeated child abuse through sophisticated developments in X-ray technology. These advances have allowed radiologists to see more clearly such things as subdural hematomas (blood clots around the brain resulting from blows to the head) and abnormal fractures. This has brought about more recognition in the medical community of the widespread incidence of child abuse, along with growing public condemnation of abuse.

In 1961, Dr. C. Henry Kempe, a pediatric radiologist, and his associates, at a symposium on the problem of child abuse under the auspices of the American Academy of Pediatrics, proposed the term "Battered Child Syndrome." The term refers to the collection of injuries sustained by a child as a result of repeated mistreatment or beatings. A year later, Dr. Kempe's findings were published (C. Henry Kempe et al., "The Battered Child Syndrome," *The Journal of the American Medical Association*, vol. 181, July 7, 1962). The term "Battered Child Syndrome" developed into "maltreatment," encompassing not only physical assault, but also other forms of abuse, such as malnourishment, failure to thrive, medical neglect, and sexual and emotional abuse.

By 1968, after Dr. Kempe's findings had gained general acceptance among health and welfare workers and the public, all 50 states had passed legislation that required the reporting of child abuse to official agencies. This was one of the most rapidly accepted pieces of legislation ever in American history. Initially, only doctors were required to report and only in cases of "serious physical injury" or "non-accidental injury." Today, all the states have laws that require most professionals who serve children to report all forms of suspected abuse (see Chapter III) and either require or permit any citizen to report child abuse.

Federal Legislation

In 1972, Congressional hearings began on child abuse and neglect. In a 1973 Congressional hearing, Dr. C. Henry Kempe outlined some of the problems researchers faced, many of which have not yet been satisfactorily resolved. He testified,

A national computerized child abuse report registry should be available. The high mobility of abusive parents makes it essential that any physician be able to ascertain whether a given child is listed in a national registry. In this way, it will be possible to discover if a child has experienced repeated injuries, thus increasing the likelihood that a correct diagnosis is made.

There is a pressing need for the development of a network of adequate foster homes for interim placement of children while parents receive help from lay therapists and Families Anonymous groups. A period of foster care placement should be seen as a temporary measure to help decrease pressure and to minimize crises while parents are learning how to cope with their problems.

It is clear that the departments of social services are not able to perform the task of preventing or treating the problems of child abuse and neglect. It is impossible to approach a multidisciplinary problem with a single-discipline service unit. We must develop a multidisciplinary service unit which can cut across many of the traditions and unworkable rules and regulations that are built into most protective service department.

In 1974, in response to the hearings, Congress passed the Child Abuse Prevention and Treatment Act (CAPTA; PL 93-247). The law stated,

[Child abuse and neglect refer to] the physical or mental injury, negligent treatment, or maltreatment of a child under the age of 18, or the age specified by the child protection law of the state in question, by a person who is responsible for the child's welfare under circumstances which indicate that the child's health or welfare is harmed or threatened thereby as determined in accordance with regulations prescribed by the Secretary of Health, Education, and Welfare.

This legislation created the National Center on Child Abuse and Neglect (NCCAN), which developed standards for handling reports of child maltreatment. NCCAN also established a nationwide network of child protective services and served as a clearinghouse for information and research on child abuse and neglect.

Since 1974, CAPTA has been amended a number of times. (See Table 1.2.) The Child Abuse Prevention, Adoption, and Family Services Act of 1988 (PL 100-294) was enacted mainly to guarantee funding through 1991. It also broadened the definition of abuse, adding a specific reference to sexual abuse and exploitation to the basic definition.

Until 1995, none of the federal child abuse legislation dealt specifically with punishing sex offenders. In December of that year, with growing acknowledgment and concern about sex crimes against minors, the Sex Crimes Against Children Prevention Act of 1995 (PL 104-71) was passed. The act increases penalties for those who sexually exploit children by engaging in illegal conduct or through computer use,

as well as those who transport children with the intent to engage in criminal sexual activity. (See Chapter VI for more information on child sexual abuse and Chapter VII for laws against sex offenders.)

Pursuant to the Child Abuse Prevention and Treatment Act Amendments of 1996 (PL 104-235), NCCAN (see above) was abolished. Its functions have subsequently been consolidated within the Children's Bureau of the U.S. Department of Health and Human Services.

CHILD ABUSE IN OTHER CULTURES: VARIATIONS ON A THEME

At 10, you are a woman.
At 20, you are an old woman.
At 30, you are dead.
— Saying in Bangkok's red-light district

From sunrise to sunset, you find them crossing the border; they are employed by "aunties" and "uncles" who are faceless…. Now that definitely is child labour in its extreme. — Paul Etiang, Ugandan Minister for Labour and Social Welfare, describing how Ugandan children were used to smuggle in sugar from Kenya to avoid payment of import taxes (at the meeting of the Organization of African Unity, Uganda, February 1998)

Child Labor

Elaine Eliah, in "Child-Labour Battle Split Over Where to Draw Line" (*Child Newsline*, UNICEF, London, 1998), reported that Africa has the largest proportion of child laborers in the world. If the trend continues, the 80 million African child laborers will increase to 100 million by the year 2015. It is

FIGURE 1.2

Source: Elaine Eliah, "Child-Labour Battle Split over Where to Draw Line," *Child Newsline*, UNICEF, February 1998

estimated that, worldwide, child laborers ages 5 to 14 number more than 250 million. (See Figure 1.2.)

The International Labor Organization (ILO) estimates that 2 of 5 (41 percent) African children ages 5 to 14 are in the workplace instead of in school where they should be. In comparison, 21 percent of Asian children and 17 percent of Latin American children are being used as laborers. (See Figure 1.2.) More than a third (37 percent) of African girls are workers, the highest percentage of female child workers in the world. Asia has slightly over a half of this proportion (20 percent) of female child laborers.

American Initiatives

Child labor in the international setting continues to be a concern for the U.S. government. In 1997, President Clinton signed the Treasury, Postal Service, and General Government Appropriations Act (PL 105-61), which limits importation into the United States of goods produced by "forced or indentured child labor." In 1998, Congress approved the Higher Education Amendments of 1998 (H.R. 6), which includes a provision "urging colleges and universities to adopt 'anti-sweatshop' policies when licensing their logos." In December 1998, on the fiftieth anniversary of the Universal Declaration of Human Rights, President Clinton announced that new immigration regulations will let children acquire political asylum more easily. The federal government has also appropriated $30 million per year, up from $3 million, to the ILO efforts to eradicate child labor.

While some developing countries agree that children should not be forced to work, they argue that the parents of these children are so destitute that they are forced to indenture their children. This way, they have one less mouth to feed and get some income from the child's earnings.

"Thrown-away" Children

In Brazil, some children from the slums escape their homes and abusive and alcoholic parents to live in the streets. Other children are abandoned by their parents. These children survive by stealing and by sniffing glue. Glue is their identity, and street children

who do not sniff are not part of the group. Young children of eight or nine years sell their bodies, contracting venereal diseases for which they rarely seek treatment. Girls give birth to babies who are not only infected with their mothers' venereal diseases but also are then neglected by their glue-addicted mothers, perpetuating the cycle of abuse and neglect. Missionaries and foreign journalists report that vigilante groups and the local police have been implicated in the murder of a growing number of Brazilian street children.

"Thrown-away" children face dangers even when their care is left to adults. In 1996, charges of maltreatment were leveled against the directors of China's state-run orphanages. New York-based Human Rights Watch accused Chinese officials of deliberately starving and neglecting children, particularly ill and deformed children, in their care. In the late 1980s and early 1990s, Shanghai's biggest orphanage, which had a constant population of 500 children, averaged annual mortality rates above 20 percent. Human Rights Watch alleges that "these astonishing death rates are the result of a deliberate policy to minimize China's population of abandoned children, many of whom have been born in violation of the country's family planning regulations and are sometimes physically or mentally handicapped."

Child Mutilation

Actions considered abusive in some cultures are often celebrated as rites of passage by others. In "Female Circumcision: Rite of Passage or Violation of Rights?" *(International Family Planning Perspectives*, The Alan Guttmacher Institute, vol. 23, no. 3, September 1997), Frances A. Althaus reported that female circumcision is not solely practiced by Muslims, as some people mistakenly believe. Christians, animists, and one Jewish sect also practice it. In patriarchal societies, where females' sexuality and fertility are controlled by men, female circumcision is a rite of passage that ushers young girls into womanhood and marriage.

Female circumcision was first called "female genital mutilation" in the international document *Programme of Action* of the International Conference on Population and Development in 1994 in Cairo, Egypt. Circumcision may be performed as early as infancy, although the procedure is usually done between 4 and 12 years. It involves the partial or complete excision of the female genitalia. In its most severe form, called infibulation, after the major mutilation of the external genitalia, the vagina is reduced to a small opening "that may be as small as a matchstick" for urination and menstruation. Due to the small vaginal opening, sexual intercourse is quite painful; the infibulation scar may have to be re-cut due to penetration difficulties.

According to the United Nations' Children's Fund (UNICEF), an estimated two million girls are circumcised each year. An estimated 100 million women worldwide have undergone the procedure. Figure 1.3 shows the countries in which female genital mutilation is most prevalent.

In some countries, the practice is almost universal — virtually every female in Djibouti and Somalia and 9 of 10 women in Eritrea, Ethiopia, Sierra Leone, and northern Sudan. In *Female Genital Cutting: Findings from the Demographic and Health Surveys Program* (Macro International, Calverton, MD, 1997), Dara Carr reported that female circumcision has been so ingrained in many cultures that women themselves support its continuing practice. In Egypt, 87 percent of women indicated they had had their daughters circumcised or planned to do so.

Some of the health implications of female circumcision include hemorrhage, shock, and death. Infections may lead to sterility and chronic pelvic pain. If a woman has been infibulated, she may have to undergo a series of cutting and resewing during her childbearing years.

Sexual Abuse

Trafficking in children for pornography and prostitution is a worldwide problem. Most of these activities go on, like the drug trade, covertly. The Japanese mafia imports young girls from the Philippines for the prostitution business that makes an estimated $1.5 million a day. In the United States, runaways are lured

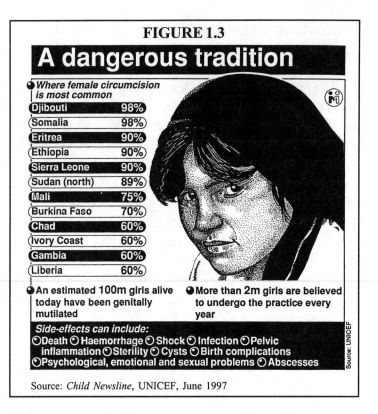

FIGURE 1.3

A dangerous tradition

● *Where female circumcision is most common*

Djibouti	98%
Somalia	98%
Eritrea	90%
Ethiopia	90%
Sierra Leone	90%
Sudan (north)	89%
Mali	75%
Burkina Faso	70%
Chad	60%
Ivory Coast	60%
Gambia	60%
Liberia	60%

● An estimated 100m girls alive today have been genitally mutilated

● More than 2m girls are believed to undergo the practice every year

Side-effects can include:
⊙ Death ⊙ Haemorrhage ⊙ Shock ⊙ Infection ⊙ Pelvic inflammation ⊙ Sterility ⊙ Cysts ⊙ Birth complications ⊙ Psychological, emotional and sexual problems ⊙ Abscesses

Source: UNICEF

Source: *Child Newsline*, UNICEF, June 1997

into the business, and in South America, street children fall victims to these activities. In Asia, poor families send their children to the city with the promise of jobs and income to help support the family, only to have the children forced into prostitution. Many young boys are also recruited to cater to pedophiles.

The United Nations reports that young children are being sold into prostitution in increasing numbers because of the mistaken belief that a 9- or 10-year-old will not be infected with AIDS. Nonetheless, many of the child prostitutes in India, Thailand, and the Philippines have tested positive for AIDS. (For more information on AIDS, see *AIDS*, Information Plus, Wylie, Texas, 1998.)

Although most European nations and the United States have laws against child prostitution and pornography, these sexual abuses continue to flourish underground because of great demand. In 1998, the British government urged that, instead of convicting child prostitutes as criminals, these children's employers and clients should be the ones prosecuted. The government believes that these children are victims of child abuse who need help.

CHAPTER II

CHILD ABUSE — A PROBLEM OF DEFINITION

WHAT IS ABUSE?

Child abuse is often a secret. Since the 1960s, however, the American people have become increasingly aware of the problems of child abuse and neglect (together referred to as child maltreatment). In 1963, only 150,000 young victims of abuse and neglect were reported to authorities (*Juvenile Court Statistics*, Children's Bureau, U.S. Department of Health, Education, and Welfare, Washington, DC, 1966). In 1996, state child protective services (CPS) agencies received more than three million reports of child maltreatment (*Child Maltreatment 1996: Reports From the States to the National Child Abuse and Neglect Data System*, Children's Bureau, U.S Department of Health and Human Services, Washington, DC, 1998). See Chapter IV for more information on this report.

There is still no agreement on what constitutes child abuse. While extreme cases are easy to label, less severe cases are viewed differently by different people. Is spanking abuse? Is spanking abuse only if the parent uses a belt and leaves welts on the child's body? Is it abuse if the marks fade in a few hours? Many parents consider it their right and duty to spank a wayward child. If a child runs into the street or is about to touch something hot, a smack on the bottom is commonly accepted as an appropriate way to teach the child not to do something dangerous.

Drs. Murray A. Straus, Richard J. Gelles, and Suzanne Steinmetz conducted two national surveys of spousal and parental-child violence and psychological abuse in 1975 (*The National Family Violence Survey*) and in 1985 (*The National Family Violence Resurvey*) (See Chapter V.) These comprehensive surveys of 8,145 households found that at least 97 percent of parents with children under 3 years of age had slapped or spanked their children at some time in the past year. This seemingly mild form of discipline obviously is not generally perceived as abuse either legally or morally by American society. Spanking is illegal, however, in the Scandinavian countries and Austria (although it is not considered a criminal act), and many of the leading researchers in the field of family violence disapprove of any physical punishment. (See Chapter V for more on corporal punishment.)

DEFINITION

Official definitions of child abuse and child neglect differ among institutions, government bodies, and experts. According to the Child Abuse Prevention and Treatment Act (CAPTA; PL 104-235), as amended in October 1996,

The term "child abuse and neglect" means, at a minimum, any recent act or failure to act, on the part of a parent or caretaker [including any employee of a residential facility or any staff person providing out-of-home care who is responsible for the child's welfare], which results in death, serious physical or emotional harm, sexual abuse or exploitation, or an act or failure to act which presents an imminent risk or serious harm. [The term "child" means a person under the age of 18, unless the child protection law of the state in which the child resides specifies a younger age for cases not involving sexual abuse.]

It should be noted that this definition of child abuse and neglect specifies that only parents and caregivers can be perpetrators of child maltreatment. Abusive and negligent behavior by other persons — strangers or persons known to the child — is considered child assault. Nonetheless, both forms of abusive behavior are crimes against children.

Based on a concern that severely disabled newborns may be denied medical care, CAPTA also considers as child abuse and neglect the "withholding of medically indicated treatment," including appropriate nutrition, hydration, and medication, which in the treating physician's medical judgment would most likely help improve or correct an infant's life-threatening conditions. This definition, however does not refer to situations where treatment of an infant, in the physician's medical judgment, would prolong dying, be ineffective in improving or correcting all the infant's life-threatening conditions, or would be futile in helping the infant to survive. In addition, this definition does not include circumstances where the infant is chronically or irreversibly comatose.

THE MAIN TYPES OF MALTREATMENT

Both the federal Child Abuse Prevention and Treatment Act of 1996 (CAPTA; see above) and state laws provide definitions of the different types of child maltreatment. CAPTA provides a foundation for states by identifying a minimum set of acts or behaviors that characterize child abuse and neglect. This law also defines the four main types of child maltreatment.

Physical Abuse

Physical abuse is the infliction of physical injury through punching, beating, kicking, slapping, biting, burning, shaking, or otherwise harming a child. Physical abuse is generally a willful act. However, there are cases in which the parent or caretaker may not have intended to hurt the child; the injury may have resulted from over-discipline or physical punishment. Nonetheless, if the child is injured, the act is considered abusive.

Sexual Abuse

Sexual abuse includes fondling a child's genitals, intercourse, incest, rape, sodomy, exhibitionism, and commercial exploitation through prostitution or the production of pornographic materials. (For more on sexual abuse, see Chapter VI.)

Emotional Abuse (Psychological Abuse, Verbal Abuse, or Mental Injury)

Emotional abuse includes acts or omissions by the parents or other caregivers that have caused, or could cause, serious behavioral, cognitive, emotional, or mental disorders. In some cases of emotional abuse, the abuser's act alone, without any harm evident in the child's behavior or condition, is enough to warrant intervention by the child protective services (CPS) agency. For example, the parent/caregiver may use extreme or bizarre forms of punishment, such as confinement of a child in a dark closet.

Other forms of emotional abuse may involve more subtle acts, such as habitual scapegoating, belittling, terrorizing, and rejection. For CPS to intervene, demonstrable harm to the child is often required. Although any of the types of child maltreatment may be found separately, they often occur in combination with one another. Nonetheless, emotional abuse is almost always present when other types are identified.

Child Neglect

Child neglect is an act of omission characterized by failure to provide for the child's basic needs. Neglect may be physical, educational, or emotional. *Physical neglect* includes failure to provide food, clothing, and shelter; refusal of or delay in seeking health care (medical neglect); abandonment; inadequate supervision; and expulsion from the home or refusal to allow a runaway to return home. *Educational neglect* includes permitting chronic truancy, failure to enroll a child of mandatory school age in school, and failure to take care of a child's special educational need. *Emotional neglect* includes substantial inattention to the child's needs for affection, the failure to provide needed psychological care, spouse abuse in the child's presence, and allowing drug or alcohol use by the child. It is very important to distinguish between willful neglect and a parent's or a caretaker's failure to provide the necessities of life because of poverty or cultural factors.

A DESCRIPTION OF
MALTREATED CHILDREN

Perhaps better than a definition of child abuse is a description of the characteristics likely to be exhibited by abused and/or neglected children. The U.S Department of Health and Human Services indicates that, in general, abused or neglected children are likely to have at least several of the following characteristics. (See Table 2.1 for more details on symptoms of abuse.)

• They appear to be different from other children in physical or emotional makeup, or their parents inappropriately describe them as being "different" or "bad."

• They seem unduly afraid of their parents.

• They may often bear welts, bruises, untreated sores, or other skin injuries.

• Their injuries seem to be inadequately treated.

• They show evidence of overall poor care.

• They are given inappropriate food, drink, or medication.

• They exhibit behavioral extremes: for example, crying often or crying very little and showing no real expectation of being comforted; being excessively fearful or seemingly fearless of adult authority; being unusually aggressive and destructive or extremely passive and withdrawn.

• Some are wary of physical contact, especially when it is initiated by an adult. They become fearful when an adult approaches another child, particularly one who is crying. Others are inappropriately hungry for affection, yet may have difficulty relating to children and adults. Based on their past experiences, these children cannot risk getting too close to others.

• They may exhibit a sudden change in behavior: for example, displaying regressive behavior — pants-wetting, thumb-sucking, frequent whining, becoming disruptive, or becoming uncommonly shy and passive.

• They take over the role of the parent, being protective or otherwise attempting to take care of the parent's needs.

• They have learning problems that cannot be diagnosed. If a child's academic IQ is average or better and medical tests indicate no abnormalities, but the child still cannot meet normal expectations, the answer may well be problems in the home — one of which may be abuse or neglect. Particular attention should be given to the child whose attention wanders and who easily becomes self-absorbed.

• They are habitually truant or late for school. Frequent or prolonged absences sometimes result when a parent keeps an injured child at home until the evidence of abuse disappears. In other cases, truancy indicates lack of parental concern or inability to regulate the child's schedule.

• In some cases, they frequently arrive at school too early and remain after classes rather than go home.

• They are always tired and often sleep in class.

• They are inappropriately dressed for the weather. Children who never have coats or shoes in cold weather are receiving subminimal care. On the other hand, those who regularly wear long sleeves or high necklines on hot days may be dressed to hide bruises, burns, or other marks of abuse.

Many of the psychological symptoms of abuse can be contradictory. One child may be excessively aggressive, while another may be too compliant. One child may be extremely dependent, while another may exhibit a clinging behavior. A child may be overly mature, attending to the emotional needs of a parent who is incapable of meeting his or her own needs. These different behaviors are possible symptoms of abuse. No one behavior on the part of a child, however, is conclusive evidence of abuse.

13

TABLE 2.1

CATEGORY	CHILD'S APPEARANCE	CHILD'S BEHAVIOR	CARETAKER'S BEHAVIOR
Physical Abuse	—Bruises and welts (on the face, lips, or mouth; in various stages of healing; on large areas of the torso, back, buttocks, or thighs; in unusual patterns, clustered, or reflective of the instrument used to inflict them; on several different surface areas). —Burns (cigar or cigarette burns; glove or sock-like burns or dough-nut shaped burns on the buttocks or genitalia indicative of immersion in hot liquid; rope burns on the arms, legs, neck or torso; patterned burns that show the shape of the item (iron, grill, etc.) used to inflict them). —Fractures (skull, jaw, or nasal fractures; spiral fractures of the long (arm and leg) bones; fractures in various states of healing; multiple fractures; any fracture in a child under the age of (two). —Lacerations and abrasions (to the mouth, lip, gums, or eye; to the external genitalia). —Human bite marks.	—Wary of physical contact with adults. —Apprehensive when other children cry. —Demonstrates extremes in behavior (e.g., extreme aggressiveness or withdrawal). —Seems frightened of parents. —Reports injury by parents.	—Has history of abuse as a child. —Uses harsh discipline inappropriate to child's age, transgression, and condition. —Offers illogical, unconvincing, contradictory, or no explanation of child's injury. —Seems unconcerned about child. —Significantly misperceives child (e.g., sees him as bad, evil, a monster, etc.). —Psychotic or psychopathic. —Misuses alcohol or other drugs. —Attempts to conceal child's injury or to protect identity of person responsible.
Neglect	—Consistently dirty, unwashed, hungry, or inappropriately dressed. —Without supervision for extended periods of time or when engaged in dangerous activities. —Constantly tired or listless. —Has unattended physical problems or lacks routine medical care. —Is exploited, overworked, or kept from attending school. —Has been abandoned.	—Is engaging in delinquent acts (e.g., vandalism, drinking, prostitution, drug use, etc.). —Is begging or stealing food. —Rarely attends school.	—Misuses alcohol or other drugs. —Maintains chaotic home life. —Shows evidence of apathy or futility. —Is mentally ill or of diminished intelligence. —Has long-term chronic illnesses. —Has history of neglect as a child.
Sexual Abuse	—Has torn, stained, or bloody underclothing. —Experience pain or itching in the genital area. —Has bruises or bleeding in external genitalia, vagina, or anal regions. —Has venereal disease. —Has swollen or red cervix, vulva, or perineum. —Has semen around mouth or genitalia or on clothing. —Is pregnant.	—Appears withdrawn or engages in fantasy or infantile behavior. —Has poor peer relationships. —Is unwilling to participate in physical activities. —Is engaging in delinquent acts or runs away. —States he/she has been sexually assaulted by parent/caretaker.	—Extremely protective or jealous of child. —Encourages child to engage in prostitution or sexual acts in the presence of caretaker. —Has been sexually abused as a child. —Is experiencing marital difficulties. —Misuses alcohol or other drugs. —Is frequently absent from the home.
Emotional Maltreatment	—Emotional maltreatment, often less tangible than other forms of child abuse and neglect, can be indicated by behaviors of the child and the caretaker.	—Appears overly compliant, passive, undemanding. —Is extremely aggressive, demanding, or rageful. —Shows overly adaptive behaviors, either inappropriately adult (e.g., parents other children) or inappropriately infantile (e.g., rocks constantly, sucks thumb, is enuretic). —Lags in physical, emotional, and intellectual development. Attempts suicide.	—Blames or belittles child. —Is cold and rejecting. —Withholds love. —Treats siblings unequally. —Seems unconcerned about child's problem.

Source: *Interdisciplinary Glossary on Child Abuse and Neglect: Legal, Medical, Social Work Terms*, DHHS Pub. No. 80-30137, Department of Health and Human Services, Washington, DC, 1980

Victims of Physical Abuse

Child victims of physical abuse often display bruises, welts, contusions, cuts, burns, fractures, lacerations, strap marks, swellings, and/or lost teeth. The list of possibilities is long and unpleasant. While internal injuries are seldom detectable without a hospital examination, anyone in close contact with children should be alert to multiple injuries, a history of repeated injuries, new injuries added to old, and untreated injuries, especially in very young children. Older children may attribute an injury to an improbable cause, lying for fear of parental retaliation. Younger children, on the other hand, may be unaware that severe beating is unacceptable and may admit to having been abused.

Physically abused children frequently have behavior problems. Especially among adolescents, chronic and unexplainable misbehavior should be investigated as possible evidence of abuse. Some children come to expect abusive behavior as the only kind of attention they can receive and so act in a way that invites abuse. Others break the law deliberately in order to come under the jurisdiction of the courts to obtain protection from their parents.

Parents of an abused child generally provide necessities such as adequate food and clean clothes, but they get angry quickly, have unrealistic expectations of the child, use inappropriate discipline, and are overly critical and rejecting of the child. While many parents were treated this way as children, alcohol and drug use are currently increasingly seen as contributing to abuse.

Victims of Physical Neglect

Physically neglected children are often hungry. They may go without breakfast and have neither food nor money for lunch. Some take the lunch money or food of other children and hoard whatever they obtain. They show signs of malnutrition — paleness, low weight relative to height, lack of body tone, fatigue, inability to participate in physical activities, and lack of normal strength and endurance.

These children are usually irritable. They show evidence of inadequate home management and are unclean and unkempt. Their clothes are torn and dirty, and they are often unbathed. They may lack proper clothing for different weather conditions, and their school attendance may be irregular. In addition, these children may frequently be ill and may exhibit a generally repressed personality, inattentiveness, and withdrawal. They are in obvious need of medical attention for such correctable conditions as poor eyesight, poor dental care, and lack of immunizations.

Children who suffer physical neglect also generally lack parental supervision at home. The child, for example, may frequently return from school to an empty house. While the need for adult supervision is, of course, relative to both the situation and the maturity of the child, it is generally held that a child younger than 12 should always be supervised by an adult or at least have immediate access to a concerned adult when necessary.

Parents of neglected children are either unable or unwilling to provide appropriate care. Some neglectful parents are mentally deficient; most lack knowledge of parenting skills and tend to be discouraged, depressed, and frustrated with their role as parents. Alcohol or drug abuse may also be involved.

Physical neglect can be a result of poverty and/or ignorance and may not be intentional. Dr. Vincent Fontana, who founded the Crisis Nursery for parents in need of support in New York, reported having seen many situations in which young mothers simply did not know what to do with a baby. One mother brought her constantly crying baby to the nursery for help because the mother could stand it no longer. Workers at the nursery concluded that the child was malnourished. The mother did not know that the baby needed to be fed several times a day every day.

Victims of Emotional Abuse and Neglect

Emotional abuse and neglect are as serious as physical abuse and neglect, although this condition is far more difficult to describe or identify. Emotional maltreatment often involves a parent's lack of love or failure to give direction or encourage the child's development. The parent may either demand far too much from the child in the area of academic, social, or athletic activity or withhold physical or verbal contact, indicating no concern for the child's successes and failures and giving no guidance or praise.

Parents who commit emotional abuse and neglect arc often unable to accept their children as fallible human beings. The effects of such abuse can often be far more serious and lasting than those of physical abuse and neglect. Emotionally abused children are often extremely aggressive, disruptive, and demanding in an attempt to gain attention and love. They are rarely able to achieve the success in school that tests indicate they can achieve.

Emotional maltreatment can be hard to determine. Is the child's abnormal behavior the result of maltreatment on the part of the parents, or is it a result of inborn or internal factors? Stuart N. Hart, Marla R. Brassard, and Henry C. Karlson ("Psychological Maltreatment," *The APSAC Handbook on Child Maltreatment,* SAGE Publications, Thousand Oaks, California, 1996) list possible behaviors associated with emotional abuse and neglect, including poor appetite, lying, low self-esteem, aggressive and antisocial behavior, insecure attachment relationships, failure to thrive, inability to be independent, and withdrawal that sometimes leads to suicide.

Victims of Medical Neglect

Medical neglect refers to the caregivers' failure to provide medical treatment for their children, including immunizations, prescribed medications, recommended surgery, and other intervention in cases of serious disease or injury. Some situations involve a parent's inability to care for a child or lack of access to health care. Other situations involve a parent's refusal to seek professional medical care, particularly due to a belief in spiritual healing.

Thorny legal issues have been raised by cases in which parents' freedom of religion clashes with the recommendations of medical professionals. Medical abuse may involve the Munchausen Syndrome by Proxy (MSBP, see below), in which psychologically disturbed parents create illnesses or injuries in children in order to gain sympathy for themselves.

Spiritual Healing

Religious beliefs sometimes prevent children from getting needed medical care. For example, Christian Scientists believe that God heals the sick and that prayer and perfect faith are the proper responses to illness. Other religions, most notably Jehovah's Witnesses, forbid blood transfusions. Religious exemption laws make it difficult to prosecute parents who do not seek treatment for a sick child because their religion forbids it, although courts generally order the emergency treatment of the children.

Rita Swan, a former Christian Scientist who lost her 16-month-old child to untreated meningitis, is the president of Children's Healthcare Is a Legal Duty, Inc. (CHILD, Inc.; an organization that seeks to "protect children from abusive religious and cultural practices, especially religion-based medical neglect"). According to CHILD, Inc., as of January 1999, 41 states have religious exemptions from child abuse and neglect charges, and 48 states (Mississippi and West Virginia are the exceptions) have religious exemptions from immunizations.

The 1996 amendments to the Child Abuse Prevention and Treatment Act (see above) provided in Sec. 113. [42 U.S.C. 5106i] that

Nothing in this Act shall be construed —

(1) as establishing a Federal requirement that a parent or legal guardian provide a child medical service or treatment against the religious belief of the parent or legal guardian; and

(2) to require that a State find, or to prohibit a State from finding, abuse or neglect in cases in which a parent or legal guardian relies solely or partially upon spiritual means rather than medical treatment, in accordance with the religious beliefs of the parent or legal guardian.

In "Child Fatalities From Religion-motivated Medical Neglect" (*Pediatrics*, vol. 101, no. 4, April 1998), Seth M. Asser and Rita Swan reviewed the deaths of children in faith-healing religious sects, where the children were denied medical care. The authors found that in 140 of the 172 deaths, the likelihood of survival was at least 90 percent had the children received medical care. Another 18 deaths would have had survival rates of more than 50 percent.

Munchausen Syndrome by Proxy

Munchausen Syndrome is a psychological disorder in which a patient fabricates the symptoms of disease or injury to get medical attention. In cases of Munchausen Syndrome by Proxy (MSBP), parents or caregivers suffering from Munchausen Syndrome call medical attention to themselves by hurting or inducing illnesses in their children. The perpetrator, usually the mother, may make up a child's medical history, alter a child's laboratory tests, or fabricate or cause an illness or injury. In some cases, caregivers sexually abuse their children so that they can claim a crime has been committed. Table 2.2 illustrates some of the medical symptoms or illnesses exhibited by MSBP victims and the methods perpetrators use to cause these conditions.

In MSBP situations, children are usually subjected to endless and often painful diagnostic tests, medications, and even surgery. Some children have had as many as 300 clinic visits and repeated hospitalizations in their first 18 months of life. The abuse is most often perpetrated against infants and toddlers before they can talk. Some older children do not reveal the deception, however, because they fear they will be abandoned by their mothers if they are no longer sick. Others come to believe that they must truly be ill.

Officially, MSBP represents fewer than 1,000 of the more than 3 million alleged cases of abuse referred for investigation each year. This figure, however, is almost certainly underestimated because of under-di-

TABLE 2.2

Common Presentations of Munchausen Syndrome by Proxy and the Usual Methods of Deception

Presentation	Mechanism
Apnea (breathing stops)	Suffocation, drugs, poisoning, lying
Seizures	Lying, drugs, poisons, asphyxiation
Bleeding	Adding blood to urine, vomit, etc.; opening intravenous line
Fevers, blood infection	Injection of feces, saliva, contaminated water into the child
Vomiting	Poisoning with drugs that cause vomiting; lying
Diarrhea	Poisoning with laxatives, salt, mineral oil

Source: *Child Neglect and Munchausen Syndrome by Proxy*, Office of Juvenile Justice and Delinquency Prevention, U.S. Department of Justice, Washington, DC, 1997

agnosis. Data that exist on MSBP reveal that mothers are the perpetrators in 98 percent of the cases. Although there are no specific numbers, many of the mothers who medically abuse their children were abused in their own childhoods. One mother who had a history of chronic abuse thought that by devoting her life to "helping" her sick child, she could be a nurturing mother, unlike her own abusive mother. She not only got the medical attention that she craved but also the sympathy of those involved in her child's care.

Many cases of MSBP go undetected because doctors feel obliged to check out any unexplained illness, and the nursing staff which spends the most time with a hospitalized child is often unaware that MSBP is a possibility. The Office of Juvenile Justice and Delinquency Prevention of the U.S. Department of Justice advises medical personnel that if MSBP is suspected, they should examine the medical records of all siblings, including autopsy reports and death certificates. The incidence of multiple alleged Sudden Infant Death Syndrome (SIDS) deaths under the same parent/caretaker warrants investigation.

A FAMILY AT RISK
FOR MALTREATMENT

While it is impossible to determine whether or not child maltreatment will occur, generally, a family may be at risk if the parent is young, has little education, has had several children born within a few years, and is highly dependent on social welfare. A family may also be at risk if the parent

- Is a "loner" — feels isolated, with no family to depend on, no real friends, or does not get along well with the neighbors.

- Has no understanding of the stages of child development and does not know what to expect of a child at a given age.

- Has a poor self-image and feels worthless, with a pervading sense of failure.

- Feels unloved, unappreciated, and unwanted, with a great fear of rejection.

- Has severe personal problems, such as ill health, alcoholism, or drug dependency.

- Feels that violence can often be the solution to life's problems, or has not learned to "blow off steam" in a socially acceptable manner.

- Is experiencing a time of severe stress — sudden unemployment, painful divorce, for example — without any coping mechanism.

- Was abused or neglected as a child.

A family may also be at risk if the child

- Is "different" — smaller than average, sicklier, disabled, or considered unattractive or was premature.

- Resembles or reminds the parent of someone the parent hates, or if the child "takes after" a disappointing spouse or former loved one.

- Is more demanding or otherwise has more problems than do other children in the family.

- Is unwanted — seen as a "mistake" or burden, having "ruined things" for the parent.

CHAPTER III

REPORTING CHILD ABUSE

In a free society, where wrong exists, some are guilty; all are responsible. — Anonymous

MANDATORY REPORTING

In 1974, Congress enacted the first Child Abuse Prevention and Treatment Act (CAPTA; PL 93-247) that set the guidelines for the reporting, investigation, and treatment of child maltreatment. States had to meet these requirements in order to receive federal funding to assist child victims of abuse and neglect. Among its many provisions, CAPTA required the states to enact mandatory reporting laws and procedures. The purpose of child abuse reporting laws is to encourage the reporting of suspected child abuse so that social service workers can take action to protect the child from further abuse.

The earliest mandatory reporting laws were directed at medical professionals, particularly physicians, because they were considered the most likely to see abused children. Currently, each state designates mandatory reporters of child maltreatment. However, any individual, whether on not he or she is a mandatory reporter, may report incidents of abuse or neglect.

Some states also require maltreatment reporting from other individuals, including firefighters, Christian Science practitioners, the clergy, animal control officers, veterinarians, commercial/private film or photograph processors, and even lawyers. As of December 1997, 20 states required all citizens to report suspected child maltreatment. Twenty-three states exempted from mandatory reporting the privileged communications of attorney/ client, clergy/penitent, and/or mental health professional/patient. (See Table 3.1.)

In 1996, more than half (51.7 percent) of all reports of alleged child maltreatment came from professionals — educators (15.6 percent), law enforcement personnel (13.3 percent), social services personnel (11.9 percent), and medical personnel (10.9 percent). Friends, parents, and other relatives comprised 25.4 percent of the reporters, while victims and self-identified perpetrators reported abuse in less than 2 percent of the cases. About 12 percent of reports were from anonymous or unknown sources. (See Figure 3.1.)

All states offer immunity to individuals who report incidents of child maltreatment "in good faith." Besides physical injury and neglect, most states include mental injury, sexual abuse, and the sexual exploitation of minors as cases to be reported.

LEGAL RESPONSIBILITY OF PROFESSIONAL REPORTERS

Identifying child maltreatment is not an easy process, since the perpetrators usually commit their acts against children in secrecy. Gary King, Robert Reece, Robert Bendel, and Vrunda Patel, in "The Effects of Sociodemographic Variables, Training, and Attitudes on the Lifetime Reporting Practices of Mandated Reporters" (*Child Maltreatment*, vol.3, no. 3, August 1998), noted that mandated reporters have to diligently determine

Mandatory Reporters of Child Abuse and Neglect

TABLE 3.1

STATE	PROFESSIONS THAT MUST REPORT					OTHERS WHO MUST REPORT		STANDARD FOR REPORTING	PRIVILEGED COMMUNI-CATIONS
	Health Care	Mental Health	Social Work	Educa-tion/Child Care	Law Enforce-ment	All Persons	Other		
ALABAMA § 26-14-3(a)	✓	✓	✓	✓	✓		▪ Any other person called upon to give aid or assistance to any child	Known or suspected	
ALASKA §§ 47.17.020(a) 47.17.023	✓	✓	✓	✓	✓		▪ Paid employees of domestic violence and sexual assault programs and drug & alcohol treatment facilities ▪ Commercial or private film or photograph processors	Have reasonable cause to suspect	
ARIZONA §§ 13-3620(A) 13-3509	✓	✓	✓	✓	✓		▪ Parents ▪ Anyone responsible for care or treatment of children ▪ Clergy	Have reasonable grounds to believe	Clergy/penitent
ARKANSAS § 12-12-507 (b)-(c)	✓	✓	✓	✓	✓		▪ Prosecutors ▪ Judges	Have reasonable cause to suspect	
CALIFORNIA § 11166	✓	✓	✓	✓	✓		▪ Firefighters ▪ Animal control officers ▪ Commercial film and photographic print processors ▪ Clergy	Have knowledge of or observe; know or reasonably suspect	Clergy/penitent
COLORADO §§ 19-3-304(1), (2), (2.5); 19-3-305(1)	✓	✓	✓	✓	✓		▪ Christian Science practitioners ▪ Veterinarians ▪ Firefighters ▪ Victim advocates ▪ Commercial film and photographic print processors	Have reasonable cause to know or suspect	

(continued)

20

Mandatory Reporters of Child Abuse and Neglect

TABLE 3.1 (Continued)

(current through December 31, 1997)

STATE	PROFESSIONS THAT MUST REPORT					OTHERS WHO MUST REPORT		STANDARD FOR REPORTING	PRIVILEGED COMMUNICATIONS
	Health Care	Mental Health	Social Work	Education/Child Care	Law Enforcement	All Persons	Other		
CONNECTICUT §§ 17a-101(b); 17a-102	✓	✓	✓	✓	✓		▪ Substance abuse counselors ▪ Sexual assault counselors ▪ Battered women's counselors ▪ Clergy	Have reasonable cause to suspect or believe	
DELAWARE tit. 16, § 903	✓	✓	✓	✓		✓		Know or reasonably suspect	
DISTRICT OF COLUMBIA § 12-1352(a), (b)	✓	✓	✓	✓	✓			Know or have reasonable cause to suspect	
FLORIDA §§ 415.504(1), (3); 415.512	✓	✓	✓	✓	✓	✓	Spiritual healers	Know or have reasonable cause to suspect	Attorney/client
GEORGIA §§ 19-7-5(c)(1), (9); 16-12-100(c), (g)(3)	✓	✓	✓	✓	✓		Persons who produce visual or printed matter	Have reasonable cause to believe	
HAWAII § 350-1.1(a)	✓	✓	✓	✓	✓		Employees of recreational or sports activities	Have reasonable cause to believe	
IDAHO § 16-1619(a),(c)	✓	✓	✓	✓	✓	✓		Have reason to believe	Clergy/penitent
ILLINOIS ch.325, para.5/4 ch.325, para.5/4.1 ch.720, para.5/11-20.2	✓	✓	✓	✓	✓		▪ Homemakers, substance abuse treatment personnel ▪ Christian Science practitioners ▪ Funeral home directors ▪ Commercial film and photographic print processors ▪ Any other person may make a report	Have reasonable cause to believe/ suspect	

(continued)

21

Mandatory Reporters of Child Abuse and Neglect

TABLE 3.1 (Continued)

(Current through December 31, 1997)

STATE	PROFESSIONS THAT MUST REPORT					OTHERS WHO MUST REPORT		STANDARD FOR REPORTING	PRIVILEGED COMMUNI-CATIONS
	Health Care	Mental Health	Social Work	Education/Child Care	Law Enforcement	All Persons	Other		
INDIANA §§ 31-6-11-3(a); 31-6-11-8						✓		Have reason to believe	
IOWA §§ 232.69(1); 728.14	✓	✓	✓	✓	✓		• Commercial film and photographic print processors • Employees of substance abuse programs	Reasonably believe	
KANSAS § 38-1522(a),(d)	✓	✓	✓	✓	✓		• Firefighters • Juvenile intake and assessment workers	Have reason to suspect	
KENTUCKY § 620.030(1); 620.050(2)	✓	✓	✓	✓	✓	✓		Know or have reasonable cause to believe	• Attorney/client • Clergy/penitent
LOUISIANA art. 603(13) art. 609 art. 610(f)	✓	✓	✓	✓	✓		Commercial film or photographic print processors	Have cause to believe; have knowledge of or observe	• Clergy/penitent • Christian Science practitioner
MAINE tit. 22, §§ 4011, 4013, 4015	✓	✓	✓	✓	✓		• Guardian *ad litems* and CASA volunteers • Fire inspectors	Know or have reasonable cause to suspect	Clergy/penitent
MARYLAND §§ 5-704, 5-705	✓		✓	✓	✓	✓		Have reason to believe	
MASSACHUSETTS ch.119, 51A ch.112, §135A ch.112, §135B ch.233, §20B	✓	✓	✓	✓	✓		Drug and alcoholism counselors	Have reasonable cause to believe	
MICHIGAN §§ 722.623(1),(8), 722.631	✓	✓	✓	✓	✓			Have reasonable cause to suspect	Attorney/client
MINNESOTA § 626.556(3)(a), (8),(9)	✓	✓	✓	✓	✓			Know or have reason to believe	Clergy/penitent

(continued)

TABLE 3.1 (Continued)

Mandatory Reporters of Child Abuse and Neglect

(Current through December 31, 1997)

STATE	PROFESSIONS THAT MUST REPORT					OTHERS WHO MUST REPORT		STANDARD FOR REPORTING	PRIVILEGED COMMUNICATIONS
	Health Care	Mental Health	Social Work	Education/Child Care	Law Enforcement	All Persons	Other		
MISSISSIPPI § 43-21-353(1)	✓	✓	✓	✓	✓	✓	■ Attorneys ■ Ministers	Have reasonable cause to suspect	
MISSOURI §§ 210.115(1),(5), 568.110, 210.140	✓	✓		✓	✓	✓	■ Persons with responsibility for care of children ■ Christian Science practitioners	Have reasonable cause to suspect	Attorney/client
MONTANA § 41-3-201(1)-(2)(4), 41-3-206(1)	✓	✓	✓	✓	✓		■ Guardian *ad litem* ■ Religious healers	Know or have reasonable cause to suspect	Clergy/penitent
NEBRASKA §§ 28-211(1), 28.813.02	✓		✓	✓		✓		Have reasonable cause to believe; have knowledge of or observe	
NEVADA §§ 432B.220(2), (4), 432B.250	✓	✓	✓	✓	✓		■ Clergy ■ Religious healers	Know or have reason to believe; have reasonable cause to believe	Clergy/penitent
NEW HAMPSHIRE §§ 169-C:29, 169-C:32	✓	✓	✓	✓	✓	✓		Have reason to suspect	Attorney/client
NEW JERSEY § 9:6-8.10						✓	Judges	Have reasonable cause to believe	
NEW MEXICO § 32A-4-3	✓	✓	✓	✓	✓	✓		Know or have reasonable suspicion	
NEW YORK §§ 413(1), 418	✓	✓	✓	✓	✓		■ Alcoholism counselors ■ Prosecutors	Know or have reasonable cause to suspect	
NORTH CAROLINA §§ 7A-543, 7A-551						✓		Have cause to suspect	Attorney/client

(continued)

TABLE 3.1 (Continued)

Mandatory Reporters of Child Abuse and Neglect

(Current through December 31, 1997)

STATE	PROFESSIONS THAT MUST REPORT					OTHERS WHO MUST REPORT		STANDARD FOR REPORTING	PRIVILEGED COMMUNICATIONS
	Health Care	Mental Health	Social Work	Education/Child Care	Law Enforcement	All Persons	Other		
NORTH DAKOTA §§ 50-25.1-03, 50-25.1-10	✓	✓	✓	✓	✓		Clergy; Religious healers; Addiction counselors	Have knowledge of reasonable cause to suspect	Clergy/penitent
OHIO § 2151.421(A)	✓	✓	✓	✓			Attorney; Religious healers	Know or suspect	Attorney/client
OKLAHOMA tit.10, §7103 tit.21, §1021.4	✓			✓		✓	Commercial film and photographic print processors	Have reason to believe; have knowledge of or observe	Mental health/patient; Clergy/penitent; Attorney/client
OREGON §§ 41913.005(3), 419B.010	✓	✓	✓	✓	✓		Attorney; Clergy; Firefighter	Have reasonable cause to believe	Mental health/patient; Clergy/penitent; Attorney/client
PENNSYLVANIA §§ 6311(a),(b), 6317	✓	✓	✓	✓	✓		Any other person who comes into contact with children through occupation or employment	Have reasonable cause to suspect	Clergy/penitent
RHODE ISLAND §§ 40-11-3(a)-(c), 40-11-3.1, 40-11-6(1), 40-11-11						✓		Have reasonable cause to suspect	Clergy/penitent
SOUTH CAROLINA §§ 20-7-510(A), 20-7-520, 20-7-550, 16-3-850	✓	✓		✓	✓		Judges; Funeral home directors and employees	Have reason to believe	Attorney/client; Priest/penitent
SOUTH DAKOTA §§ 26-8A-3, 26-8A-	✓	✓	✓	✓	✓		Abuse counselors; Religious healers	Have reasonable cause to suspect	
TENNESSEE §§ 37-1-403(a), (c), 37-1-605(a)	✓	✓	✓	✓	✓	✓	Judges; Neighbors; Relatives; Friends	Know or have reasonable cause to suspect	

(continued)

TABLE 3.1 (Continued)

Mandatory Reporters of Child Abuse and Neglect

(Current through December 31, 1997)

STATE	PROFESSIONS THAT MUST REPORT					OTHERS WHO MUST REPORT		STANDARD FOR REPORTING	PRIVILEGED COMMUNICATIONS
	Health Care	Mental Health	Social Work	Education/Child Care	Law Enforcement	All Persons	Other		
TEXAS §§ 261.101(a), (c), 261.102						✓		Have cause to believe	
UTAH §§ 62A-4a-403 (1)–(3) 62A-4a-404, 62A-4a-405	✓					✓		Have reason to believe	Clergy/penitent
VERMONT tit.33, §4913(a)	✓	✓	✓	✓	✓		Camp administrators and counselors	Have reasonable cause to believe	
VIRGINIA § 63.1-248.3(A)	✓	✓	✓	✓	✓		• Mediators • Christian Science practitioners	Have reason to suspect	
WASHINGTON §§ 26.44.030 (1), (2) 5.60.060(3),(4), 18.83.110, 9.68A.080, 18.53.200, 9.69.100	✓	✓	✓	✓	✓	✓	Commercial photographic film processors	Have reasonable cause to believe	
WEST VIRGINIA §§ 49-6A-2, 49-6A-3, 49-6A-7	✓	✓	✓	✓	✓		• Clergy • Religious healers • Judges	Know reasonable cause to suspect	Attorney/client
WISCONSIN § 48,981(2), (2m)(c),(d)	✓	✓	✓	✓	✓		• Abuse counselors • Mediators • Financial and employment planners	Have reasonable cause to suspect; have reason to believe	
WYOMING §§ 14-3-205(a), 14-3-207						✓		Know or have reasonable cause to believe or suspect	
TOTALS, ALL STATES	44	37	40	43	37	20	34	N/A	23

Source: *Statutes at a Glance: Mandatory Reporters of Child Abuse and Neglect*, National Clearinghouse on Child Abuse and Neglect Information, Washington, DC, 1998

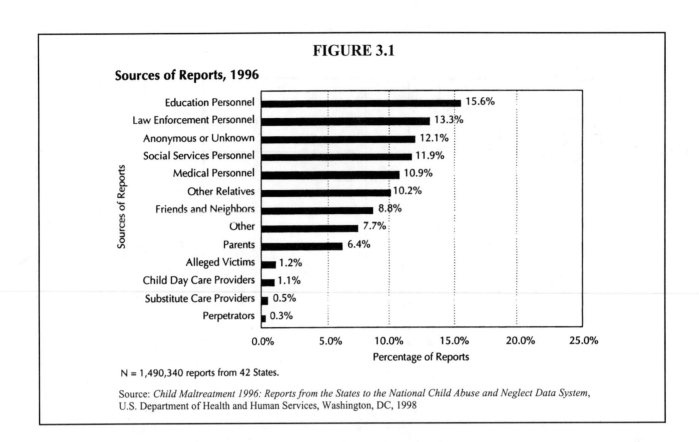

FIGURE 3.1

Sources of Reports, 1996

Sources of Reports (y-axis):
- Education Personnel 15.6%
- Law Enforcement Personnel 13.3%
- Anonymous or Unknown 12.1%
- Social Services Personnel 11.9%
- Medical Personnel 10.9%
- Other Relatives 10.2%
- Friends and Neighbors 8.8%
- Other 7.7%
- Parents 6.4%
- Alleged Victims 1.2%
- Child Day Care Providers 1.1%
- Substitute Care Providers 0.5%
- Perpetrators 0.3%

Percentage of Reports (x-axis): 0.0% 5.0% 10.0% 15.0% 20.0% 25.0%

N = 1,490,340 reports from 42 States.

Source: *Child Maltreatment 1996: Reports from the States to the National Child Abuse and Neglect Data System,* U.S. Department of Health and Human Services, Washington, DC, 1998

whether abuse has actually occurred. Factors that come into play may include the mandated reporter's training and experience, attitudes regarding child discipline, own experience of abuse, and beliefs regarding what official intervention would accomplish and what adverse consequences may result from the reporting.

Teachers

While all 50 states require educators to report suspected child maltreatment, a study of teachers' knowledge of the signs of child sexual abuse found that 75 percent could not recognize even the most obvious signs (*The Harvard Education Letter*, March/April 1995). Most teachers in the study reported they had never had an abused or neglected child in their classes. Nonetheless, in 1996, most reports of abuse and neglect came from educators (15.6 percent). (See Figure 3.1.)

Pediatricians

Many pediatricians fail to report suspected abuse, often because of disagreements about what constitutes appropriate parental discipline. Many physicians do not consider discipline as abusive unless the consequences are serious. An official with the Mayor's Task Force on Child Abuse and Neglect in New York City thinks that private pediatricians, because of their poor record of recognizing and reporting child abuse, are part of the problem, not the solution.

A pediatrician may be afraid to offend the parents who pay the bill and who may spread rumors about the doctor's competence, potentially damaging his or her practice. Some doctors think that the problem can best be dealt with privately and choose to take care of it by discussing it with the parents. Many doctors fear the time lost in reporting abuse and the possibility of being sued by an outraged parent or having to testify in court.

Some pediatricians may believe that child protective services (CPS) agencies are not very effective in doing their jobs. Gary King et al. (see above) reported that their survey of pediatricians, master's level social workers, and physician assistants (PAs) showed that those who had never received feed-

TABLE 3.2

Professional Opinion and the Mean Number of Ever-Suspected Cases and Lifetime Reporting Proportion[a]

Independent Variable	Mean of Ever-Suspected Cases	Lifetime Reporting Proportion (LRP)
Overall mean	23.95	68.51
CPS adequately protects children	25.16	69.25
Receive feedback from Child Protective Services (CPS)	29.40**[b]	72.27**
Lack of sufficient evidence	24.21	68.52**
Unwilling to jeopardize relationship with family	24.17	68.76*[b]
Respect for cultural differences	24.19	68.89**
Concern about maintaining anonymity	24.26	68.89**
Reporting process is too time-consuming	24.19	68.89
Reluctance to get involved with courts	24.19	68.89*[b]
CPS interventions not effective	24.36	68.77**
Reporting may harm child	24.11	69.13***
Reporting may result in removal of child	24.38	69.11***
Child already known to CPS	24.19	68.89

a. Levels within categories were compared by an ANOVA. Sample sizes ranged from 237 to 274 for all variables.
b. Not significant with a Bonferonni adjustment.
*$p \leq .05$. **$p \leq .01$. ***$p \leq .001$.

Source: Gary King et al., "The Effects of Sociodemographic Variables, Training, and Attitudes On the Lifetime Reporting Practices of Mandated Reporters," *Child Maltreatment*, vol. 3, no. 3, August 1998, pp. 276-283, copyright © 1998 by Sage Publications, Inc. Reprinted by permission of Sage Publications, Inc.

TABLE 3.3

Role in Cases of Suspected Child Maltreatment (in percentages)

Role	Nurse Practitioners (n = 65)	Registered Nurses (n = 34)	Physician Assistants (n = 5)	Total Sample (N = 104)
Perform physical evaluations in suspected child maltreatment				
Sexual abuse	96.9	91.2	100.0	95.2
Physical abuse	74.4	58.8	80.0	70.0
Neglect	55.4	50.0	60.0	54.0
Collection of evidence for cases of suspected child sexual abuse	92.3	91.2	100.0	92.3
Colposcope examinations	83.1	67.6	60.0	76.9
Interpretation of colposcopic findings	81.5	50.0	60.0	70.2
Use of telemedicine for consultation	0.0	9.1	0.0	2.9
Prescription writing privileges	81.3	0.0	80.0	54.9
Practice settings in CM[a]				
Clinic	78.0	47.0	80.0	70.0
Emergency department	35.4	55.9	20.0	41.4
Child abuse program	20.0	41.2	40.0	27.9
Child advocacy center	29.2	11.8	20.0	23.4
Inpatient unit	15.4	14.7	40.0	16.4
Public health	9.2	23.5	20.0	14.4
Member of a child abuse protection team	73.0	60.0	60.0	68.0
Member of a child fatality review team	10.9	11.8	00.0	10.7
Number of years experience in child maltreatment				
M	6.0	6.1	4.7	6.0
SD	5.1	5.2	3.5	5.0

a. Total is greater than 100% because of multiple practice settings.

Source: Susan J. Kelley and Beatrice Crofts Yorker, "The Role of Nonphysician Health Care Providers in the Physical Assessment and Diagnosis of Suspected Child Maltreatment: Results of a National Survey," *Child Maltreatment*, vol. 2, no. 4, November 1997, pp. 331-340, copyright © 1998 by Sage Publications, Inc. Reprinted by permission of Sage Publications, Inc.

back from CPS after they had reported suspected maltreatment indicated a smaller proportion of lifetime reporting practices (58.4 percent) than those who sometimes (76.3 percent) or always/almost always (74 percent) received feedback from CPS.

Other factors that influenced the professionals' decision to report child maltreatment and the resulting percentages of lifetime reporting practices are illustrated on Table 3.2.

Howard Dubowitz, in "Neglect of Children's Health Care" (*Neglected Children: Research, Practice, and Policy*, SAGE Publications, Thousand Oaks, California, 1999), noted that very few cases of neglected medical care are reported to CPS. Although physicians are mandated reporters, they have varying levels of suspicion. The author offers physicians two guidelines:

- Rcport if the actual or potential harm is serious.

- Report if less intrusive interventions have failed and moderate or serious, actual or potential, harm remains a concern.

Nonphysician Health Care Providers

Traditionally, physicians perform the physical evaluation and treatment of child abuse and neglect. However, registered nurses (RNs), nurse practitioners (NPs), and physician assistants (PAs) trained in child maltreatment are increasingly performing the physical evaluation of suspected cases. Susan J. Kelley and Beatrice Crofts Yorker, in "The Role of Nonphysician Health Care Providers in the Physical Assessment and Diagnosis of Suspected Child Maltreatment: Results of a National Survey" (*Child Maltreatment*, vol. 2, no. 4, November 1997), found that among a national sample of 104 RNs, NPs, and PAs from 44 states and the District of Columbia, over 9 in 10 (95.2 percent) had performed physical evaluations in suspected sexual abuse, 7 in 10 (70 percent) diagnosed suspected physical abuse, and over half (54 percent) evaluated suspected child neglect. (See Table 3.3.)

These nonphysician health care providers (92.3 percent) also collected evidence for cases of suspected sexual abuse, with three-quarters (76.9 percent) performing colposcope examinations, and 70.2 percent interpreting the results of these examinations. (A colposcope examination involves visual inspection of the cervix and vagina under magnification.) The health care providers were most likely to practice their child maltreatment specialty in clinics (70 percent), followed by emer-

gency departments (41.4 percent), child abuse programs (27.9 percent), child advocacy centers (23.4 percent), inpatient units (16.4 percent), and public health agencies (14.4 percent). More than two-thirds (68 percent) of RNs, NPs, and PAs were members of a child abuse prevention team, and these professionals reported they had practiced their specialty an average of six years. (See Table 3.3.)

A NEED FOR CHILD MALTREATMENT SPECIALISTS

Although child abuse is a well-documented social and public health problem in the United States, the U.S. Department of Health and Human Services (HHS) has found that few medical schools and residency training programs include child abuse education and other family violence education in their curricula. The Centers for Disease Control and Prevention (CDC) of the HHS reported on an effort by the Virginia Commission on Family Violence to identify the presence of family violence education in the curricula of medical school-based residency programs in the state. The commission created the Task Force on Violence Education and Awareness to survey these residency programs.

The CDC, in "Family Violence Education in Medical School-Based Residency Programs — Virginia, 1995" (*Morbidity and Mortality Weekly Report*, vol. 45, no. 31, August 9, 1996), reported on the task force survey of 69 residency programs within Virginia's three medical schools (Eastern Virginia Medical School, the Medical College of Virginia, and the University of Virginia). Of the 48 residency programs that responded, 20 programs (42 percent) covered child abuse in their curricula. Sixteen of the 20 programs offered required courses. In some cases, child abuse education programs were offered as electives (not required courses).

This study illustrates the need for integrating family violence education into the nation's medical school and internship/residency programs.

However, there is a shortage of medical specialists to provide such education. Carol Jenny, a child abuse doctor, in "Pediatric Fellowships in Child Abuse and Neglect: The Development of a New Subspecialty" (*Child Maltreatment*, vol. 2, no. 4, November 1997), pointed out that recently, when 14 medical school and academic teaching hospitals advertised faculty positions for specialists in child abuse, many positions could not be filled.

Dr. Jenny cited four advantages for developing formal fellowship training and board certification for physicians who primarily care for child abuse victims.

The primary objective of fellowship training is to create the next generation of medical school faculty.... With child abuse specialists on faculties, students are more likely to receive a carefully defined education in recognizing and caring for abused and neglected children. Another objective is to train young physicians to do research on child abuse.... [M]ore trained researchers with specific interests in child abuse will be needed to advance the field. A third advantage ... is to develop a pool of credible expert witnesses for legal proceedings. A final advantage ... is that pooling of clinical experience leads to excellence in care.

THE HOSPITAL'S ROLE

A child suffers different types of injuries from accidental trauma than from intentional trauma, often allowing doctors to determine whether the child was abused regardless of the parent's report of the cause of injury. Figure 3.2 shows the different locations on a child's body of typical accidental injuries compared to abuse-related injuries.

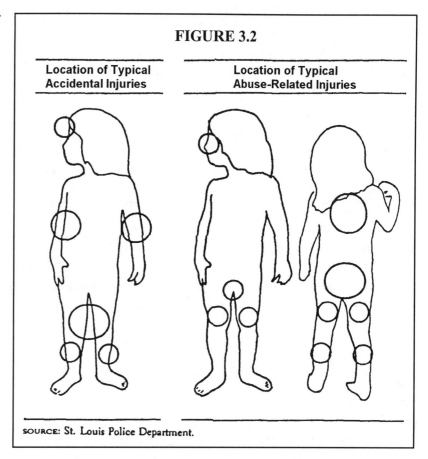

FIGURE 3.2

| Location of Typical Accidental Injuries | Location of Typical Abuse-Related Injuries |

SOURCE: St. Louis Police Department.

The emergency room is often where serious abuse first comes to the attention of the authorities. The American Academy of Pediatrics (AAP) believes that the hospital inpatient unit is the right place for the "initial assessment" of suspected victims of child maltreatment. The Committee on Hospital Care and the Committee on Child Abuse and Neglect of the AAP recommend that, in communities where no crisis intervention centers exist, hospitals have the obligation to admit children suspected of being abused ("Medical Necessity for the Hospitalization of the Abused and Neglected Child [RE9737]," *Pediatrics*, vol. 101, no. 4, April 1998).

The AAP observes that, while managed care and peer-review organizations may deny reimbursement of the child's hospital stay or limit the length of stay, their actions in no way minimize the treating physician's medical judgment. (A peer-review group consists of physicians who review the work and clinical decisions of other physicians.) According to the AAP, peer-review personnel may feel that hospital admission of the alleged child victim may not have been medically necessary, since child maltreatment is a social and not a medical problem.

The AAP, however, believes that the hospital setting affords the medical team and the authorities a first-person observation of parent-child interaction. Moreover, at the time of the child's visit to the emergency room, the hospital may provide the only safe place until child protective services (CPS) has the chance to decide whether to return the child to a potentially dangerous home situation.

FAILURE TO REPORT MALTREATMENT

Many states impose penalties, either a fine and/or imprisonment, for failure to report child maltreatment. A mandated reporter, such as a physician, may also be sued for negligence because he or she has failed to protect the child from harm. The landmark case, *Landeros v. Flood* (551 P.2d 389, 1976), illustrates such a case. Eleven-month-old Gita Landeros was brought by her mother to the San Jose Hospital for treatment of injuries. Besides a fractured lower leg, the girl had bruises on her back and abrasions on other parts of her body. She also appeared scared when anyone approached her. At the time, Landeros was also suffering from a fractured skull, but this was never diagnosed by the attending physician, A. J. Flood.

Gita Landeros returned home with her mother and subsequently suffered further serious abuse in the hands of her mother and the mother's boyfriend. Three months later, Landeros was brought to another hospital for medical treatment, where the doctor diagnosed "Battered Child Syndrome" and reported the abuse to the proper authorities. After surgery, the child was placed with foster parents. The mother and boy friend were eventually convicted of the crime of child abuse. The guardian *ad litem* (a court-appointed special advocate) for Gita Landeros filed a malpractice suit against Dr. Flood and the hospital — "as a proximate (direct) results of defendants' negligence, plaintiff suffered painful permanent physical injuries and great mental distress, including the probable loss of use or amputation of her left hand."

The California Supreme Court agreed, stating that the "Battered Child Syndrome" (see Chapter I) was a recognized medical condition that Dr. Flood should have been aware of and diagnosed. The court ruled that the doctor's failure to do so contributed to the child's continued suffering, and Dr. Flood and the hospital were liable for this. While this case applied specifically to a medical doctor, the principles reached by the court are applicable to other professionals. Most professionals are familiar with the court's decision in *Landeros*.

CHILD PROTECTIVE SERVICES (CPS)

Local government agencies generally referred to as child protective services (CPS) receive and investigate reports of child maltreatment. Partly funded by the federal government, CPS agencies were first established in response to the 1974 Child Abuse and Prevention Act (PL 93-247), which mandated that all states establish procedures to investigate suspected incidents of child maltreatment.

Upon receipt of a report of suspected child maltreatment, CPS screens the case to determine if it falls within their jurisdiction. For example, if it has been determined that the alleged perpetrator of sexual abuse was the victim's parent or caretaker, CPS conducts further investigation. On the other hand, if the alleged perpetrator was a stranger or someone who was not the parent or caregiver of the victim, the case is referred to the police. Cases of reported child abuse or neglect typically undergo a series of steps through CPS and the child welfare system. (See Figure 3.3.)

Court Involvement

The civil or juvenile court hears the allegations of child maltreatment and decides if the child has been abused and/or neglected. The court then de-

FIGURE 3.3

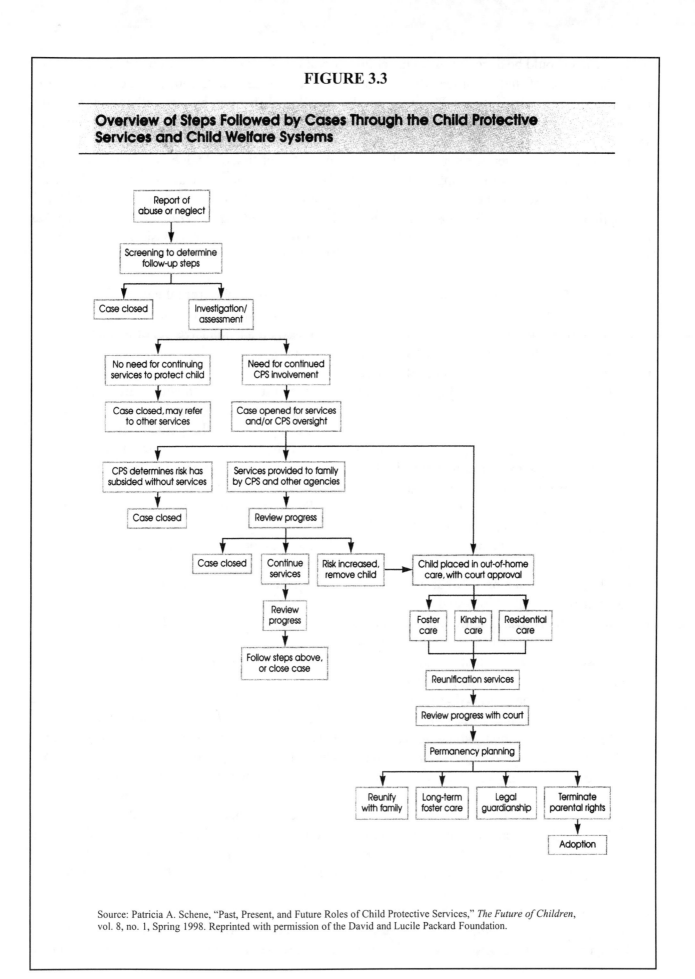

Overview of Steps Followed by Cases Through the Child Protective Services and Child Welfare Systems

Report of abuse or neglect

Screening to determine follow-up steps

Case closed

Investigation/ assessment

No need for continuing services to protect child

Need for continued CPS involvement

Case closed, may refer to other services

Case opened for services and/or CPS oversight

CPS determines risk has subsided without services

Services provided to family by CPS and other agencies

Case closed

Review progress

Case closed

Continue services

Risk increased, remove child

Child placed in out-of-home care, with court approval

Review progress

Foster care

Kinship care

Residential care

Follow steps above, or close case

Reunification services

Review progress with court

Permanency planning

Reunify with family

Long-term foster care

Legal guardianship

Terminate parental rights

Adoption

Source: Patricia A. Schene, "Past, Present, and Future Roles of Child Protective Services," *The Future of Children*, vol. 8, no. 1, Spring 1998. Reprinted with permission of the David and Lucile Packard Foundation.

termines what should be done to protect the child. The child may be left in the home with his or her parents under the supervision of CPS, or the child may be placed in a foster home. If the child is removed from the home and it is later determined that the child should never be returned to the parents, the court can begin proceedings to terminate the parental rights so that the child can be put up for adoption. The state may also prosecute the abusive parent or caretaker when a crime has been allegedly committed.

Family Preservation

Critics frequently charge that CPS too often returns children to homes where their lives are at risk. The Adoption Assistance and Child Welfare Act of 1980 (PL 96-272, Sec. 471a 15, p.503) required that

> In each case, reasonable efforts will be made (A) prior to the placement of a child in foster care, to prevent or eliminate the need for removal of the child from his home, and (B) to make it possible for the child to return to his home.

The law was a reaction to what was seen as over-zealousness in the 1960s and 1970s, when children, especially Black children, were taken from their homes because their parents were poor. Today, however, many agree that the circumstances have changed. They feel that the problems of drug or substance abuse can mean that returning the child to the home is a likely guarantee of further abuse. In addition, situations where, for example, there is a live-in partner who has no emotional attachment to the child may also present risks to the child.

Richard J. Gelles, co-director of the Family Research Laboratory of the University of New Hampshire, Durham, believes professionals were naive to think that a mother who hurts her child is similar to one who cannot keep house and that, with enough supervision, both can be turned into good parents. Once a vocal advocate of family pres-

ervation, Dr. Gelles had a change of heart after studying the case of 15-month-old David Edwards, who was suffocated by his mother after the child welfare system failed to rescue him from his abusive parent. Although David's parents had lost custody of their first child due to abuse, and although there were reports of David's abuse, CPS made "reasonable efforts" to let the parents keep David. In *The Book of David: How Preserving Families Can Cost Children's Lives* (BasicBooks, New York, 1996), Dr. Gelles stated,

> We must escape from the trap of the "one size fits all" theories and interventions based on an exclusive belief in social and environmental causes of abuse. We need to abandon the notion that one intervention or treatment can help "cure" all abusers, and recognize that in the most serious cases of abuse, the parents are probably constitutionally different from those who do not seriously abuse or kill their children.

> Reasonable efforts become unreasonable when they are applied to individuals or families for whom the services cannot work or who are simply not amenable to changing their dangerous and harmful behaviors.

A System Under Siege

Increased Caseloads

The U.S. Government Accounting Office (GAO), in *Child Protective Services: Complex Challenges Require New Strategies* (Washington, DC, July 1997), concluded that the CPS system is in crisis. Reports of child maltreatment continue to rise, resulting in heavier caseloads for CPS workers. The increasing number of maltreatment reports is due in part to child abuse by drug-dependent parents and caretakers, the mandatory reporting by certain professionals, and the stresses of poverty among families.

The GAO cited the U.S. Advisory Board on Child Abuse and Neglect finding, which revealed that, for several years, CPS caseworkers have been besieged with severe problems in dealing with the increasing reports of child maltreatment. According to the Advisory Board,

> In many jurisdictions, caseloads are so high that CPS response is limited to taking the complaint call, making a single visit to the home, and deciding whether or not the complaint is valid, often without any subsequent monitoring of the family.

Problem of Substance Abuse

Substance abuse by the parent or caretaker has been associated with child maltreatment. The National Committee to Prevent Child Abuse, in *Current Trends in Child Abuse Reporting and Fatalities: The Results of the 1997 Annual Fifty State Survey* (Chicago, Illinois, 1998), asked the state liaisons for child maltreatment about the major problems they encountered in their caseloads. Of the 41 states that responded, 36 states (88 percent) cited substance abuse as one of the two major problems of abusive families, up 12 percentage points from 1996.

According to the U.S. Department of Health and Human Services, the number of CPS cases that involve substance abuse can run anywhere from 20 to 90 percent, depending on the area of the country. The National Institute for Mental Health's Epidemiologic Catchment Area survey found that substance-abusing parents are 2.9 times more likely to abuse and 3.24 times more likely to neglect their children than non-substance abusers.

Many children experience neglect when their parent is under the influence of alcohol or is out of the home looking for drugs. Even when the parent is at home, he or she may be psychologically unavailable to the children. (See Neglect in Chapters II and V.) The growing number of women who abuse drugs has not only resulted in many infants being exposed to illegal substances before birth (see Chapter VII), but has further contributed to the rising incidence of child maltreatment.

Weaknesses in the System

CPS agencies are continually plagued by weaknesses in the system. The tasks of protecting children from maltreatment can be quite complex. CPS agencies often have difficulties attracting and retaining qualified caseworkers. The low pay not only makes it difficult to attract qualified workers but also contributes to employees leaving for better-paying jobs. In some jurisdictions, due to deficient hiring policies, employees have college degrees that may not necessarily be related to social work. In addition, limited funds preclude sufficient in-service training needed to help workers keep abreast of the changing environments in which child maltreatment occurs.

Some jurisdictions maintain automated data for federal and state reporting purposes. Unfortunately, caseworkers find that these data do not help in their day-to-day management of cases. Many workers rely on paper files, which may be misfiled or lost. Retrieving previous information on repeat cases can be time-consuming and sometimes impossible. In addition, supervisors have difficulty monitoring cases that may be handwritten on 5"-by-8" cards that may not be accessible when needed. Currently, some state programs are undergoing computerization designed to provide more systematic case management.

The increasing number of reported child maltreatment cases has also strained the court system. The overcrowded court schedules, judges who may be ignorant of child welfare laws, and overworked lawyers, among other factors, have made the CPS worker's job even harder. The inefficient system of scheduling cases may result in caseworkers spending long hours in court when they could be performing other tasks.

Lives Saved

Although CPS agencies have had many problems and are often unable to perform as effectively as they should, many thousands of maltreated children have been identified, many lives have been saved, and many more have been taken out of dangerous environments. It is impossible to tally the number of child abuse cases that might have ended in death. These children have been saved by changes in the laws, by awareness and reporting, and by the efforts of the professionals who intervened in their lives.

REFORM OF THE REPORTING AND INVESTIGATING PROCESS

Over the years, child advocates and critics of CPS have called for the reform of child maltreatment reporting and investigation procedures. The Harvard Executive Session was the most recent group to suggest a new model for child protection. Jane Waldfogel, in "Rethinking the Paradigm (model) for Child Protection" (*The Future of Children: Protecting Children from Abuse and Neglect*, vol. 8, no. 1, Spring 1998), described the proposal by this task force of child welfare administrators, practitioners, policymakers, and experts.

The Harvard model of child protection calls for a sharing of responsibilities between CPS and the community. CPS will respond to cases involving higher-risk cases of maltreatment, while other public or private agencies in the community will respond to lower-risk cases. "This would help ensure that the system acts aggressively to protect children at high risk, while not intervening coercively with families at lower risk."

The Harvard model also stressed the importance of recruiting "informal helpers" to support at-risk families. The task force felt that, since abusive or neglectful parents may have been child maltreatment victims themselves, the extended family members may not be ideal protectors for the children. In addition, there may be few social supports within poor neighborhoods for at-risk children. The larger community can provide the support and protection these children need.

Preventing Inappropriate Reporting

Douglas J. Besharov, first director of the U.S. National Center on Child Abuse and Neglect and currently a member of New York City's Child Fatality Review Panel, believes that "abused and neglected children are dying, both because they are not being reported to the authorities and because the authorities are being overwhelmed by the need to investigate inappropriate reports." In "Four Commentaries: How We Can Better Protect Children from Abuse and Neglect" (*The Future of Children: Protecting Children from Abuse and Neglect*, vol. 8, no.1, Spring 1998), Besharov suggested various steps to overhaul the child protection system:

- Rewrite child maltreatment laws to clarify the reportable parental behaviors that put children at risk of abuse and neglect.

- Provide comprehensive continuing public education and training concerning conditions that warrant reporting as well as those that do not.

- Put in place policies and procedures for screening reports of maltreatment.

- Modify liability laws to address "good-faith" reporters as well as those who have failed to report what may later turn out to be actual child maltreatment.

- Let reporters know the outcome of their personal involvement, which in a later situation may help them assess the presence of maltreatment.

- Set up formal reporting policies for such public and private agencies as schools and child care centers.

Public Involvement in Preventing Child Maltreatment

The National Committee to Prevent Child Abuse national survey, *Public Opinion and Behaviors Regarding Child Abuse Prevention: 1998 Survey* (Dr. Deborah Daro, Chicago, Illinois, 1998), found that nearly three-quarters (73 percent) of all parents with children under age 18 living at home felt they could do a lot or something to prevent

TABLE 3.4

Public Perception of How Much They Can Do To Prevent Child Abuse
(In Percentages)

	1998	1997	1996	1995	1994	1993	1992	1991	1990	1989	1988	1987
PARENTS	%	%	%	%	%	%	%	%	%	%	%	%
A lot/some	73	70	73	68	68	71	77	68	68	77	80	76
Only a little	18	22	19	21	21	20	17	24	22	18	14	19
Nothing	5	6	4	6	6	7	4	6	6	4	4	4
n =	433	470	445	470	474	468	445	480	460	513	490	500
NON-PARENTS	%	%	%	%	%	%	%	%	%	%	%	%
A lot	54	59	55	52	55	56	57	51	52	54	55	55
Only a little	30	25	28	30	28	26	29	31	31	26	30	25
Nothing	11	12	13	14	13	15	11	14	12	14	10	13
n =	817	781	829	793	776	782	809	770	790	737	760	750
FULL SAMPLE	%	%	%	%	%	%	%	%	%	%	%	%
A lot	61	63	61	58	61	61	64	57	58	63	66	66
Only a little	26	24	25	27	26	24	25	28	27	22	24	24
Nothing	9	9	10	11	10	12	9	11	10	10	8	8
n =	1250	1253	1274	1263	1250	1250	1254	1250	1250	1250	1250	1250

Source: Deborah Daro, *Public Opinion and Behaviors Regarding Child Abuse Prevention: 1998 Survey*. Reprinted with permission from the National Committee to Prevent Child Abuse, Chicago, IL, 1998.

child abuse, compared to just over half (54 percent) of individuals with no children living at home (Table 3.4).

The survey also found that the public behavior towards helping prevent child abuse has remained unchanged during the past 12 years. In 1998, overall, just a quarter (25 percent) of the general public indicated they took personal action to prevent child abuse. Parents (36 percent) with children under age 18 living at home were more likely than non-parents (19 percent) were to be personally involved with child abuse prevention. (See Table 3.5.)

VAGUE LAWS

Child maltreatment laws, in their effort to reach all abused and neglected children, are purposely vague. A child can be taken from the parents and put in foster care if the child's "condition or environment is such as to warrant the state, in the interests of the child, in assuming his guardianship" (Ohio) or if the parent "does not provide the proper or necessary support ... for a child's well-being" (Illinois).

The distinction between poverty and neglect is sometimes blurred. Many of the states' definitions can fit any of several situations. For example, the Connecticut maltreatment law, which defines a maltreated child as one who "is being permitted to live under conditions, circumstances, or associations injurious to his well-being" can fit many inner-city ghetto children if CPS chooses to apply the definition.

TABLE 3.5

Took Personal Action to Prevent Child Abuse
(Percentage responding yes)

	1998	1997	1996	1995	1994	1993	1992	1991	1990	1989	1988	1987
	%	%	%	%	%	%	%	%	%	%	%	%
PARENTS	36	36	38	34	36	35	37	37	32	39	35	32
NON-PARENTS	19	20	21	18	21	20	20	20	17	15	18	17
FULL SAMPLE	25	26	27	24	27	25	26	27	23	25	25	23
n =	1250	1253	1274	1263	1250	1250	1254	1250	1250	1250	1250	1250

Source: Deborah Daro, *Public Opinion and Behaviors Regarding Child Abuse Prevention: 1998 Survey*. Reprinted with permission from the National Committee to Prevent Child Abuse, Chicago, IL, 1998.

IMPROPER ACCUSATION

Although people are outraged by stories about horribly abused and/or neglected children missed by the authorities, there is also a backlash movement against the intrusiveness of CPS and wrongs committed when parents are unjustly accused of abuse. Some parents claim they keep their children home from school if they have a bruise for fear the teacher will report the parents and have them investigated for abuse.

In *Wounded Innocents: The Real Victims of the War Against Child Abuse* (Prometheus Books, Buffalo, New York, 1995), Richard Wexler wrote that after a teacher in Waukeegan, Illinois, was charged with sexual abuse and sued by two parents, the Chicago Teachers' Union provided "self-defense" guidelines to its teachers. Educators were told to use public areas when holding conferences with students and to "use discretion when touching children for purposes of praise, reward, or comfort."

Wexler, a former newsman who covered child abuse and foster care, also noted that the panic created by unwarranted accusations is driving away the relatively few men who might be willing to work in day care centers. Some day care centers preferred not to hire men at all. He added, "Even some fathers have become more hesitant to show normal affection, especially divorced fathers taking their children on visits."

Other critics of the CPS system point out that large proportions of reports to CPS are not substantiated. For example, the U.S. Department of Health and Human Services survey, *Child Maltreatment 1996: Reports from the States to the National Child Abuse and Neglect Data System* (Washington, DC, 1998) reported that 57.7 percent of the reports were not substantiated. (See Figure 4.1 in Chapter IV.)

Hotlines for reporting abuse and neglect accept all calls, even when the reporter cannot give a reason why he or she thinks the child is being maltreated. In addition, CPS is called to handle cases that previously would have been handled by other agencies, but cutbacks in funding have pushed problems of poverty, homelessness, truancy, and delinquency on CPS because it is known as a social agency that will at least investigate the problem.

It is also important to remember that just because a report has not been substantiated does not mean that the child is not at risk, only that CPS either could not determine that the child was suffering from maltreatment or chose not to pursue the case. (See Chapter IV for a more complete discussion of substantiation.)

Overreporting Needs to Be Controlled

Richard Wexler (*Wounded Innocents*, see above) claimed that one reason the number of abuse reports is deceptive is that in the majority of reports, the children have not been maltreated at all. He explained that reports of child maltreatment are sometimes made when a parent is guilty of nothing more than poverty. For example, child abuse was reported in the following cases:

- A woman's home was in disrepair.

- A man could not pay his utility bill.

- A woman could not afford to buy a pair of eyeglasses for her child.

- A woman was kicked out of two apartments because of "no children allowed" rules.

The Problem Is Underreporting

David Finkelhor and Donileen Loseke, in "The Main Problem Is Still Underreporting, Not Overreporting" (*Current Controversies on Family Violence*, SAGE Publications, Newbury Park, 1993), asserted that the problem is underreporting, not overreporting. One proof they offered to show that a great deal of abuse is still being missed is that, when adults are asked whether they were abused as children, the percentages are far higher than the number of children who are reported each year. If, for example, 15 percent of women and 5 percent of men were sexually abused in childhood (a low estimate according to some experts), this would translate to yearly rates of child abuse two to three times higher than the rates reported today. (See Chapter VI for more on rates of sexual abuse.)

Finkelhor and Loseke also rejected claims that many reports of abuse are "minor situations." They offered examples of cases that they said would be dismissed by critics but which they insisted are part of the crucial effort to discover an abusive situation before serious injury occurs. These include situations such as emotional abuse, when a child is locked in a room or threatened with death; physical neglect, when a parent leaves young children alone but who are rescued before they suffer any harm; or physical abuse, such as when a child is shot at but missed.

In defense of CPS investigations of what may turn out to be an unfounded case of child maltreatment, the authors compared the investigation process to the criminal justice system in which only about 55 percent of the persons arrested are ever convicted. (A difference Finkelhor and Loseke ignored is that the perpetrator of a crime is often unknown, while the child abuser can nearly always be identified.) They believed that Americans tolerate inefficiencies in the criminal justice system that are remarkably similar to the deficiencies in the child protective system — charges that cannot be proven, technicalities that prevent prosecution, and overworked investigators.

Furthermore, according to the authors, Americans accept the intrusions of tax audits and airline security measures because the overall goals of catching tax evaders and ensuring airline safety outweigh the inconveniences. If Americans can live with these systems, they surely can accept an occasional false accusation for the benefit of saving children.

Harassment

Small proportions of reports are false or ill-considered, either because the reporter was in er-

ror or because the reporter was deliberately lying to get the alleged abuser in trouble. Sexual abuse is the most common form of false accusation because it is such a heinous crime and does not require physical evidence.

False, vindictive reports are sometimes made anonymously to CPS to harass parents. Richard Wexler (*Wounded Innocents*, see above) reported how in one case, social workers demanded entry to a woman's house more than five times in a two-year period. They ordered her to wake up her sleeping children and strip them naked while social workers examined them for signs of abuse. All of the reports turned out to be false, but the caller, whose anonymity was protected by the law, could start the process again with a simple phone call.

IS THERE BIAS IN REPORTING?

Some critics claim that reporting of child abuse and neglect is biased against parents and caretakers in the lower socioeconomic classes. Brett Drake and Susan Zuravin, in "Bias in Child Maltreatment Reporting: Revisiting the Myth of Classlessness" (*American Journal of Orthopsychiatry*, 68 [2], April 1998), discussed four forms of potential bias that may be responsible for the overrepresentation of child maltreatment among the poor in CPS caseloads.

Visibility bias, also called "exposure bias," is the belief that poor families, who are more likely to use such public services as welfare agencies and public hospitals, tend to be noticed by potential reporters. The researchers reported that, to date, no scientific studies have ever been done to investigate the visibility bias theory.

Drake and Zuravin surmised that if the visibility bias does exist, it will follow that mandated reporters who have more contact with the poor will file more reports of abuse among poor children. They studied six Missouri sites with the lowest percentage of families living below the poverty line. When they compared the mandated reports about child maltreatment among upper middle-class suburban families (44.4 percent) and among inner-city poor families (49.2 percent), they did not find a large overrepresentation of the poor.

The researchers also noted that mandated reporters (for example, law enforcement, medical, and social services personnel), who are more likely to come in contact with a larger proportion of poor families than with non-poor families, accounted for one-third of all referrals. This proportion could not possibly be responsible for the overrepresentation of maltreatment reports of poor families.

Labeling bias refers to the predisposition to look for and find maltreatment among certain groups of individuals. Review of empirical studies showed no such bias exists among mandated reporters. Drake and Zuravin found, in one study, that Head Start personnel were not likely to look for signs of maltreatment among the children in their care just because they were from a lower socioeconomic status.

Reporting bias implies a person's failure to report what he or she suspects to be child maltreatment among certain groups. In the late 1970s and early 1980s, studies found that professionals were very likely not to report child maltreatment among the higher-income families. The authors have found that, currently, mandated professionals are more likely to report maltreatment because of the legal ramifications associated with failure to comply with child maltreatment laws. Hence, the reporting bias theory does not hold true.

Substantiation bias describes any tendency on the part of CPS investigators to base substantiation conclusions on such factors as a family's socioeconomic status. Empirical studies show that this is not the case.

The researchers concluded that, although a large percentage of child abuse and neglect occurs among the poor, empirical studies have shown that this overrepresentation is not a result of reporting biases. Finally, they suggested,

If child maltreatment is born largely of the stresses and wants associated with being poor, then primary intervention efforts might best target the underlying political, social, and economic structures that perpetuate poverty.

ABUSE IN FOSTER HOMES

Many foster parents develop a nurturing, loving relationship with the children left in their care and spend a great deal of time and their own money trying to help the children; some foster parents legally adopt the children. While there are many success stories in the foster care system, there are, unfortunately, many failures as well. Because there are far more foster children than foster parents, children are often placed with adults who have had little training or background investigation. Few studies have been conducted to determine the rates of abuse in foster homes. The number of children living in foster homes is unclear. Many foster children live in numerous foster homes, sometimes over a period of just a few months.

One of the most comprehensive studies of foster care abuse was conducted in the late 1980s by Trudy Festinger, chairwoman of the Department of Research at New York University School of Social Work. She and a team of researchers reviewed the case histories of 149 foster children from Baltimore, Maryland, and found that 42 of the children (28 percent) had been abused in foster care.

In addition, the average foster child in Baltimore had at least a better than one-in-four chance of being abused each time he or she was placed; 35 percent of the foster children were placed at least four times. "Foster care is like Russian roulette," said a former CPS worker from New York City. "The [foster] home could be 100 percent worse than where they are."

Abuse of Gay Youth in Foster Care

On January 15, 1999, a federal class-action suit, the first of its kind in the United States, was filed against the New York City child welfare system. The Urban Justice Center, an advocacy group for the homeless, and a private law firm brought the lawsuit before the U.S. District Court in Manhattan. The lawsuit charged that, because of their sexual orientation, gay, lesbian, and bisexual youths are subjected to abuses in foster care. The abusive acts included harassment, psychological abuse, physical violence, and rape by other residents in foster care. The suit also charged that staff members not only failed to protect the children from the abuse but also themselves inflicted psychological abuse through threats and humiliating comments.

An Urban Justice Center lawyer noted that research indicates gay and lesbian children are overrepresented in foster care because they are more likely to be rejected by their families. Gay and lesbian adolescents are two to three times more likely than heterosexual adolescents to attempt suicide, making suicide the leading cause of death among these young people. A large number also become runaways. Nationwide, only two foster programs exist for gay and lesbian children — one in New York City and the other in Los Angeles. These programs are able to serve only a small number of older teenagers.

Not Enough Foster Homes

The number of available foster homes has been declining. This decline has been attributed to a number of factors — the growing number of women working outside the home, the rise in single-parent households, and the increasing divorce rates.

Patrick T. Murphy, in *Wasted: The Plight of America's Unwanted Children* (Ivan R. Dee, Inc., Chicago, Illinois, 1997), claims that there are available foster homes, but some social workers are "prevent[ing] the neediest children from being united with a potential pool of foster and adoptive parents. The foster and adoptive parents are white, and the kids needing services are black." Since the 1960s, Murphy, a Public Guardian ("an office unique in the United States") of Cook County, Illinois, has been representing abused and neglected children in court, including the U.S. Supreme Court.

Murphy noted that, while poverty and substance abuse have led to a growing number of Black children being removed from their homes and needing placement in foster homes, the proportion of Blacks in the population has generally remained constant. Currently, 88 percent of the 40,000 children in the Cook County Department of Children and Family Services are Black, although only a third of the county residents are Black.

Some caseworkers believe that it is in the best interests of a Black child to be placed with a Black family, and they have been known to discourage interested White prospective parents. Despite the amendment to the Multiethnic Placement Act of 1994 (PL 103-382), which requires that the adoption process be free from discrimination and delays based on the race, culture and ethnicity of the child or the prospective parents, some caseworkers have found a loophole in the law that allows exceptions where the best interests of the child should be served first.

CHAPTER IV

HOW MANY CHILDREN ARE MALTREATED?

Statistics on child abuse are difficult to interpret and compare because there is very little consistency in how information is collected. The definitions of abuse vary from study to study, as do the methods of counting incidents of abuse. Some methods count only the number of reported cases of abuse. Some statistics are based on estimates projected from a small study; others are based on interviews. In addition, it is virtually impossible to know what child maltreatment occurs in the privacy of the home.

PREVALENCE AND INCIDENCE OF CHILD MALTREATMENT

According to Diana J. English, in "The Extent and Consequences of Child Maltreatment" (*The Future of Children: Protecting Children From Abuse and Neglect*, Center for the Future of Children, Los Altos, California, vol. 8, no. 1, 1998), two terms are usually used to describe the estimates of the number of victims of child abuse and neglect.

- Prevalence — refers to the number of people who have had at least one experience of child maltreatment in their lifetime. These experiences may or may not have been reported to child protective services (CPS) agencies, which receive and respond to reports of maltreatment.

- Incidence — refers to the number of child abuse and neglect cases reported to CPS. The rate of incidence

includes only those cases reported and not the number of children who have actually been maltreated.

To measure the *prevalence* of child maltreatment, researchers use self-report surveys of parents and child victims. Examples of self-report surveys are the landmark 1975 and 1985 *National Family Violence Surveys* conducted by Murray A. Straus and Richard J. Gelles (see Chapter V).

Major sources of *incidence* of child maltreatment include surveys based on official reports of child maltreatment by CPS and by community professionals. Private national organizations, such as the National Committee to Prevent Child Abuse (NCPCA), also collect and analyze incidence rates of child abuse and neglect (see below).

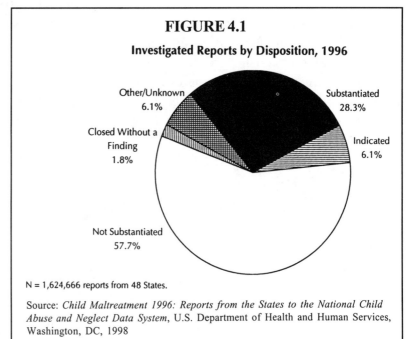

FIGURE 4.1

Investigated Reports by Disposition, 1996

Other/Unknown 6.1%
Substantiated 28.3%
Closed Without a Finding 1.8%
Indicated 6.1%
Not Substantiated 57.7%

N = 1,624,666 reports from 48 States.

Source: *Child Maltreatment 1996: Reports from the States to the National Child Abuse and Neglect Data System*, U.S. Department of Health and Human Services, Washington, DC, 1998

Official Reports

Studies based on official reports depend on a number of things happening before an incident of abuse can be recorded. The child abuse victim must be seen by people outside the home; these people must recognize that the child has been abused. Once they have recognized this fact, they must then decide whether to report the abuse and know to whom to report it. CPS receives the report, screens it for appropriateness, and then takes action.

Funding influences what cases are investigated and how broad the definition of abuse may be. In some cases, the initial call to CPS is prompted by a problem that actually needs to be handled by a different agency. It may be a case of neglect due to poverty rather than abuse, although the initial report is still recorded as abuse.

For the data to become publicly available, CPS must keep records on its cases and then pass them on to a national group that collects those statistics. Consequently, final reported statistics are understated estimates, valuable as indicators but not definitive findings. It is very unlikely that accurate statistics on child abuse will ever be available.

SOURCES OF REPORTS

The 1974 Child Abuse Prevention and Treatment Act (CAPTA; PL 93-247) created the National Center on Child Abuse and Neglect (NCCAN) to coordinate the nationwide efforts to protect children from abuse and neglect (see Chapter II). As part of the former U.S. Department of Health, Education, and Welfare, NCCAN commissioned the American Humane Association (AHA) to collect data from the states. In 1976, the first time the AHA collected data,

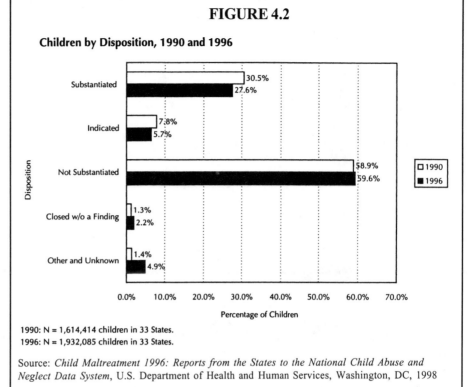

FIGURE 4.2

Children by Disposition, 1990 and 1996

1990: N = 1,614,414 children in 33 States.
1996: N = 1,932,085 children in 33 States.

Source: *Child Maltreatment 1996: Reports from the States to the National Child Abuse and Neglect Data System*, U.S. Department of Health and Human Services, Washington, DC, 1998

it recorded approximately 669,000 reports of child maltreatment. Between 1980 and 1985, the AHA reported a 12 percent annual increase in maltreatment reports to CPS agencies.

In 1985, the federal government stopped funding data collection of child maltreatment. In 1986, the National Committee to Prevent Child Abuse (NCPCA), a private organization dedicated to the prevention of all forms of child abuse, picked up where the government left off. The NCPCA started collecting detailed information from the states on "the number and characteristics of child abuse reports, the number of child abuse fatalities, and changes in the funding and scope of child welfare services." The NCPCA continues to conduct annual surveys of child maltreatment in each state and the District of Columbia (see below).

In 1988, the Child Abuse Prevention, Adoption, and Family Services Act (PL 100-294) replaced the 1974 CAPTA. The new law mandated that NCCAN, as part of the U.S. Department of Health and Human Services (HHS), establish a national data collection program on child maltreatment. In 1990, the National Child Abuse and Neglect Data System (NCANDS),

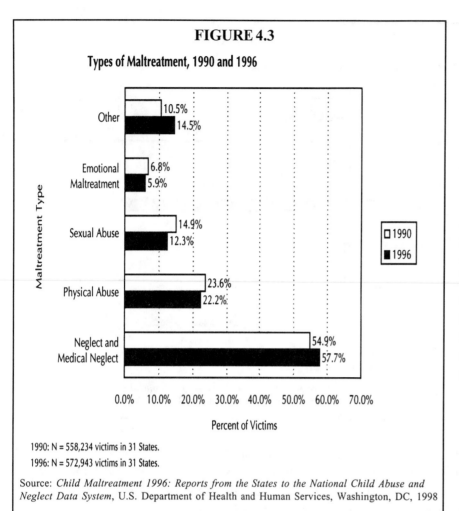

FIGURE 4.3

Types of Maltreatment, 1990 and 1996

1990: N = 558,234 victims in 31 States.

1996: N = 572,943 victims in 31 States.

Source: *Child Maltreatment 1996: Reports from the States to the National Child Abuse and Neglect Data System*, U.S. Department of Health and Human Services, Washington, DC, 1998

analyzes the characteristics of child abuse and neglect that are known to community-based professionals, including those not reported to CPS. (See below for the *Third National Incidence Study of Child Abuse and Neglect [NIS-3]*.)

In 1996, pursuant to the Child Abuse Prevention and Treatment Act Amendments (CAPTA; PL 104-23), NCCAN ceased operating as a separate agency. Since then, all child maltreatment prevention functions have been consolidated within the Children's Bureau of the HHS.

MALTREATMENT REPORTS TO CPS AGENCIES

Child Maltreatment 1996: Reports From the States to the National Child Abuse and Neglect Data System (Children's Bureau, HHS, Washington, DC, 1998) is the seventh consecutive survey conducted by NCANDS. It is the primary source of national information on the incidence of child maltreatment known to state CPS agencies.

designed to fulfill this mandate, began collecting and analyzing child maltreatment data from CPS agencies in the 50 states, the District of Columbia, the territories, and the Armed Services. The first three surveys were known as *Working Paper 1*, *Working Paper 2*, and *Child Maltreatment 1992*. *Child Maltreatment 1996* is the latest NCANDS survey (see below).

As part of the 1974 Child Abuse Prevention and Treatment Act, Congress also mandated NCCAN to conduct a periodic *National Incidence Study of Child Abuse and Neglect (NIS)*. Data on maltreated children were collected not only from CPS agencies but also from professionals in community agencies, such as law enforcement, public health, juvenile probation, hospitals, schools, day care, mental health, and voluntary social services. The *NIS* is the single most comprehensive source of information about the incidence of child maltreatment in the United States because it

Collecting child maltreatment data from the states is difficult because each state has its own method of gathering and classifying the information. Most states collect data on an incident basis; that is, they count each time a child is reported for abuse or neglect. If the same child is reported several times in one year, each incident is counted. Consequently, there may be more incidents of child maltreatment than the number of maltreated children.

Reports of Maltreated Children

In 1996, approximately 3 million children were reported as alleged victims of child abuse and neglect.

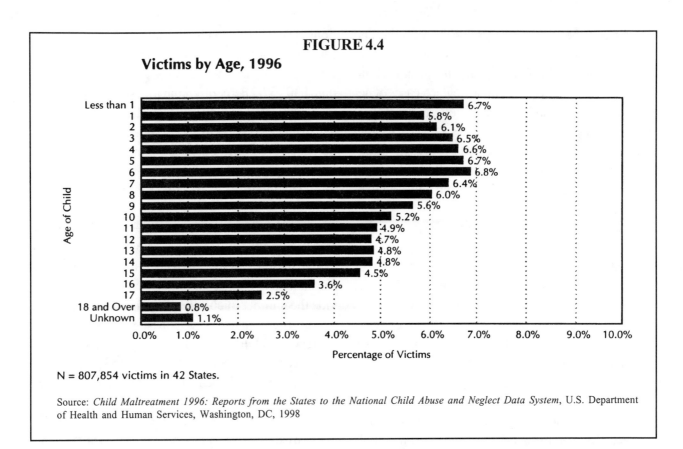

FIGURE 4.4

Victims by Age, 1996

N = 807,854 victims in 42 States.

Source: *Child Maltreatment 1996: Reports from the States to the National Child Abuse and Neglect Data System*, U.S. Department of Health and Human Services, Washington, DC, 1998

(As discussed above, some children may have been reported and counted more than once.) In 1996, the national rate of reported children younger than 18 years of age was 44 per 1,000 children, up from 41 per 1,000 children in 1990.

States may vary in the rates of child maltreatment reported. There are differences in the state definitions of maltreatment — for example, in 1996, Vermont's child abuse laws did not consider the lack of supervision of a child as neglect. State public agencies may

TABLE 4.1

Type of Maltreatment by Age of Victim, DCDC

Age Group	Type of Maltreatment					Totals
	Physical Abuse	Neglect	Medical Neglect	Sexual Abuse	Emotional Maltreatment	
0–3	12.010 (20.0%)	50.400 (33.7%)	5.339 (51.7%)	2.873 (10.3%)	1.644 (15.7%)	72.266 (28.0%)
4–7	15.454 (25.7%)	43.559 (29.2%)	2.169 (21.0%)	7.932 (28.4%)	2.710 (26.0%)	71.824 (27.8%)
8–11	13.681 (22.8%)	30.370 (20.3%)	1.501 (14.5%)	7.123 (25.5%)	2.905 (27.8%)	55.580 (21.5%)
12 and Over	18.960 (31.5%)	25.096 (16.8%)	1.313 (12.7%)	10.037 (35.9%)	3.182 (30.5%)	58.588 (22.7%)
Totals	60.105 (100.0%)	149.425 (100.0%)	10.322 (100.0%)	27.965 (100.0%)	10.441 (100.0%)	258.258 (100.0%)

Source: *Child Maltreatment 1996: Reports from the States to the National Child Abuse and Neglect Data System*, U.S. Department of Health and Human Services, Washington, DC, 1998

also differ in their policies regarding the receiving and investigating of reports — for instance, in 1996, Pennsylvania's child abuse registry did not collect statistics on cases involving general neglect; cases of neglect were processed through a general protective services agency. Although the states varied in the rate of children reported and referred for investigation, about two-thirds of the states reported a rate between 30 and 59 children per 1,000 children under age 18.

Dispositions of Investigated Reports

State CPS agencies have three main categories for investigation dispositions of child maltreatment.

- Substantiated or founded — means that the allegation of abuse is supported or founded on the basis of state law or policy.

- Indicated or reason to suspect — means that the abuse and/or neglect cannot be substantiated, but there is reason to suspect that the child was maltreated or was at risk of maltreatment.

- Not substantiated or unfounded — means there is insufficient evidence on the basis of state law to conclude that the child was maltreated.

Forty-eight states provided information on substantiated and unsubstantiated investigation dispositions. These states conducted about 1.6 million investigations of alleged maltreatment. In some cases, an investigation may include more than one child. More than half (57.7 percent) of the investigated reports of maltreatment were judged not substantiated, more than a quarter (28.3 percent) were substantiated, and 6.1 percent were indicated. (See Figure 4.1.)

Dispositions of Alleged Child Victims

In 1996, 43 states provided data on substantiated and unsubstantiated dispositions of children. Because of their practice of destroying records of unsubstantiated reports, some states were unable to provide the number of children for whom maltreatment was unsubstantiated. About one-third (34 percent) of the reported children were victims of substantiated or indicated maltreatment, and over half (59 percent) had investigations resulting in unsubstantiated dispositions.

Disposition data were available from 33 states for comparison of 1990 and 1996 victims. The percentage of children with substantiated dispositions declined from 30.5 percent in 1990 to 27.6 percent in 1996, and indicated dispositions decreased from 7.8 to 5.7 percent. On the other hand, unsubstantiated dispositions remained about the same at 58.9 percent in 1990 and 59.6 percent in 1996. (See Figure 4.2.) (Figures 4.1 and 4.2 differ because Figure 4.1 concerns reports and Figure 4.2 concerns the number of children.)

TABLE 4.2
Type of Maltreatment by Sex of Victim, DCDC

Sex	Type of Maltreatment					Totals
	Physical Abuse	Neglect	Medical Neglect	Sexual Abuse	Emotional Maltreatment	
Male	31,316 (51.6%)	76,955 (51.2%)	5,386 (52.0%)	6,454 (22.8%)	4,989 (47.0%)	125,100 (48.0%)
Female	29,367 (48.4%)	73,426 (48.8%)	4,975 (48.0%)	21,867 (77.2%)	5,622 (53.0%)	135,257 (52.0%)
Totals	60,683 (100.0%)	150,381 (100.0%)	10,361 (100.0%)	28,321 (100.0%)	10,611 (100.0%)	260,357 (100.0%)

Source: *Child Maltreatment 1996: Reports from the States to the National Child Abuse and Neglect Data System*, U.S. Department of Health and Human Services, Washington, DC, 1998

Types of Maltreatment

In 1996, 48 states reported on the types of maltreatment suffered by 968,748 children. More than half (52 percent) suffered neglect. Nearly a quarter (24 percent) were physically abused, and 12 percent were sexually molested. About 6 percent were subjected to emotional maltreatment, and 3 percent, to medical neglect. Approximately 16 percent suffered "other" types of maltreatment, including abandonment, congenital drug addiction, and threats to harm a child. Some victims suffered more than one type of maltreatment.

Data from 31 states were used to compare types of maltreatment suffered by children in 1990 and 1996. Between 1990 and 1996, the proportion of victims who suffered neglect and medical neglect rose by almost 3 percentage points (from 54.9 percent in 1990 to 57.7 percent in 1996), and that of victims of "other" types of maltreatment (see above) increased by 4 percentage points (from 10.5 to 14.5 percent). On the other hand, the proportion of children emotionally, physically, and sexually abused declined slightly. (See Figure 4.3.)

Characteristics of Abused Children

Age

In 1996, younger children accounted for most maltreated children. As the children got older, they made up a smaller and smaller proportion of victims — those 18 and over comprised just 0.8 percent of all maltreated children. (See Figure 4.4.)

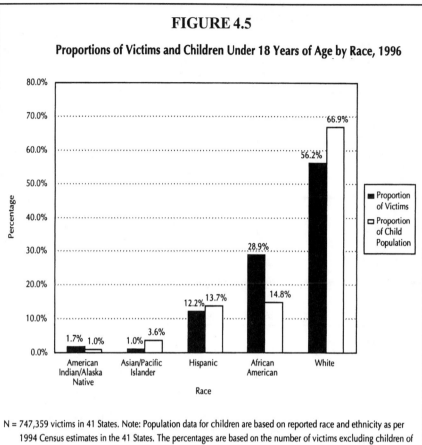

FIGURE 4.5

Proportions of Victims and Children Under 18 Years of Age by Race, 1996

N = 747,359 victims in 41 States. Note: Population data for children are based on reported race and ethnicity as per 1994 Census estimates in the 41 States. The percentages are based on the number of victims excluding children of "Other" or "Unknown" race.

Source: *Child Maltreatment 1996: Reports from the States to the National Child Abuse and Neglect Data System*, U.S. Department of Health and Human Services, Washington, DC, 1998

TABLE 4.3

Type of Maltreatment by Race/Ethnicity of Victim, DCDC

Race/Ethnicity	Type of Maltreatment					Totals
	Physical Abuse	Neglect	Medical Neglect	Sexual Abuse	Emotional Maltreatment	
White	33,181 (56.1%)	76,967 (52.3%)	4,224 (41.3%)	17,978 (64.8%)	7,130 (68.9%)	139,480 (54.8%)
African American	16,406 (27.7%)	50,401 (34.3%)	4,509 (44.0%)	5,339 (19.2%)	1,684 (16.3%)	78,339 (30.8%)
Hispanic	8,053 (13.6%)	16,447 (11.2%)	1,299 (12.7%)	3,901 (14.1%)	1,265 (12.2%)	30,965 (12.2%)
American Indian/Alaska Native	670 (1.1%)	2,018 (1.4%)	145 (1.4%)	349 (1.3%)	167 (1.6%)	3,349 (1.3%)
Asian/Pacific Islander	842 (1.4%)	1,275 (0.9%)	61 (0.6%)	198 (0.7%)	104 (1.0%)	2,480 (1.0%)
Totals	59,152 (100.0%)	147,108 (100.0%)	10,238 (100.0%)	27,765 (100.0%)	10,350 (100.0%)	254,613 (100.0%)

Source: *Child Maltreatment 1996: Reports from the States to the National Child Abuse and Neglect Data System*, U.S. Department of Health and Human Services, Washington, DC, 1998

TABLE 4.4

Perpetrators by Sex and Age, DCDC

Age Group	Sex Male	Sex Female	Totals
19 and Younger	5,727 (10.4%)	6,205 (7.2%)	11,932 (8.5%)
20–29	13,468 (24.5%)	33,464 (39.0%)	46,932 (33.3%)
30–39	21,241 (38.6%)	33,516 (39.1%)	54,757 (38.9%)
40–49	9,984 (18.2%)	8,885 (10.4%)	18,869 (13.4%)
50 and Older	4,586 (8.3%)	3,681 (4.3%)	8,267 (5.9%)
Totals	55,006 (100.0%)	85,751 (100.0%)	140,757 (100.0%)

Source: *Child Maltreatment 1996: Reports from the States to the National Child Abuse and Neglect Data System*, U.S. Department of Health and Human Services, Washington, DC, 1998

The Detailed Case Data Component (DCDC) of the NCANDS provided more detailed case-level information on each victim.

DCDC information collected from 11 states (in which the total child population made up about one-third of the total U.S. population under 18) showed that the type of maltreatment was generally associated with the child's age. The proportion of children who suffered neglect and medical neglect decreased with age — while over half (51.7 percent) of medical neglect victims were younger than four, only 12.7 percent were children age 12 and older. In contrast, the percentage of children who were physically, sexually, and emotionally abused increased with age — for example, while 10.3 percent of sexual abuse victims were younger than four years, 35.9 percent were age 12 and older. (See Table 4.1.)

Gender

The child victims of abuse were nearly equally divided between males (48 percent) and females (52 percent), although girls made up 77.2 percent of sexual abuse victims, compared to 22.8 percent of boys. (See Table 4.2.)

Race and Ethnicity

More than half (53 percent) of the victims were White; one-quarter (27 percent), Black; and 11 percent, Hispanic. American Indians/Alaska Natives comprised 2 percent of victims, and Asians accounted for 1 percent.

Based on their proportions in the total child population, Black and American Indian/Alaska Native children were twice as likely to be victimized as Whites, Hispanics, and Asians/Pacific Islanders. (See Figure 4.5.)

Children of different races suffered different types of maltreatment. Overall, White children made up over half (54.8 percent) of all maltreatment victims. White

TABLE 4.5
Type of Maltreatment by Sex of Perpetrator, DCDC

Sex	Maltreatment Type Physical Abuse	Neglect	Medical Neglect	Sexual Abuse	Emotional Maltreatment	Totals
Male	17,590 (44.7%)	20,617 (28.1%)	1,893 (21.7%)	16,448 (71.5%)	2,586 (43.0%)	59,134 (39.3%)
Female	21,757 (55.3%)	52,675 (71.9%)	6,818 (78.3%)	6,571 (28.5%)	3,429 (57.0%)	91,250 (60.7%)
Totals	39,347 (100.0%)	73,292 (100.0%)	8,711 (100.0%)	23,019 (100.0%)	6,015 (100.0%)	150,384 (100.0%)

Source: *Child Maltreatment 1996: Reports from the States to the National Child Abuse and Neglect Data System*, U.S. Department of Health and Human Services, Washington, DC, 1998

TABLE 4.6
Child Fatality Victims by Sex and Age, DCDC

Age Group	Child Sex		Totals
	Male	Female	
0–3	128 (74.4%)	106 (78.5%)	234 (76.2%)
4–7	23 (13.4%)	21 (15.6%)	44 (14.3%)
8–11	15 (8.7%)	4 (3.0%)	19 (6.2%)
12 and Over	6 (3.5%)	4 (3.0%)	10 (3.3%)
Totals	172 (100.0%)	135 (100.0%)	307 (100.0%)

Source: *Child Maltreatment 1996: Reports from the States to the National Child Abuse and Neglect Data System*, U.S. Department of Health and Human Services, Washington, DC, 1998

children were also about two-thirds of all victims of sexual abuse (64.8 percent) and of emotional maltreatment (68.9 percent). Black children comprised nearly a third (30.8 percent) of all maltreatment victims, accounting for a smaller percentage of sexual abuse (19.2 percent) and emotional maltreatment (16.3 percent) victims. However, Black children made up nearly half (44 percent) of medical neglect victims. (See Table 4.3.)

Perpetrators

In 1996, 43 states reported that 77 percent of perpetrators were parents, while other relatives of the victims accounted for another 11 percent. Caretakers, such as foster parents, child care providers, and facility staff, made up 2 percent of perpetrators.

About 4 of 5 perpetrators (80.7 percent) were under age 40. Perpetrators were more likely to be 20 to 29 years old (33.3 percent) and 30 to 39 years old (38.9 percent) and female (60.9 percent). (See Table 4.4.) While about three-quarters of neglect and medical neglect were committed by female perpetrators, nearly three-quarters of sexual abuse were committed by male perpetrators (Table 4.5).

Fatalities

In 1996, 41 states reported a total of 971 deaths from abuse and neglect. The estimated total count for the 50 states and the District of Columbia was closer to 1,100. There were likely more deaths due to abuse than were reported to CPS agencies.

TABLE 4.7

	1988	1989	1990	1991	1992	1993	1994	1995	1996	1997
Estimated Number of Children Reported for maltreatment	2,265,000	2,435,000	2,559,000	2,684,000	2,909,000	2,967,000	3,074,000	3,126,000	3,142,000	3,195,000
Per 1,000 U.S. Child	35	38	40	42	45	45	46	46	46	47

	1993	1994	1995	1996	1997
Average Indicated/ Substantiated Rate	34%	33%	33%	32%	33%
Est. # of children confirmed as victims of maltreatment	1,009,000	1,014,000	1,032,000	1,005,000	1,054,000
Per 1,000 U.S. Children	15	15	15	15	15

Source: Ching-Tung Wang and Deborah Daro, *Current Trends in Child Abuse Reporting and Fatalities: The Results of the 1997 Annual Fifty State Survey.* Reprinted with permission from the National Committee to Prevent Child Abuse, Chicago, IL, 1998.

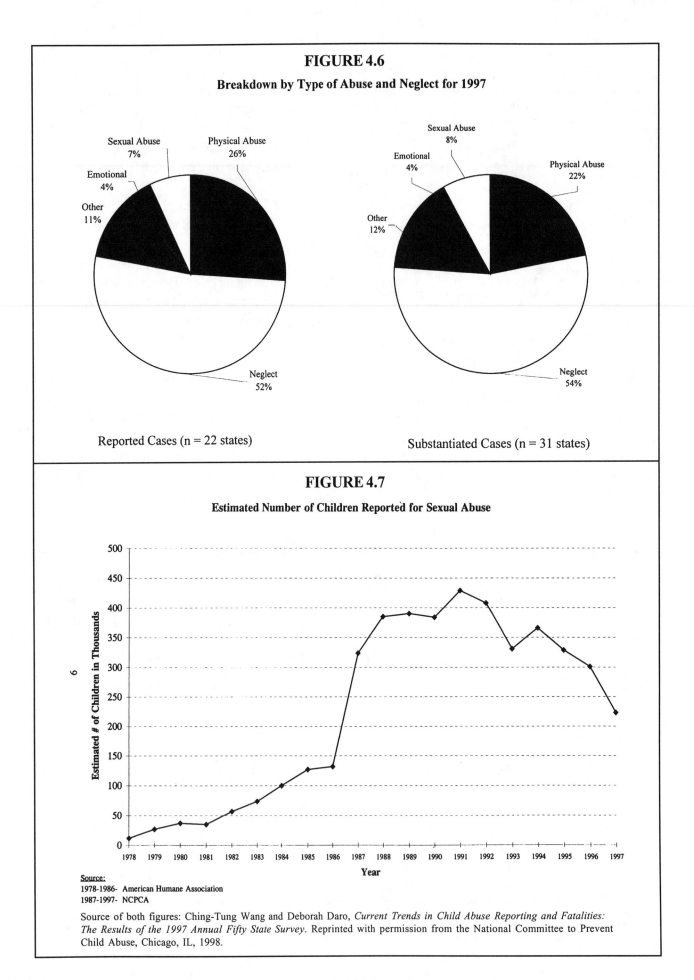

FIGURE 4.6

Breakdown by Type of Abuse and Neglect for 1997

Reported Cases (n = 22 states)

Substantiated Cases (n = 31 states)

FIGURE 4.7

Estimated Number of Children Reported for Sexual Abuse

Source:
1978-1986- American Humane Association
1987-1997- NCPCA

Source of both figures: Ching-Tung Wang and Deborah Daro, *Current Trends in Child Abuse Reporting and Fatalities: The Results of the 1997 Annual Fifty State Survey*. Reprinted with permission from the National Committee to Prevent Child Abuse, Chicago, IL, 1998.

Fatality data from 40 states that reported child maltreatment in both 1990 and 1996 were compared. In 1990, there were 1.9 deaths per 100,000 children, compared to 1.6 deaths per 100,000 children under age 18 in 1996. Deaths occurred mostly among very young victims of abuse and neglect. Children under four accounted for three-quarters (76.2 percent) of all deaths. (See Table 4.6.)

TABLE 4.8

Breakdown of Child Maltreatment Fatalities: % Distribution by Category

	1995	1996	1997	Average
Prior or Current Contact with CPS	42% (18 states)	40% (20 states)	41% (16 states)	41%
Deaths Due to Neglect	43% (27 states)	43% (28 states)	45% (20 states)	44%
Deaths Due to Abuse	54% (27 states)	52% (28 states)	48% (20 states)	51%
Deaths Due to Neglect and Abuse	3% (27 states)	5% (28 states)	7% (20 states)	5%
Deaths to Children Under Five Yrs. Old	76% (27 states)	78% (25 states)	79% (19 states)	78%
Deaths to Children Under One Yr. Old	37% (27 states)	39% (25 states)	38% (18 states)	38%

Source: Ching-Tung Wang and Deborah Daro, *Current Trends in Child Abuse Reporting and Fatalities: The Results of the 1997 Annual Fifty State Survey.* Reprinted with permission from the National Committee to Prevent Child Abuse, Chicago, IL, 1998.

TABLE 4.9

National Incidence of Maltreatment under the Harm Standard in the NIS–3 (1993), and Comparison with the NIS–2 (1986) and the NIS–1 (1980) Harm Standard Estimates.

Harm Standard Maltreatment Category	NIS–3 Estimates 1993 Total No. of Children	NIS–3 Estimates 1993 Rate per 1,000 Children	NIS–2: 1986 Total No. of Children	NIS–2: 1986 Rate per 1,000 Children		NIS–1: 1980 Total No. of Children	NIS–1: 1980 Rate per 1,000 Children	
ALL MALTREATMENT	1,553,800	23.1	931,000	14.8	*	625,100	9.8	*
ABUSE:								
ALL ABUSE	743,200	11.1	507,700	8.1	m	336,600	5.3	*
Physical Abuse	381,700	5.7	269,700	4.3	m	199,100	3.1	*
Sexual Abuse	217,700	3.2	119,200	1.9	*	42,900	0.7	*
Emotional Abuse	204,500	3.0	155,200	2.5	ns	132,700	2.1	m
NEGLECT:								
ALL NEGLECT	879,000	13.1	474,800	7.5	*	315,400	4.9	*
Physical Neglect	338,900	5.0	167,800	2.7	*	103,600	1.6	*
Emotional Neglect	212,800	3.2	49,200	0.8	*	56,900	0.9	*
Educational Neglect	397,300	5.9	284,800	4.5	ns	174,000	2.7	*

* The difference between this and the NIS–3 estimate is significant at or below the p<.05 level.

m The difference between this and the NIS–3 estimate is statistically marginal (i.e., .10>p>.05).

ns The difference between this and the NIS—3 estimate is neither significant nor marginal (p>.10).

Note: Estimated totals are rounded to the nearest 100.

Source: *The Third National Incidence Study of Child Abuse and Neglect,* National Center on Child Abuse and Neglect, Washington, DC, 1996

TABLE 4.10

National Incidence of Maltreatment under the Endangerment Standard in the NIS–3 (1993), and Comparison with the NIS–2 (1986) Endangerment Standard Estimates.

Endangerment Standard Maltreatment Category	NIS–3 Estimates 1993		Comparison With NIS–2 1986		
	Total No. of Children	*Rate per 1,000 Children*	Total No. of Children	*Rate per 1,000 Children*	
ALL MALTREATMENT	2,815,600	*41.9*	1,424,400	*22.6*	*
ABUSE:					
ALL ABUSE	1,221,800	*18.2*	590,800	*9.4*	*
Physical Abuse	614,100	*9.1*	311,500	*4.9*	*
Sexual Abuse	300,200	*4.5*	133,600	*2.1*	*
Emotional Abuse	532,200	*7.9*	188,100	*3.0*	*
NEGLECT:					
ALL NEGLECT	1,961,300	*29.2*	917,200	*14.6*	*
Physical Neglect	1,335,100	*19.9*	507,700	*8.1*	*
Emotional Neglect	584,100	*8.7*	203,000	*3.2*	*
Educational Neglect	397,300	*5.9*	284,800	*4.5*	ns

* The difference between this estimate and the NIS–3 estimate is significant at or below the p<.05 level.

Note: Estimated totals are rounded to the nearest 100.

Source: *The Third National Incidence Study of Child Abuse and Neglect*, National Center on Child Abuse and Neglect, Washington, DC, 1996

THE NATIONAL COMMITTEE TO PREVENT CHILD ABUSE SURVEY

The National Committee to Prevent Child Abuse (NCPCA) provides annual estimates of the number of children reported and substantiated as victims of maltreatment and the number of deaths from child abuse nationwide. The committee's most recent annual report, *Current Trends in Child Abuse Reporting and Fatalities: The Results of the 1997 Annual Fifty State Survey* (Ching-Tung Wang and Deborah Daro, Chicago, Illinois, 1998), is based on information received from every state, but Maine and Nevada, and the District of Columbia. Of the 49 respondents, 35 knew or were able to project their child abuse reporting statistics for 1997; 29 respondents provided 1997 statistics on child abuse fatalities.

Reported and Substantiated Cases of Abuse

In 1997, state CPS agencies received reports of an estimated 3.2 million child victims of maltreatment. Thirty-three percent (1,054,000) or 15 per 1,000 children under 18 were confirmed as maltreated. The NCPCA found that the nationwide rate of children reported as victims of abuse or neglect increased 4 percent, from 45 per 1,000 children in 1992 to 47 per 1,000 in 1997. Overall, since 1988, the total number of child victims reported nationwide has increased 41 percent. (See Table 4.7.)

Factors Affecting Reporting Trends

The survey's principal researcher, Ching-Tung Wang, Ph.D., and the director, Deborah Daro, D.S.W., noted that states with increased reporting trends attributed the increase in reporting rates to heightened public awareness. Mandated reporters, as well as the public, have become more aware of their responsibility to report suspicions

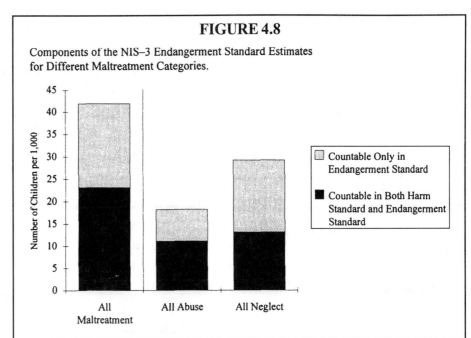

FIGURE 4.8

Components of the NIS–3 Endangerment Standard Estimates for Different Maltreatment Categories.

Legend:
- ▢ Countable Only in Endangerment Standard
- ■ Countable in Both Harm Standard and Endangerment Standard

TABLE 4.11

Sex Differences in Incidence Rates per 1,000 Children for Maltreatment under the Harm Standard in the NIS–3 (1993).

Harm Standard Maltreatment Category	Males	Females	Significance of Difference
ALL MALTREATMENT	21.7	24.5	m
ABUSE:			
All Abuse	9.5	12.6	*
Physical Abuse	5.8	5.6	ns
Sexual Abuse	1.6	4.9	*
Emotional Abuse	2.9	3.1	ns
NEGLECT:			
All Neglect	13.3	12.9	ns
Physical Neglect	5.5	4.5	ns
Emotional Neglect	3.5	2.8	ns
Educational Neglect	5.5	6.4	ns
SEVERITY OF INJURY:			
Fatal	0.04	0.01	ns
Serious	9.3	7.5	m
Moderate	11.3	13.3	ns
Inferred	1.1	3.8	*

* The difference is significant at or below the p<.05 level.

m The difference is statistically marginal (i.e., .10>p>.05).

ns The difference is neither significant nor marginal (p>.10).

Source of figure and table: *The Third National Incidence Study of Child Abuse and Neglect*, National Center on Child Abuse and Neglect, Washington, DC, 1996

of child abuse. Similarly, those states with decreased reporting trends claimed that people understand better when they should report suspected child abuse. States agreed that an improved reporting system, including standardized screening and centralized intake and referral units, contributed to more accurate reporting. In addition, four states attributed the rising reports of maltreatment to substance abuse.

Case Characteristics

The NCPCA asked each state to provide a breakdown of all reported and substantiated cases by type of maltreatment. Twenty-two states responded that 52 percent of all reported cases involved neglect; 26 percent involved physical abuse; 7 percent, sexual abuse; 4 percent, emotional maltreatment; and 11 percent, other (see below). For all substantiated cases, 31 states reported that 54 percent involved neglect; 22 percent involved physical abuse; 8 percent, sexual abuse; 4 percent, emotional maltreatment; and 12 percent, other. In 1997, since the states used more detailed classifications of the types of maltreatment, the category "other" was expanded to include "abandonment, multiple types of maltreatment, imminent risk, medical and educational neglect, substance and alcohol abuse, dependency, threat of harm, and lack of supervision or bizarre discipline." (See Figure 4.6.)

Reports of Sexual Abuse

Wang and Daro noted a decline in the proportion of reported

TABLE 4.12

Sex Differences in Incidence Rates per 1,000 Children for Maltreatment under the Endangerment Standard in the NIS–3 (1993).

Endangerment Standard Maltreatment Category	Males	Females	Significance of Difference
ALL MALTREATMENT	40.0	42.3	ns
ABUSE:			
All Abuse	16.1	20.2	*
Physical Abuse	9.3	9.0	ns
Sexual Abuse	2.3	6.8	*
Emotional Abuse	8.0	7.7	ns
NEGLECT:			
All Neglect	29.2	27.6	ns
Physical Neglect	19.7	18.6	ns
Emotional Neglect	9.2	7.8	*
Educational Neglect	5.5	6.4	ns
SEVERITY OF INJURY:			
Fatal	0.04	0.01	ns
Serious	9.4	7.6	m
Moderate	14.1	15.3	ns
Inferred	2.1	4.6	*
Endangered	14.5	14.8	ns

* The difference is significant at or below the p<.05 level.

m The difference is statistically marginal (i.e., .10>p>.05).

ns The difference is neither significant nor marginal (p>.10).

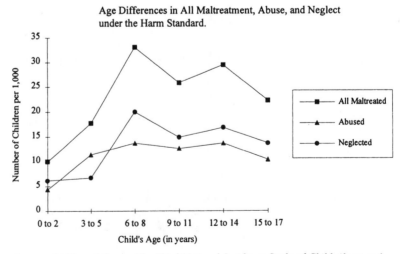

FIGURE 4.9

Age Differences in All Maltreatment, Abuse, and Neglect under the Harm Standard.

Source of table and figure: *The Third National Incidence Study of Child Abuse and Neglect*, National Center on Child Abuse and Neglect, Washington, DC, 1996

cases of child sexual abuse. In 1986, sexual abuse made up 16 percent of all reports. By 1995, the percentage reported was down to around 10 percent. In 1997, reported sexual abuse comprised only 7 percent of all cases. Child sexual abuse, which had been ignored in the past, gained public attention in the 1980s. The authors surmised that many of the cases reported in the 1980s involved long-term abuse, and "After over ten years of attention to this problem, it is possible that the reservoir of cases involving years of abuse have been reduced...." Nonetheless, the number of

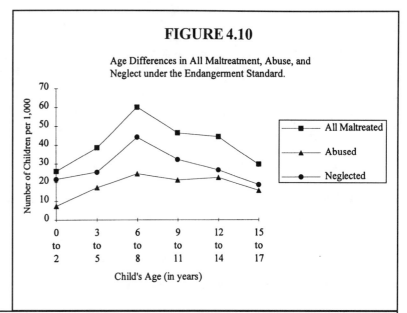

FIGURE 4.10

Age Differences in All Maltreatment, Abuse, and Neglect under the Endangerment Standard.

TABLE 4.13

Incidence Rates per 1,000 Children for Maltreatment under the Harm Standard in the NIS–3 (1993) for Different Family Structures.

Harm Standard Maltreatment Category	Both Parents	Single Parent			Neither Parent	Significance of Differences
		Either Mother or Father	Mother-only	Father-only		
ALL MALTREATMENT	15.5	27.3	26.1	36.6	22.9	A, C, D
ABUSE:						
All Abuse	8.4	11.4	10.5	17.7	13.7	D, e
Physical Abuse	3.9	6.9	6.4	10.5	7.0	a, D, e
Sexual Abuse	2.6	2.5	2.5	2.6	6.3	ns
Emotional Abuse	2.6	2.5	2.1	5.7	5.4	ns
NEGLECT:						
All Neglect	7.9	17.3	16.7	21.9	10.3	A, C, D
Physical Neglect	3.1	5.8	5.9	4.7	4.3	A, C
Emotional Neglect	2.3	4.0	3.4	8.8	3.1	a, G
Educational Neglect	3.0	9.6	9.5	10.8	3.1	A, B, f
SEVERITY OF INJURY:						
Fatal	0.019	0.015	0.017	0.005	0.016	ns
Serious	5.8	10.5	10.0	14.0	8.0	A, C
Moderate	8.1	15.4	14.7	20.5	10.1	A
Inferred	1.6	1.4	1.3	2.1	4.8	ns

A   Difference between "Both Parents" and "Either Mother or Father" is significant at or below the p < .05 level.
a   Difference between "Both Parents" and "Either Mother or Father" is statistically marginal (i.e., .10 > p > .05).
B   Difference between "Either Mother or Father" and "Neither Parent" is significant at or below the p < .05 level.
C   Difference between "Both Parents" and "Mother only" is significant at or below the p < .05 level.
D   Difference between "Both Parents" and "Father only" is significant at or below the p < .05 level.
e   Difference between "Mother only" and "Father only" is statistically marginal (i.e., .10 > p > .05).
f   Difference between "Mother only" and "Neither Parent" is statistically marginal (i.e., .10 > p > .05).
G   Difference between "Father only" and "Neither Parent" is significant at or below the p < .05 level.
ns No between-group difference is significant or marginal (all p's > .10).

Source of figure and table: *The Third National Incidence Study of Child Abuse and Neglect*, National Center on Child Abuse and Neglect, Washington, DC, 1996

TABLE 4.14

Incidence Rates per 1,000 Children for Maltreatment under the
Endangerment Standard in the NIS–3 (1993) for Different Family Structures.

Endangerment Standard Maltreatment Category	Both Parents	Single Parent			Neither Parent	Significance of Differences
		Either Mother or Father	Mother-only	Father-only		
ALL MALTREATMENT	26.9	52.0	50.1	65.6	39.3	A, C, D, G
ABUSE:						
All Abuse	13.5	19.6	18.1	31.0	17.3	a
Physical Abuse	6.5	10.6	9.8	16.5	9.2	d
Sexual Abuse	3.2	4.2	4.3	3.1	6.6	ns
Emotional Abuse	6.2	8.6	7.7	14.6	7.1	ns
NEGLECT:						
All Neglect	17.6	38.9	37.6	47.9	24.1	A, C, D, G
Physical Neglect	10.8	28.6	27.5	36.4	17.1	A, c, D
Emotional Neglect	6.4	10.5	9.7	16.2	8.3	a
Educational Neglect	3.0	9.6	9.5	10.8	3.1	A, B, C, f
SEVERITY OF INJURY:						
Fatal	0.020	0.015	0.017	0.005	0.016	ns
Serious	5.9	10.5	10.0	14.0	8.0	A, C
Moderate	9.6	18.5	17.7	24.8	11.5	A, b
Inferred	2.1	2.5	2.0	6.0	4.7	ns
Endangered	9.3	20.5	20.4	20.7	15.1	A, C

A   Difference between "Both Parents" and "Either Mother or Father" is significant at or below the p<.05 level.
a   Difference between "Both Parents" and "Either Mother or Father" is statistically marginal (i.e., .10>p>.05).
B   Difference between "Either Mother or Father" and "Neither Parent" is significant at or below the p<.05 level.
b   Difference between "Either Mother or Father" and "Neither Parent" is statistically marginal (i.e., .10>p>.05).
C   Difference between "Both Parents" and "Mother only" is significant at or below the p<.05 level.
c   Difference between "Both Parents" and "Mother only" is statistically marginal (i.e., .10>p>.05).
D   Difference between "Both Parents" and "Father only" is significant at or below the p<.05 level.
d   Difference between "Both Parents" and "Father only" is statistically marginal (i.e., .10>p>.05)
f   Difference between "Mother only" and "Neither Parent" is statistically marginal (i.e., .10>p>.05).
G   Difference between "Father only" and "Neither Parent" is significant at or below the p<.05 level.
ns No between-group difference is significant or marginal (all p's>.10).

Source: *The Third National Incidence Study of Child Abuse and Neglect*, National Center on Child Abuse and Neglect, Washington, DC, 1996

children reported for sexual abuse in 1997 was still far higher than those reported in the 1970s and 1980s. (See Figure 4.7.)

Deaths Due to Child Abuse

States also provided the NCPCA with data on the types of maltreatment that caused child fatalities from 1995 through 1997. An average of 2 in 5 (41 percent) of children who died had prior or current contact with CPS agencies. About 44 percent died from neglect; 51 percent, from abuse; and 5 percent, from a combination of abuse and neglect. Children under age five were at the highest risk of dying from maltreatment. Between 1995 and 1997, three-quarters (78 percent) of children who died from maltreatment were under five years old, and more than one-third (38 percent) were under one year old. (See Table 4.8.)

THE THIRD NATIONAL INCIDENCE STUDY (NIS-3)

The *Third National Incidence Study of Child Abuse and Neglect* (NIS-3; U.S. Department of Health and Human Services, Washington, DC, 1996) differed from the *Child Maltreatment 1996* survey (see above) because NIS-3 findings were based on a nationally representative sample of more than 5,600 professionals in 842 agencies serving 42 counties. The NIS-3 included not only child victims investigated by CPS agencies, but also children who were seen by community professionals but not reported to CPS or who were reported to CPS but not investigated. In addition, estimates were unduplicated, which means that each estimate counted each child only once.

Definition Standards

The NIS-3 used two standardized definitions of abuse and neglect:

- Harm Standard — required that an act or omission must have resulted in demonstrable harm in order to be considered as abuse or neglect. This standard was also used in NIS-1 (1980) and NIS-2 (1986).

- Endangerment Standard — allowed children who have not yet been harmed by maltreatment to be counted in the estimates of maltreated children if a non-CPS professional considered them to be at risk of harm or if their maltreatment was substantiated or indicated in a CPS investigation. This standard was also used in NIS-2.

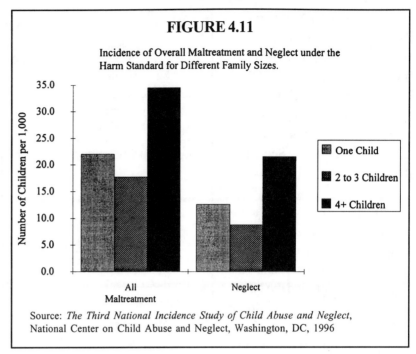

FIGURE 4.11

Incidence of Overall Maltreatment and Neglect under the Harm Standard for Different Family Sizes.

Source: *The Third National Incidence Study of Child Abuse and Neglect*, National Center on Child Abuse and Neglect, Washington, DC, 1996

Incidence of Maltreatment

In 1993, under the Harm Standard, an estimated 1,553,800 children were victims of maltreatment, a 67 percent increase from the NIS-2 estimate (931,000 children) and a 149 percent increase from the NIS-1 estimate (625,100 children). Significant increases occurred for all types of abuse and neglect as compared

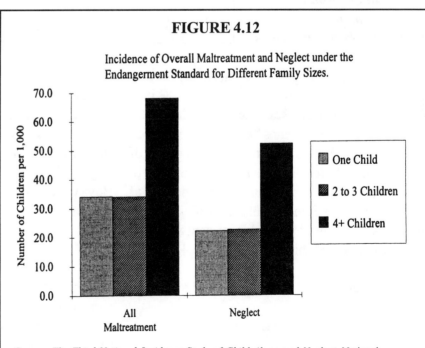

FIGURE 4.12

Incidence of Overall Maltreatment and Neglect under the Endangerment Standard for Different Family Sizes.

Source: *The Third National Incidence Study of Child Abuse and Neglect*, National Center on Child Abuse and Neglect, Washington, DC, 1996

to the two earlier NIS surveys. The over 1.5 million child victims of maltreatment in 1993 reflected a yearly incidence rate of 23.1 children per 1,000 children under 18 in the general population nationwide, or 1 of 43 children in the United States. (See Table 4.9.)

In 1993, under the Endangerment Standard, an estimated 2,815,600 children experienced some type of maltreatment. This figure nearly doubled the NIS-2 estimate of 1,424,400 children in 1986. As with the Harm Standard, marked increases occurred for all types of abuse and neglect using the Endangerment Standard. The incidence rate for 1993 was 41.9 children per 1,000 children under 18 in the general population, or 1 of 24 children in the United States. (See Table 4.10.)

Comparison of Maltreatment Estimates Under the Two Definitions

TABLE 4.15

Incidence Rates per 1,000 Children for Maltreatment under the Harm Standard in the NIS–3 (1993) for Different Levels of Family Income.

Harm Standard Maltreatment Category	<$15K/yr	$15-29K/yr	$30K+/yr	Significance of Differences
ALL MALTREATMENT	47.0	20.0	2.1	a
ABUSE:				
All Abuse	22.2	9.7	1.6	a
Physical Abuse	11.0	5.0	0.7	a
Sexual Abuse	7.0	2.8	0.4	b
Emotional Abuse	6.5	2.5	0.5	b
NEGLECT:				
All Neglect	27.2	11.3	0.6	a
Physical Neglect	12.0	2.9	0.3	a
Emotional Neglect	5.9	4.3	0.2	ns
Educational Neglect	11.1	4.8	0.2	a
SEVERITY OF INJURY:				
Fatal	0.060	0.002	0.001	ns
Serious	17.9	7.8	0.8	a
Moderate	23.3	10.5	1.3	a
Inferred	5.7	1.6	0.1	b

a All between-group differences are significant at or below the p<.05 level.

b The highest income group ($30,000 or more) differs significantly from the others (p's<.05), but the difference between the <$15,000 group and the $15,000 to $29,999 group is statistically marginal (i.e., .10>p>.05).

ns No between-group difference is significant or marginal (all p's>.10).

Source: *The Third National Incidence Study of Child Abuse and Neglect*, National Center on Child Abuse and Neglect, Washington, DC, 1996

In 1993, the Endangerment Standard included an additional 1,261,800 children under 18 (an 81 percent increase) beyond those counted under the stricter Harm Standard. This means that children included under the Harm Standard represented 55 percent of those counted under the Endangerment Standard. Harm Standard children accounted for 61 percent of the Endangerment Standard total of all abused children and 45 percent of the Endangerment Standard total of all neglected children. (See Figure 4.8.)

Characteristics of Abused Children

Gender

Under both the Harm and Endangerment Standards, more girls were subjected to maltreatment than boys. Girls were sexually abused about three times more often than boys. Boys, on the other hand, were more likely to experience physical and emotional neglect under the Endangerment Standard. Under both standards, boys suffered more physical and emotional neglect, while girls suffered more educational neglect. Boys were at a somewhat greater risk of serious injury and death than girls. (See Tables 4.11 and 4.12.)

Age

The NIS-3 found a lower incidence of maltreatment among younger children, particularly 0- to 5-year-olds. This may be due to the fact that, prior to reaching school age, children are less observable to community professionals, especially educators — the group most likely to report suspected maltreatment.

In addition, the NIS-3 noted a disproportionate increase in the incidence of maltreatment among children between the ages of 6 and 14. (See Figures 4.9 and 4.10.) Andrea J. Sedlak and Diane D. Broadhurst, the authors of the NIS-3, noted a lower incidence of maltreatment among children older than 14 years. If the maltreatment became more prevalent or severe, older children were more likely to escape. They were also more able to defend themselves and/or fight back.

Under the Harm Standard, only 10 per 1,000 children in the age group 0 to 2 years experienced overall maltreatment. Among those age six and over, the incidence rate was 22 per 1,000 children. Under the Endangerment Standard, 26 per 1,000 children ages 0 to 2 years were subjected to overall maltreatment, compared to 44 per 1,000 children ages 6 to 14. Among the oldest age group, ages 15 to 17, 29.7 per 1,000 children suffered maltreatment of some type. (See Figures 4.9 and 4.10.)

Race

The NIS-3 found no significant differences in race in the incidence of maltreatment. The authors noted that this finding may be somewhat surprising, considering the overrepresentation of Black children in the child welfare population and in those served by public agencies. They attributed this lack of race differences in maltreatment incidence to the broader range of children identified by the NIS-3, compared to the smaller number investigated by public agencies and the even smaller number receiving child protective and other welfare services. The NIS-2 also had not found any disproportionate differences in race in relation to maltreatment incidence.

Family Characteristics

Family Structure

The NIS-3 found that, under the Harm Standard, among children living with single parents, an estimated 27.3 per 1,000 children under 18 suffered some type of maltreatment, almost twice the incidence rate for children living with both parents (15.5 percent). The same ratio held true for all types of abuse and neglect.

TABLE 4.16

Incidence Rates per 1,000 Children for Maltreatment under the Endangerment Standard in the NIS–3 (1993) for Different Levels of Family Income.

Endangerment Standard Maltreatment Category	<$15K/yr	$15-29K/yr	$30K+/yr	Significance of Differences
ALL MALTREATMENT	95.9	33.1	3.8	*
ABUSE:				
All Abuse	37.4	17.5	2.5	*
Physical Abuse	17.6	8.5	1.5	*
Sexual Abuse	9.2	4.2	0.5	*
Emotional Abuse	18.3	8.1	1.0	*
NEGLECT:				
All Neglect	72.3	21.6	1.6	*
Physical Neglect	54.3	12.5	1.1	*
Emotional Neglect	19.0	8.2	0.7	*
Educational Neglect	11.1	4.8	0.2	*
SEVERITY OF INJURY:				
Fatal	0.060	0.002	0.003	ns
Serious	17.9	7.9	0.8	*
Moderate	29.6	12.1	1.5	*
Inferred	7.8	2.7	0.2	*
Endangered	40.5	10.3	1.3	*

* All between-group differences are significant at or below the p<.05 level.
ns No between-group difference is significant or marginal (all p's>.10).

Source: *The Third National Incidence Study of Child Abuse and Neglect*, National Center on Child Abuse and Neglect, Washington, DC, 1996

Children living with single parents also had a greater risk of suffering serious injury (10.5 per 1,000 children) than those living with both parents (5.8 per 1,000 children). (See Table 4.13.)

As defined by the Endangerment Standard, an estimated 52 per 1,000 children living with single parents suffered some type of maltreatment, compared to 26.9 per 1,000 children living with both parents.

TABLE 4.17

Distribution of Perpetrator's Relationship to Child and Severity of Harm by the Type of Maltreatment.

Category	Percent Children in Maltreatment Category	Total Maltreated Children	Percent of Children in Row with Injury/Impairment...		
			Fatal or Serious	Moderate	Inferred
ABUSE:	100%	743,200	21%	63%	16%
Natural Parents	62%	461,800	22%	73%	4%
Other Parents and Parent/substitutes	19%	144,900	12%	62%	27%
Others	18%	136,600	24%	30%	46%
Physical Abuse	100%	381,700	13%	87%	+
Natural Parents	72%	273,200	13%	87%	+
Other Parents and Parent/substitutes	21%	78,700	13%	87%	+
Others	8%	29,700	*	82%	+
Sexual Abuse	100%	217,700	34%	12%	53%
Natural Parents	29%	63,300	61%	10%	28%
Other Parents and Parent/substitutes	25%	53,800	19%	18%	63%
Others	46%	100,500	26%	11%	63%
Emotional Abuse	100%	204,500	26%	68%	6%
Natural Parents	81%	166,500	27%	70%	2%
Other Parents and Parent/substitutes	13%	27,400	*	57%	24%
Others	5%	10,600	*	*	*
NEGLECT:	100%	879,000	50%	44%	6%
Natural Parents	91%	800,600	51%	43%	6%
Other Parents and Parent/substitutes	9%	78,400	35%	59%	*
Others	^	^	^	^	^
Physical Neglect	100%	338,900	64%	15%	21%
Natural Parents	95%	320,400	64%	16%	20%
Other Parents and Parent/substitutes	5%	18,400	*	*	*
Others	^	^	^	^	^
Emotional Neglect	100%	212,800	97%	3%	+
Natural Parents	91%	194,600	99%	*	+
Other Parents and Parent/substitutes	9%	*	*	*	+
Others	^	^	^	^	+
Educational Neglect	100%	397,300	7%	93%	+
Natural Parents	89%	354,300	8%	92%	+
Other Parents and Parent/substitutes	11%	43,000	*	99%	+
Others	^	^	^	^	+
ALL MALTREATMENT:	100%	1,553,800	36%	53%	11%
Natural Parents	78%	1,208,100	41%	54%	5%
Other Parents and Parent/substitutes	14%	211,200	20%	61%	19%
Others	9%	134,500	24%	30%	46%

[+] This severity level not applicable for this form of maltreatment.
[*] Fewer than 20 cases with which to calculate estimate; estimate too unreliable to be given.
[^] These perpetrators were not allowed by countability requirements for cases of neglect.

Source: *The Third National Incidence Study of Child Abuse and Neglect*, National Center on Child Abuse and Neglect, Washington, DC, 1996

Children in single-parent households were abused at a 45 percent higher rate than those in two-parent households (19.6 versus 13.5 per 1,000 children) and suffered over twice as much neglect (38.9 per 1,000 children) as those in two-parent households (17.6 per 1,000 children). Children living with single parents (10.5 per 1,000 children) were also more likely to suffer serious injuries than those living with both parents (5.9 per 1,000 children). (See Table 4.14.)

Family Size

The number of children in the family was related to the incidence of maltreatment. Additional children

TABLE 4.18

Distribution of Perpetrator's Sex by Type of Maltreatment and Perpetrator's Relationship to Child.

Category	Percent Children in Maltreatment Category	Total Maltreated Children	Percent of Children in Row with Perpetrator Whose Sex was . . .		
			Male	Female	Unknown
ABUSE:	100%	743,200	67%	40%	*
Natural Parents	62%	461,800	56%	55%	*
Other Parents and Parent/substitutes	19%	144,900	90%	15%	*
Others	18%	136,600	80%	14%	*
Physical Abuse	100%	381,700	58%	50%	*
Natural Parents	72%	273,200	48%	60%	*
Other Parents and Parent/substitutes	21%	78,700	90%	19%	*
Others	8%	29,700	57%	39%	*
Sexual Abuse	100%	217,700	89%	12%	*
Natural Parents	29%	63,300	87%	28%	*
Other Parents and Parent/substitutes	25%	53,800	97%	*	*
Others	46%	100,500	86%	8%	*
Emotional Abuse	100%	204,500	63%	50%	*
Natural Parents	81%	166,500	60%	55%	*
Other Parents and Parent/substitutes	13%	27,400	74%	*	*
Others	5%	10,600	*	*	*
ALL NEGLECT:	100%	879,000	43%	87%	*
Natural Parents	91%	800,600	40%	87%	*
Other Parents and Parent/substitutes	9%	78,400	76%	88%	*
Others	^	^	^	^	^
Physical Neglect	100%	338,900	35%	93%	*
Natural Parents	95%	320,400	34%	93%	*
Other Parents and Parent/substitutes	5%	18,400	*	90%	*
Others	^	^	^	^	^
Emotional Neglect	100%	212,800	47%	77%	*
Natural Parents	91%	194,600	44%	78%	*
Other Parents and Parent/substitutes	9%	18,200	*	*	*
Others	^	^	^	^	^
Educational Neglect	100%	397,300	47%	88%	*
Natural Parents	89%	354,300	43%	86%	*
Other Parents and Parent/substitutes	11%	43,000	82%	100%	*
Others	^	^	^	^	^
ALL MALTREATMENT:	100%	1,553,800	54%	65%	1%
Natural Parents	78%	1,208,100	46%	75%	*
Other Parents and Parent/substitutes	14%	211,200	85%	41%	*
Others	9%	134,500	80%	14%	7%

*Fewer than 20 cases with which to calculate, estimate too unreliable to be given
^These perpetrators were not allowed by countability requirements for cases of neglect.

Source: *The Third National Incidence Study of Child Abuse and Neglect*, National Center on Child Abuse and Neglect, Washington, DC, 1996

meant additional tasks and responsibilities for the parents; therefore, it followed that the rates of child maltreatment were higher in these families. Among children in families with four or more children, an estimated 34.5 children per 1,000 children under the Harm Standard and 68.1 per 1,000 children under the Endangerment Standard suffered some type of maltreatment (See Figures 4.11 and 4.12.)

Surprisingly, households with an only child had a higher maltreatment incidence rate than households with 2 to 3 children (22 versus 17.7 per 1,000 children under the Harm Standard and 34.2 versus 34.1 per 1,000 children under the Endangerment Standard). (See Figures 4.11 and 4.12.) The authors thought that an only child might have been in a situation where parental expectations were all focused on that one child. Another explanation was that "only" children may be in households where the parents, who were just starting a family, were relatively young and inexperienced.

Family Income

Family income was significantly related to the incidence rates of child maltreatment. Under the Harm Standard, children in families with annual incomes less than $15,000 had the highest rate of maltreatment — 47 per 1,000 children. The figure is almost twice as high (95.9 per 1,000 children) using the Endangerment Standard. Incidence rates of abuse and neglect were also significantly higher among families with incomes of less than $15,000. (See Tables 4.15 and 4.16.)

Characteristics of Perpetrators

Relationship to the Child

Most child victims (78 percent) were maltreated by their birth parents. Parents accounted for the maltreatment of 72 percent of physically abused children and 81 percent of emotionally abused children. On the other hand, almost half (46 percent) of sexually abused children were violated by someone other than a parent or parent-substitute. More than a quarter (29 percent) were sexually abused by a birth parent, and 25 percent were sexually abused by a parent-substitute, such as a stepparent or a father's girlfriend. In addition, sexually abused children were more likely to sustain fatal or serious injuries or impairments when birth parents were the perpetrators. (See Table 4.17.) See Chapter VI for more information on sexual abuse.

Perpetrator's Sex

Overall, children were somewhat more likely to be maltreated by female perpetrators (65 percent of children) than by males (54 percent of children). Among children maltreated by their parents, most (75 percent) were maltreated by their mothers, but almost half (46 percent) were maltreated by their fathers. (Children who were maltreated by both parents were included in both "male" and "female" counts). Children who were maltreated by other parents and parent-substitutes were more likely to have been maltreated by a male (85 percent) than by a female (41 percent). Four of 5 children (80 percent) were maltreated by other adults who were males, and only 14 percent were maltreated by other adults who were females. (See Table 4.18. Note that the numbers will not add to 100 percent because many children were maltreated by both parents.)

Neglected children differed from abused children with regard to the sex of the perpetrators. Because mothers or other females tend to be the primary caretakers, children were more likely to suffer all forms of neglect by female perpetrators (87 percent versus 43 percent by male perpetrators). In contrast, children were more often abused by males (67 percent) than by females (40 percent). (See Table 4.18.)

CHAPTER V

CAUSES AND EFFECTS OF CHILD ABUSE

Raising a child is not easy. Everyday stresses, strains, and sporadic upheavals in family life, coupled with the normal burdens of child care, cause most parents to feel angry at times. People who would not dream of hitting a colleague or an acquaintance when they are angry with that person think nothing of hitting their children. Some feel remorse after hitting a loved one; nevertheless, when they are angry, they still resort to violence. The deeper intimacy and greater commitment in a family make emotionally charged disagreements more frequent and more intense.

Drs. Murray A. Straus and Richard J. Gelles, experts in child abuse research who are affiliated with the Family Research Laboratory of the University of New Hampshire, Durham (see below), believe that cultural standards permit violence in the family. The family, which is the center of love and security in most children's lives, is also the place where the child is punished, often physically.

In addition to this accepted violence, some parents go further and actually threaten their children's health and safety. What pushes parents over the edge? Detailed interviews conducted by Straus and Gelles in their 1975 and 1985 *National Family Violence Surveys* and by Glenda Kaufman Kantor in the *1992 National Alcohol and Family Violence Survey* (Institute for Survey Research of Temple University, Philadelphia, 1994) have provided considerable information on the factors that seem to increase the chances of abuse or neglect.

The 1975 and 1985 *National Family Violence Surveys* are the most complete studies of spousal

and parent-child abuse yet prepared in the United States. The major difference between these two surveys and most other surveys discussed in Chapter IV is that the data from the former came from detailed interviews with the general population, not just those cases that came to the attention of official agencies. Straus and Gelles had a more intimate knowledge of the families and an awareness of incidences of child abuse that were not reported to the authorities. (Straus and Gelles incorporated researches from the *National Family Violence Surveys* and additional chapters into the book *Physical Violence in American Families: Risk Factors and Adaptations to Violence in 8,145 Families*, Transaction Publishers, New Brunswick, NJ, 1990; see below.)

CHARACTERISTICS OF ABUSIVE FAMILIES

The factors contributing to child maltreatment are complex. The *Third National Incidence Study of Child Abuse and Neglect* (*NIS-3*; Andrea J. Sedlak and Diane D. Broadhurst, U.S. Department of Health and Human Services [HHS], Washington, DC, 1996), the most comprehensive federal source of information about the current incidence of child maltreatment in the United States, found that family structure and size, poverty, alcohol and substance abuse, domestic violence, and community violence are contributing factors to child abuse and neglect.

Under the Harm Standard of the *NIS-3*, children in single-parent households were at a higher risk of physical abuse and of all types of neglect than were children in other family structures. Children living with only their fathers were more likely to suffer the highest incidence rates of physical abuse and emotional and educational neglect (Figure 5.1). Under the Endangerment Standard, higher incidence rates of physical and emotional neglect occurred among children living with only their fathers than those living in other family structures (Figure 5.2). (See Chapter IV for more on the *NIS-3* Harm and Endangerment Standards and findings related to family size and income.)

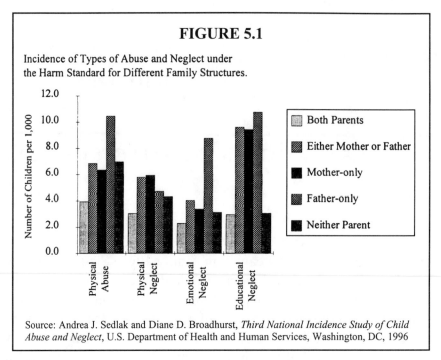

FIGURE 5.1

Incidence of Types of Abuse and Neglect under the Harm Standard for Different Family Structures.

Source: Andrea J. Sedlak and Diane D. Broadhurst, *Third National Incidence Study of Child Abuse and Neglect*, U.S. Department of Health and Human Services, Washington, DC, 1996

Sedlak and Broadhurst noted that the increase in illicit drug use since the 1986 *NIS-2* study may have contributed to the increased child maltreatment incidence reported in *NIS-3*. Children whose parents are alcohol and substance abusers are at very high risk of abuse and neglect because of the physiological, psychological, and sociological nature of the addiction.

While several factors increase the likelihood of maltreatment, they do not necessarily lead to abuse. It is important to understand that the causes of child abuse and the characteristics of families in which child abuse occurs are only indicators. The vast majority of parents, even under the most stressful and demanding situations and even with a personal history that might predispose them to be more violent than parents without such a history, do not abuse their children. Murray A. Straus and Christine Smith noted, in "Family Patterns and Child Abuse" (*Physical Violence in American*

Families: Risk Factors and Adaptions to Violence in 8,145 Families, see above), that one cannot simply single out an individual factor as the cause of the abuse.

The authors found that a combination of several factors is more likely to result in child abuse rather than a single factor by itself. Also, the sum of the effects of individual factors taken together does not necessarily add up to what Straus and

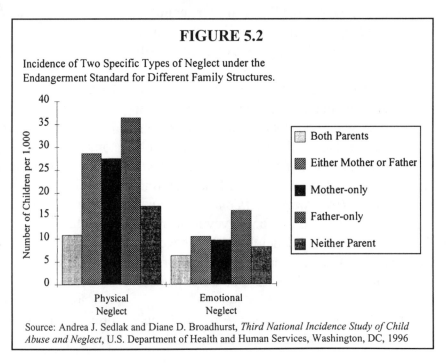

FIGURE 5.2

Incidence of Two Specific Types of Neglect under the Endangerment Standard for Different Family Structures.

Source: Andrea J. Sedlak and Diane D. Broadhurst, *Third National Incidence Study of Child Abuse and Neglect*, U.S. Department of Health and Human Services, Washington, DC, 1996

Smith called the "explosive combinations" of several factors interacting with one another. Nonetheless, even "explosive combinations" do not necessarily lead to child abuse.

Less Physical Abuse by Fathers

In 1975, Straus found the overall child maltreatment rate by fathers to be 10.1 per 100 children, compared to a rate by mothers of 17.7 per 100 children. The 1985 rates, however, were nearly the same for both parents, with maltreatment rate by fathers of 10.2 per 100 children and by mothers of 11.2 per 100 children. According to *Trends in Physical Abuse by Parents From 1975 to 1992: A Comparison of Three National Surveys*, a paper presented by Murray A. Straus and Glenda Kaufman Kantor at the annual meeting of the American Society of Criminology, Boston, in November 1995, the rates declined specifically for physical abuse. In the 1975 *National Family Violence Survey*, the rate for physical abuse by fathers was 12.1 per 100 children, while the rate by mothers was 20.1 per 100 children. In 1985, the physical abuse rate was 10.5 per 100 children by fathers and 14.2 per 100 children by mothers. By 1992, the physical abuse rates were 8.6 and 10.6 per 100 children by fathers and mothers, respectively. (See Figure 5.3.)

The authors attributed the downward trend in physical abuse to economic change. Child abuse is known to be associated with unemployment and economic stress (see Socioeconomic Status below). The rates of unemployment and inflation were lower in 1985 and 1992 than in 1975. Thus, Straus and Kantor believed that the lower level of economic stress when the latter studies were conducted might have contributed to the reported decline in physical abuse.

The three national surveys found a decrease in physical abuse as children grew older. The biggest decrease between 1975 and 1985 was for children 3 to 5 years old and 6 to 9 years old (though it edged up somewhat for this latter age group in the 1992 survey). Teenagers suffered the least abuse.

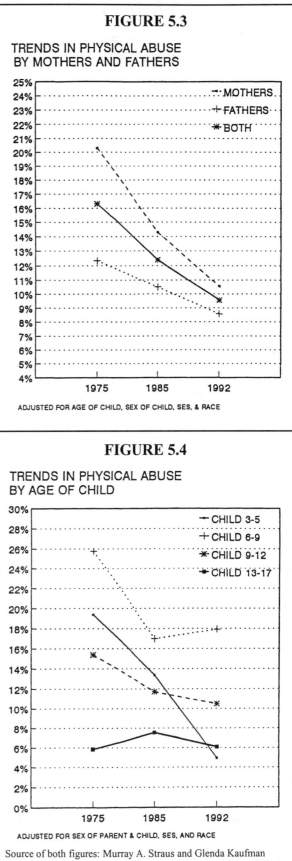

FIGURE 5.3

TRENDS IN PHYSICAL ABUSE
BY MOTHERS AND FATHERS

ADJUSTED FOR AGE OF CHILD, SEX OF CHILD, SES, & RACE

FIGURE 5.4

TRENDS IN PHYSICAL ABUSE
BY AGE OF CHILD

ADJUSTED FOR SEX OF PARENT & CHILD, SES, AND RACE

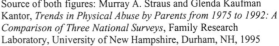

Source of both figures: Murray A. Straus and Glenda Kaufman Kantor, *Trends in Physical Abuse by Parents from 1975 to 1992: A Comparison of Three National Surveys*, Family Research Laboratory, University of New Hampshire, Durham, NH, 1995

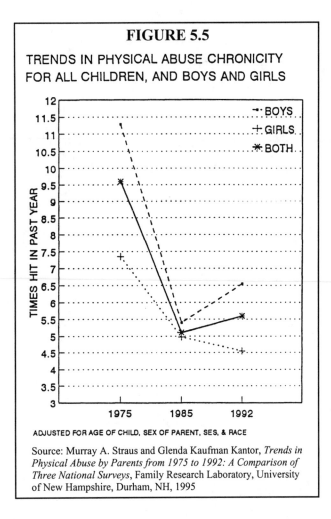

FIGURE 5.5

TRENDS IN PHYSICAL ABUSE CHRONICITY
FOR ALL CHILDREN, AND BOYS AND GIRLS

ADJUSTED FOR AGE OF CHILD, SEX OF PARENT, SES, & RACE

Source: Murray A. Straus and Glenda Kaufman Kantor, *Trends in Physical Abuse by Parents from 1975 to 1992: A Comparison of Three National Surveys*, Family Research Laboratory, University of New Hampshire, Durham, NH, 1995

(See Figure 5.4.) The surveys also showed that chronicity (frequency) of physical child abuse decreased dramatically from 1975 to 1985. The downward trend continued between 1985 and 1992, decreasing from 5 times to 4.5 times a year for girls. The number of times boys were physically abused, however, increased from 5.5 times per year in 1985 to 6.5 times per year in 1992. (See Figure 5.5.)

Abusive Mothers

Straus and Smith, in "Family Patterns and Child Abuse" (see above), found that women are as likely, if not more likely, as men to abuse their children. The authors believed child abuse by women could be explained in terms of social factors rather than psychological factors. Women are more likely to abuse their children because they are more likely to have much greater responsibility for raising the children, which means that they are more exposed to the trials and frustrations of child-rearing.

Women spend more "time at risk" while tending to their children. "Time at risk" refers to the time a potential abuser spends with the victim. This would apply to any form of domestic violence, such as wife abuse and elder abuse. For example, elderly people are more likely to experience abuse from each other, not from a caregiver, if one is present. This is not because elderly couples are more violent than caregivers, but because they spend more time with each other. (See *Violent Relationships: Battering and Abuse Among Adults*, Information Plus, Wylie, Texas, 1999.)

To illustrate the "time at risk" factor, the authors noted the reduction in the difference in child abuse rates between mothers and fathers from the 1975 to the 1985 *National Family Violence Survey*. Since fathers had taken on some responsibility for child care between this time period, men and women had shared more equally in the "time at risk" spent with the children.

The researchers believe two other factors may contribute to the problem of high abuse rates among mothers. Generally, the mother is blamed if the child misbehaves or does not do as well as expected. Since all children misbehave at some time or other, and since standards of children's accomplishments are sometimes not clear, "almost all mothers tend to feel anxiety, frustration, and guilt about their children and their adequacy as mothers. This is true not because women are any more anxiety prone than men, but because our society creates a situation in which a high level of anxiety and frustration is almost inevitable in the maternal role."

Working Mothers and Stay-at-home Mothers

A third factor that may predispose mothers to abuse their children has to do with the roles society has imposed on women — caretakers and homemakers — that some women may resent. Straus and Smith advanced two theories regarding this factor. Although many more women are working outside the home than a generation ago, the attitudes among many families toward who is responsible for the children have not changed. Con-

64

sequently, the working mother comes home to most of the responsibility for raising the children and maintaining the household, even though she may be just as physically, emotionally, and mentally exhausted from a day at work as her husband. The woman may, as a result, be more vulnerable to losing control of herself when the children frustrate her.

Straus and Smith noted that, on the other hand, more women working outside of the home might instead have contributed to the decrease in the incidence of abuse between the 1975 and 1985 surveys. Mothers who work outside the home spend less "time at risk," because they are exposed to the children for less time and therefore have fewer opportunities for abusive confrontations. Furthermore, they can often escape the stress and frustrations that sometimes accompany child-rearing. The decrease in the abuse rate may reflect social changes — women who do not want to be homemakers no longer feel society's pressure to stay home with the children, while women who are full-time homemakers are usually there by choice.

The 1975 and 1985 *National Family Violence Surveys* confirmed this second theory. The 1975 survey found that full-time homemakers had a considerably higher rate of child abuse (15.7 per 100 children) than did mothers with jobs outside the home (10.3 per 100 children). This latter rate was virtually the same as that for men (10.1 per 100 children). In the 1985 survey (by which time, in theory, women who did not want to be full-time homemakers had gotten jobs), the child abuse rate among homemakers dropped sharply to 11 per 100 children, almost the same rate as that for mothers with jobs outside the home (10.3 per 100 children). The authors surmised that earning a salary might have increased women's self-esteem and their power in the family.

Socioeconomic Status

Which Comes First — Poverty or Abuse?

Candace Kruttschnitt et al., in "The Economic Environment of Child Abuse" (*Social Problems*,

vol. 41, no. 2, 1994), examined the interaction between poverty and abuse and concluded that the relationships between the two are more complicated than previously thought. The researchers found that, overall, poor children were abused more severely than non-poor children were and that this was the result of higher rates of both current poverty and severe abuse in Black families.

Blacks were found to be more likely to hit their children with an object such as a belt than were White parents, which categorizes abuse by Black parents as more severe. Sociologists have suggested that perhaps Blacks are more likely to use an object to beat a child because poor, Black, single mothers lack family support, or perhaps a cultural history of slavery has taught them that harsh discipline is necessary for survival. Sociologists also theorize that because more Black children live in dangerous ghetto neighborhoods, Black parents place greater value on conformity in an effort to protect their children from outside dangers.

Kruttschnitt et al. also found links between spousal violence and parental criminality and between poverty and abuse, but it is not clear if the poverty caused the violence and the criminality or if the reverse was true. Researchers found that children who were repeatedly abused lived in very different circumstances from other children. They were more likely to live in families with a generalized history of violence, which in some cases explained their parents' criminal histories. They were also more likely to live in families with intergenerational histories of poverty. The authors concluded that "conditions of economic deprivation are often intertwined with other negative stressors which, in turn, explain inadequate parenting. We can only conclude that family violence may be both a consequence of, and create continuities in, economic disadvantage and antisocial behavior."

Unemployment and Socioeconomic Status

The 1975 *National Family Violence Survey* found child abuse considerably higher among families suffering from unemployment than among

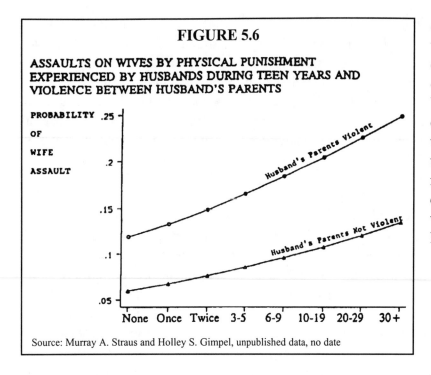

FIGURE 5.6

ASSAULTS ON WIVES BY PHYSICAL PUNISHMENT EXPERIENCED BY HUSBANDS DURING TEEN YEARS AND VIOLENCE BETWEEN HUSBAND'S PARENTS

PROBABILITY OF WIFE ASSAULT

Husband's Parents Violent

Husband's Parents Not Violent

None Once Twice 3-5 6-9 10-19 20-29 30+

Source: Murray A. Straus and Holley S. Gimpel, unpublished data, no date

those in which the husband was working full-time. Families in which the husband was not working had a significantly higher rate of child abuse than other families (22.5 versus 13.9 per 100 children). This finding did not recur, however, in the 1985 survey, although wives of unemployed husbands did have a higher rate of abuse than wives of husbands working full-time (16.2 versus 11.0 per 100 children).

The rate of abuse in the 1985 survey was considerably higher in families where the husband was a blue-collar rather than a white-collar worker. Blue-collar fathers committed abuse at a rate of 11.9 per 100 children, compared to 8.9 per 100 children among white-collar workers. The abuse rate for the wives of blue-collar workers was even greater, 13.9 per 100 children versus 8.1 per 100 children among wives of white-collar workers.

Straus and Smith, in "Family Patterns and Child Abuse" (see above), proposed several factors that contribute to the class differences in the child abuse rate. Blue-collar parents tend to be more authoritarian with their children, are more likely to use physical punishment as a means of child-rearing, and generally have less understanding of child psychology. Furthermore, blue-collar families are more likely to emphasize conformity and be less permissive. In addition, low-income areas of Ameri-

can cities have much higher rates of violence and are more crowded, increasing stress and setting a pattern of aggressive response to conflicts. Workers in the lower-economic class also face greater stress because they often have less control over their employment situation, are more likely to find themselves unemployed, and have fewer resources with which to cope with these problems.

THE VIOLENT FAMILY

Power and Family Violence

Richard J. Gelles and Murray A. Straus, in *Intimate Violence: The Definitive Study of the Causes and Consequences of Abuse in the American Family* (Simon and Schuster, New York, 1988), pointed out that the greater the inequality of power in a family, the greater the risk of violence. "Power, power confrontation, and perceived threats to domination, in fact, are underlying issues in almost all acts of family violence." They quoted a woman whose husband became enraged when he felt he did not get any respect from his daughter.

My husband wanted to think of himself as the head of the household. He thought that the man should wear the pants in the family. Trouble was, he couldn't seem to get his pants on. He had trouble getting a job and almost never could keep one. If I didn't have my job as a waitress, we would have starved. Even though he didn't make no money, he still wanted to control the house and the kids.

Family Conflicts and Violence

Spousal Conflicts

Child abuse is sometimes a reflection of other forms of severe family conflict. Violence in one aspect of family life often flows into other aspects.

Parents may have an excessive dependence on physical punishment because they do not know any other way to deal with conflicts. Figure 5.6 illustrates the higher probability of wife assaults among husbands who were subjected to physical punishment as teens and who witnessed violence between their parents.

Communications are poor among members of violent families. Abusive parents talk to their children less, and when they do, it is often in a negative manner, not in a praising, positive way that builds the self-confidence of the child. They touch their children less. Some of this behavior is a product of the individual parent, but much has been learned from the parent's parents.

Straus and Smith ("Family Patterns and Child Abuse" [see above]) found, in the 1985 *National Family Violence Survey*, that parents who were in constant conflict were also more likely to abuse their children. The researchers measured the level of husband-wife conflict over such issues as money, sex, social activities, housekeeping, and children. The child abuse rate for fathers involved in high marital conflict was 13 per 100 children, compared to 7.4 per 100 children for other men. Mothers in high-conflict relationships reported an even higher child abuse rate — 13.6 per 100 children versus 8 per 100 children among mothers in lower-conflict homes.

Spousal Verbal Aggression and Child Abuse

Husbands and wives sometimes use verbal aggression to deal with their conflicts. The 1985 survey found that spouses who verbally attacked each other were also more likely to abuse their children. Among verbally aggressive husbands, the child abuse rate was 11.2 per 100 children, compared to 4.9 per 100 children for other husbands. Verbally aggressive wives had a child abuse rate of 12.3 per 100 children, compared to 5.3 per 100 children for other wives. The researchers believed that verbal attacks between spouses, rather than clearing the air, tended to mask the reason for the dispute. The resulting additional tension made it even harder to resolve the original source of the conflict.

Spousal Physical Aggression and Child Abuse

Straus and Smith reported, in "Family Patterns and Child Abuse" (see above), that one of the most distinct findings of the two *National Family Violence Surveys* is that "violence in one family relationship is related to violence in other family relationships." In the 1985 survey, in families in which the husband struck his wife, the child abuse rate was much higher (22.3 per 100 children) than in other families (8.0 per 100 children). Similarly, in families where the wife hit the husband, the child abuse rate was also considerably higher (22.9 per 100 children), compared to families where the wife did not hit the husband (9.2 per 100 children).

In "Risk of Physical Abuse to Children of Spouse Abusing Parents" (*Child Abuse and Neglect*, vol. 20, no. 7, January 1996), Susan Ross, who did further research based on the 1985 *National Family Violence Survey*, reported that marital violence is a statistically significant predictor of physical child abuse. The researcher noted that the probability of child abuse by a violent husband increases from 5 percent with one act of marital violence to near certainty with 50 or more acts of spouse abuse. The percentages were similar for violent wives.

Ross found that, of those husbands who had been violent with their wives, 22.8 percent had engaged in violence toward their children. Similarly, 23.9 percent of violent wives had engaged in at least one act of physical child abuse. These rates of child abuse were much higher than those of parents who were not violent towards each other (8.5 percent for fathers and 9.8 percent for mothers). In other words, the more frequent the spousal violence, the higher the probability of child abuse.

Child Witnesses of Parental Violence

Azmaira Hamid Maker, Markus Kemmelmeier, and Christopher Peterson, in "Long-Term Psychological Consequences in Women of Witnessing Parental Physical Conflict and Experiencing Abuse in Childhood" (*Journal of Interpersonal Violence*, vol. 13, no. 5, October 1998), found that in distressed families, child witnesses of physical violence between parents experienced other childhood risk factors. In a survey of community college women ages 18 to 43, child maltreatment, specifically sexual abuse and physical abuse, were found to have co-existed with domestic violence.

Women who had witnessed parental violence as children reported being involved in violent dating relationships, both as victims and perpetrators. Witnesses of severe parental violence not only were victims of violence by their dating partners but also exhibited violence towards their dating partners. The risk factors of childhood maltreatment that co-existed with parental violence also accounted for long-term psychological problems, such as depression, antisocial behaviors, and trauma symptoms.

Verbal Abuse of Children

Parents who verbally abused their children were also more likely to physically abuse their children. In 1975, parents in the *National Family Violence Survey* who verbally abused their children reported a child abuse rate six times that of other parents (21 versus 3.6 per 100 children). A decade later, in 1985, verbally abusive mothers physically abused their children nearly 10 times more than other mothers (16.3 versus 1.8 per 100 children). Verbally aggressive fathers physically abused their children three and a half times as much as other fathers (14.3 versus 4.2 per 100 children).

Woman Battering and Child Maltreatment

Some experts believe that a link exists between woman battering and child maltreatment. According to the Advisory Board on Child Abuse and Neglect (*A Nation's Shame: Fatal Child Abuse and Neglect in the United States*, U.S. Department of Health and Human Services, Washington, DC, 1995), domestic violence is the single major precursor to child abuse and neglect deaths in the United States.

Jeffrey L. Edleson, in "The Overlap Between Child Maltreatment and Woman Battering" (*Violence Against Women*, vol. 5, no. 2, February 1999), found that 30 to 60 percent of families in 29 studies dealing with either child maltreatment or adult domestic violence showed a co-occurrence of the two forms of violence, with the mothers as the victims of battering. Ironically, in child maltreatment reports, child protective services (CPS) records often just list the mother's name and the steps that mothers should take to ensure their children's safety. Abusive males are "invisible" in CPS caseload data.

Sibling Abuse

Vernon R. Wiehe, in "Sibling Abuse" (*Understanding Family Violence*, SAGE Publications, Thousand Oaks, California, 1998), claimed that "[A]busive behavior between siblings is excused as sibling rivalry, and mandatory reporting of these incidents is not required." The author conducted a nationwide survey of survivors of sibling abuse who had sought professional counseling for problems resulting from physical, emotional, and sexual abuse by a brother or sister.

The respondents were generally victims of more than one type of abuse — 71 percent reported being physically, emotionally, and sexually abused. An additional 7 percent indicated being just emotionally abused, pushing the total of emotionally abused victims to 78 percent. Emotional abuse took the forms of "name-calling, ridicule, degradation, exacerbating a fear, destroying personal possessions, and torturing or destroying a pet."

As far as the victims of sibling incest could remember, they were sexually abused at ages 5 to 7. However, the author believed, it was possible that the abuse started at an earlier age. The perpetrators were often an older sibling, about 3 to 10 years older. The incest generally occurred over an extended period of time. (See Chapter VI for more on sexual abuse.)

TABLE 5.1

Prevalence of Reported Maltreatment Prior to Age 12 by Demographic Characteristics

	Reported Maltreatment	No Maltreatment
Total Sample	14%	86%
Demographic Characteristics		
Sex		
Male	13%	87%
Female	14%	86%
Race		
White	16%	84%
African American	14%	86%
Hispanic	9%	91%
Disadvantaged Family		
Yes	20%	80%
No	8%	92%
Family Structure		
Two Biological Parents	3%	97%
Other Family Structures	19%	81%

Source: Barbara Tatem Kelley et al., "In the Wake of Childhood Maltreatment," *OJJDP Juvenile Justice Bulletin*, August 1997

Adolescent Victims

The Council on Scientific Affairs of the American Medical Association (AMA), in "Adolescents as Victims of Family Violence" (*The Journal of the American Medical Association,* vol. 270, no. 15, October 20, 1993), issued a recommendation that physicians ask all their teen patients a series of questions designed to elicit information about the possibility of abuse. Their research found that the rates of abuse and neglect in adolescents were as high or higher than the rates for young children.

Adolescents are less likely to be identified as abused, however, for several reasons. Their injuries are frequently less severe than an abused infant's, and so they are less likely to come to the attention of medical authorities. Adolescents are also more likely to be served by agencies other than child protective services — runaway centers and shelters — which are not surveyed for cases of abuse. Numerous reporting studies have found that less than 40 percent of adolescent maltreatment cases were reported to child protective services, compared to more than 75 percent for younger children.

One of the most important factors distinguishing adolescents from children is the perception that abused adolescents are not necessarily innocent victims. Studies have found that many abuse incidents involving teens are preceded by the teen's arguing with or disobeying the parent. Because of this, many teens feel they deserve the beating and do not identify the behavior as abuse.

Two parenting styles have been associated with physical abuse that begins in adolescence — authoritarian and overindulgent. Authoritarian parenting is characterized by harsh, rigid patterns of discipline, and incidents of abuse typically occur when the adolescent challenges the parent by acting out. Overindulgent parents make few demands and have few rules for their children but seek emotional closeness and gratification. When teens start to look outside the family for emotional relationships, some parents respond with excessive force.

CHILDHOOD MALTREATMENT, DELINQUENCY, AND CRIMINAL BEHAVIOR

Consequences During Adolescence

The Office of Juvenile Justice and Delinquency Prevention of the U.S. Department of Justice, in "In the Wake of Childhood Maltreatment" (Barbara Tatem Kelley, Terence P. Thornberry, and Carolyn A. Smith, *Juvenile Justice Bulletin*, Washington DC, 1997), studied the relationship between childhood maltreatment and subsequent adolescent problem behaviors. The *Rochester Youth Development Study* included a sample of 1,000 seventh and eighth graders from the Rochester, New York, public schools. The longitudinal study was conducted until the students were in grades 11 and 12.

Demographic Characteristics

Substantiated child maltreatment was reported for 14 percent of the students. While no significant differences were reported in the prevalence of maltreatment by sex or race, the youth's socioeconomic status had a bearing on the prevalence of maltreatment — 20 percent of the children from disadvantaged families had been maltreated, compared to 8 percent of those from nondisadvantaged families. (A disadvantaged family was described as one in which the main wage earner was unemployed, welfare was received, or income was below the poverty level.) A marked difference in the prevalence of maltreatment involved the family structure — only 3 percent of the youth who lived with both biological parents had been maltreated, while 19 percent of those in other family structures were victims of maltreatment. (See Table 5.1.)

Delinquency

The Rochester researchers measured the prevalence of delinquency by examining official police records and self-reported offenses. Self-reported delinquency was determined during the face-to face interviews with the children at intervals of six months for a total of seven interviews, using the questions in Table 5.2. Figure 5.7 illustrates the relationship between childhood maltreatment and later delinquency.

Other Negative Outcomes

The *Rochester Youth Development Study* also measured other negative outcomes during adolescence as a result of childhood maltreatment. (See Figure 5.8.)

- Pregnancy — there was no difference between the maltreated and nonmaltreated boys in the rates of impregnating a female. However, maltreated girls (52 percent) were more likely than nonmaltreated girls (34 percent) to get pregnant.

- Drug use — the risk of drug use was about one-third higher among maltreated youth (43 percent), compared to nonmaltreated youth (32 percent).

- Low academic achievement — a lower GPA (Grade Point Average) during middle or junior high school was evident in 33 percent of maltreated youth, compared to 23 percent of those who had no history of maltreatment. The researchers found that "students performing poorly in middle school are considered at increased risk for continued academic failure in high school, low educational aspirations, premature school dropout, and reduced educational and economic opportunities."

- Mental health problems — 26 percent of childhood maltreatment victims, compared to 15 percent of nonmaltreated youth exhibited externalized conduct problems (aggression, hostility, hyperactivity) and internalized problems (social isolation, anxiety, physical distress).

Adult Criminality

The National Institute of Justice, in "The Cycle of Violence" (Cathy Spatz Widom, Washington, DC, 1992), found that being abused and neglected as a child increased the likelihood not only of delinquency (see also above) but also of adult criminality. The arrest records of a study group of 908 children with substantiated abuse or neglect were compared with those of 667 children who were not abused but were matched with the study group for gender, age, race, and socioeconomic status. The children were 11 years old or younger at the time the abuse or neglect occurred. The study was conducted over a 15- to 20-year period.

Table 5.3 shows the percentages of subjects involved in juvenile delinquency, adult criminality, and violent criminal behaviors (murder, forc-

TABLE 5.2

Interview Items for Self-Reported Delinquency Indexes

Since we interviewed you last time, have you . . .	Minor Delinquency	Moderate Delinquency	Serious Delinquency	Violent Delinquency
1. Carried a hidden weapon?				
2. Been loud or rowdy in a public place where someone complained and you got in trouble?	■			
3. Been drunk in a public place?		■		
4. Damaged, destroyed, marked up, or tagged somebody else's property on purpose?		■		
5. Set fire or tried to set fire to a house, building, or car on purpose?				
6. Gone into or tried to go into a building to steal or damage something?			■	
7. Tried to steal or actually stolen money or things worth $5 or less?	■			
8. Tried to steal or actually stolen money or things worth $5–$50?		■		
9. Tried to steal or actually stolen money or things worth $50–$100?			■	
10. Tried to steal or actually stolen money or things worth more than $100?			■	
11. Tried to buy or sell things that were stolen?				
12. Taken someone else's car or motorcycle for a ride without the owner's permission?		■		
13. Stolen or tried to steal a car or other motor vehicle?				
14. Forged a check or used fake money to pay for something?				
15. Used or tried to use a credit card, bank card, or automatic teller card without permission?				
16. Tried to cheat someone by selling them something that was not what you said it was or that was worthless?				
17. Attacked someone with a weapon or with the idea of seriously hurting or killing them?			■	■
18. Hit someone with the idea of hurting them?		■		■
19. Been involved in gang or posse fights?		■		■
20. Thrown objects such as rocks or bottles at people?		■		■
21. Used a weapon or force to make someone give you money or things?			■	■
22. Made obscene phone calls?		■		
23. Been paid for having sexual relations with someone?				
24. Physically hurt or threatened to hurt someone to get them to have sex with you?			■	■
25. Sold marijuana/reefer/pot?				
26. Sold hard drugs such as crack, heroin, cocaine, or LSD/acid?				
Total Number of Items	**2**	**9**	**8**	**6**

Source: Barbara Tatem Kelley et al., "In the Wake of Childhood Maltreatment," *OJJDP Juvenile Justice Bulletin*, August 1997

ible rape, robbery, and aggravated assault). Those individuals who had been subjected to physical abuse as children were the most likely to be arrested later for violent offenses (15.8 percent). This group was followed by victims of neglect (12.5 percent). (See Table 5.4.)

CORPORAL PUNISHMENT

Widespread Acceptance

The 1985 *National Family Violence Resurvey* found that over 90 percent of parents of children 3 to 4 years old used some form of corporal punishment, ranging from a slap on the hand to severe spanking. While spanking generally decreased as the child got older, 48 percent of 13-year-olds were still being physically punished.

In 1997, the Gallup Organization found that 65 percent of the general public and 66 percent of parents approved of spanking children. This proportion is the same as that of the 1990 survey. Fifty years ago, in 1946, three-quarters (74 percent) of parents approved of spanking children. (See Table 5.5.) About 4 in 5 of all respondents (81 to 82 percent) said that they had been spanked as a child, about the same percentage (84 percent) as those who said so in 1947. (See Table 5.6.)

In the United States, hitting a child with "reasonable force" for purposes of discipline is not considered criminal assault. This means that objects such as belts may be used as long as the child does not suffer injury. When states passed child abuse laws in the 1960s, provisions allowing parents to use corporal punishment helped facilitate passage of the legislation. Ironically, as Dr. Murray A. Straus of the Family Research Laboratory observed, "Legislation intended to protect children from physical abuse contained provisions that further legitimated a practice that increases the risk of physical abuse."

Prevalence and Chronicity of Corporal Punishment

Murray A. Straus and Julie H. Stewart, in *Corporal Punishment by American Parents: National Data on Prevalence, Chronicity, Severity, and Duration, in Relation to Child and Family Characteristics* (Family Research Laboratory, University of New Hampshire, Durham, NH; a paper presented at the 14th World Congress of Sociology, Montreal, Canada, 1998), reported on a national survey of American parents regarding their use of corporal punishment. The researchers defined corporal punishment as "the use of physical force with the intention of causing a child to experience pain, but not injury, for the purpose of correction or control of the child's behavior." This is the same definition used by all states to exempt parents from prosecution from criminal assault when they use physical force on their children.

Overall, based on the chronological age of the children, over a third (35 percent) of the parents used corporal punishment on their infants, reaching a peak of 94 percent of parents hitting their children who were 3 and 4 years old. The prevalence rate of parents hitting their children decreased after age 5, with just over 50 percent of parents hitting their children at age 12, one-third (33 percent) at age 14, and 13 percent at age 17. (See Figure 5.9.) The survey also found that "corporal punishment was more prevalent among African American and low

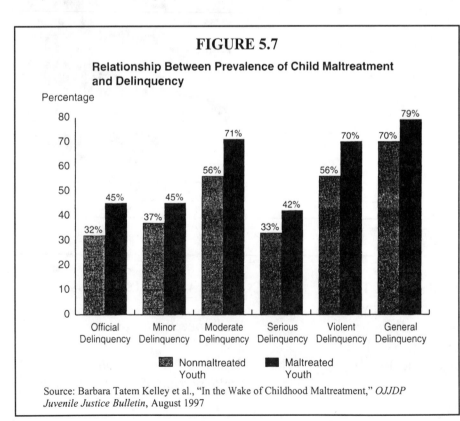

FIGURE 5.7

Relationship Between Prevalence of Child Maltreatment and Delinquency

Percentage

Official Delinquency: Nonmaltreated 32%, Maltreated 45%
Minor Delinquency: Nonmaltreated 37%, Maltreated 45%
Moderate Delinquency: Nonmaltreated 56%, Maltreated 71%
Serious Delinquency: Nonmaltreated 33%, Maltreated 42%
Violent Delinquency: Nonmaltreated 56%, Maltreated 70%
General Delinquency: Nonmaltreated 70%, Maltreated 79%

Nonmaltreated Youth
Maltreated Youth

Source: Barbara Tatem Kelley et al., "In the Wake of Childhood Maltreatment," *OJJDP Juvenile Justice Bulletin*, August 1997

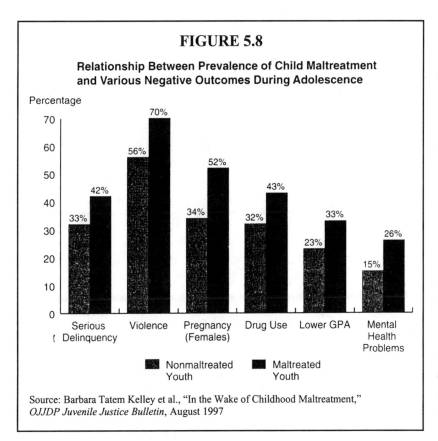

FIGURE 5.8

**Relationship Between Prevalence of Child Maltreatment
and Various Negative Outcomes During Adolescence**

Percentage

- Serious Delinquency: Nonmaltreated 33%, Maltreated 42%
- Violence: Nonmaltreated 56%, Maltreated 70%
- Pregnancy (Females): Nonmaltreated 34%, Maltreated 52%
- Drug Use: Nonmaltreated 32%, Maltreated 43%
- Lower GPA: Nonmaltreated 23%, Maltreated 33%
- Mental Health Problems: Nonmaltreated 15%, Maltreated 26%

■ Nonmaltreated Youth   ■ Maltreated Youth

Source: Barbara Tatem Kelley et al., "In the Wake of Childhood Maltreatment," *OJJDP Juvenile Justice Bulletin*, August 1997

Corporal Punishment and Antisocial Behavior of Children

Murray A. Straus, David B. Sugarman, and Jean Giles-Sims, in "Spanking by Parents and Subsequent Antisocial Behavior of Children" (*Archives of Pediatrics and Adolescent Medicine*, vol. 151, no. 8, August 1997), analyzed over 900 children ages 6 to 9 whose mothers reported using corporal punishment. The researchers found that regardless of the child's socioeconomic status, sex, and ethnic group and regardless of whether or not the parents provided emotional support, mental stimulation, and satisfactory socialization environment, corporal punishment was linked to an increase in the children's antisocial behavior between the start of the study to two years later. The antisocial behavior included cheating or lying, bullying of or cruelty to others, lack of remorse for misbehavior, deliberate destruction of things, disobedience in school, and trouble in getting along with their teachers.

The researchers pointed out that frequent physical punishment does not always result in a child's exhibiting antisocial behavior. However, physical punishment, if used through the teen years, has been associated with adult behavior problems (see below).

socioeconomic-status parents, in the South, for boys, and by mothers."

Chronicity refers to the frequency of the infliction of corporal punishment during the year. Corporal punishment was most frequently used by parents of two-year-olds, averaging 18 times during the year. After age 2, chronicity declined, averaging six times a year for teenagers. (See Figure 5.10.)

Corporal Punishment and Criminal Violence

Murray A. Straus, in *Spanking and the Making of a Violent Society* (a report to the American Academy of Pediatrics, Elk Grove, Illinois, February 1996), indicated that while corporal

TABLE 5.3

Extent of Involvement in Delinquency, Adult Criminality, and Violent Criminal Behavior

Type of arrest	Abused and Neglected (n = 908) (%)	Comparison Group (n = 667) (%)
Juvenile	26.0	16.8
Adult	28.6	21.1
Violent crime	11.2	7.9

Note: All differences significant.

Source: Cathy Spatz Widom, "The Cycle of Violence," *National Institute of Justice Research in Brief*, October 1992

TABLE 5.4

Childhood Maltreatment and Arrests for Violent Crime

Abuse Group	Number	Percent Arrested for Violent Offense
Physical abuse only	76	15.8%
Neglect only	609	12.5
Physical abuse and neglect	70	7.1
Sexual abuse and other abuse or neglect	28	7.1
Sexual abuse only	125	5.6
Comparison group	667	7.9

Source: Cathy Spatz Widom, "The Cycle of Violence," *National Institute of Justice Research in Brief*, October 1992

punishment alone does not cause a violent society, it increases the probability of societal violence. In explaining the connection between corporal punishment and criminal violence, Straus pointed out that almost all corporal punishment is carried out to control or correct behavior, and almost all assaults and about two-thirds of homicides are committed to correct a wrong action or behavior.

Straus noted that several studies have shown that the more corporal punishment experienced in middle childhood or early adolescence, the greater the probability of crime and violence. Figure 5.11 is a graphic summary of various studies that have linked corporal punishment to delinquency, criminal arrests and assault of family and non-family members. The second arrow from the top (Criminal Arrests, McCord, 1991) refers to a 33-year study of individuals who experienced corporal punishment as boys. Their conviction records were examined when they reached middle age. Even after controlling for the criminality of the boys' fathers, corporal punishment was linked to the doubling of the proportion of sons who were convicted of serious crimes (Figure 5.12).

Straus noted four unintended consequences of physical punishment:

The first of these unintended consequences is the association of love with violence. Parents are the first and usually the only ones to hit an infant. The child therefore learns that his or her primary love objects are also those who hit. Second, since physical punishment is used to train the child or to teach about which dangerous things are to be avoided, it establishes the moral rightness of hitting other family members. The third unintended consequence is the principle that when something is really important, it justifies the use of physical force. Fourth is the idea that when one is under stress, tense, or angry, hitting — although wrong — is "understandable," i.e., to a certain extent legitimate.

Corporal Punishment and Cognitive Development

Murray A. Straus and Mallie J. Paschall, in *Corporal Punishment By Mothers and Child's*

TABLE 5.5

Do you approve or disapprove of spanking children?

	Approve	Disapprove	No opinion
1997			
National adults	65%	32	3
All parents	66%	31	3
1990			
National adults	65%	25	10
1946			
All parents	74%	24	2

Spanking — Trend

TABLE 5.6

Were you spanked as a child?

	Yes	No	No opinion
1997			
National adults	81%	18	1
All parents	82%	17	1
1947			
All parents	84%	15	1

Spanked as Child — Trend

Source of both tables: *The Gallup Poll Monthly*, March 1997

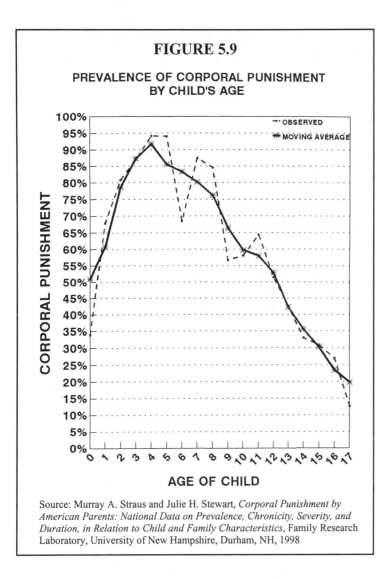

FIGURE 5.9

PREVALENCE OF CORPORAL PUNISHMENT
BY CHILD'S AGE

Source: Murray A. Straus and Julie H. Stewart, *Corporal Punishment by American Parents: National Data on Prevalence, Chronicity, Severity, and Duration, in Relation to Child and Family Characteristics*, Family Research Laboratory, University of New Hampshire, Durham, NH, 1998

Cognitive Development: A Longitudinal Study (Family Research Laboratory, University of New Hampshire, Durham, NH; a paper presented at the 14th World Congress of Sociology, Montreal, Canada, 1998), found that "corporal punishment is associated with [a child's failure] to keep up with the average pattern of cognitive development."

Straus and Paschall followed the cognitive development of 960 children born to mothers who participated in the *National Longitudinal Study of Youth*. The women were 14 to 21 years old at the start of the study. In 1986, when they were between the ages of 21 and 28, those with children were interviewed regarding the way they were raising these children. The children underwent cognitive, psychosocial, and behavioral assessments. Children ages 1 to 4 were selected, among other rea-

sons, because "the development of neural connections is greatest at the youngest ages." The children were tested again in 1990.

High Incidence and Long Duration

About 7 in 10 (71 percent) of mothers reported spanking their toddlers during the past week, with 6.2 percent hitting the child during the course of their interview for this study. Those who used corporal punishment reported using it an average of 3.6 times per week. This amounted to an estimated 187 spankings a year.

Cognitive Development

Straus and Paschall found that the more prevalent the corporal punishment, the greater the decrease in cognitive ability (Figure 5.13). Considering other studies, which showed that talking to children, including infants, is associated with increased neural connections in the brain and cognitive functioning, the researchers hypothesized that if parents are not using corporal punishment to discipline their child, they are very likely verbally interacting with that child, thus positively affecting cognitive development.

Moreover, corporal punishment has been found to affect cognitive development in other ways. It is believed that experiencing corporal punishment can be very stressful to a child. Stress hampers a child's ability to process events, which is important for his or her cognitive development. And since corporal punishment generally occurs over a long period of time, a child's bonding with his parents may be minimized to the point that he or she will not be motivated to learn from them.

Other Findings

Straus and Paschall also found that, contrary to some beliefs that corporal punishment is acceptable if the parent provides emotional support to the child, the adverse effects of physical punishment on cognitive development remained the same whether or not there was maternal support. The results of the study also debunked the general belief among Blacks that corporal punishment benefits children. The adverse consequences on cognitive development held true for all racial and ethnic groups.

Intergenerational Violence — Parents Who Were Victims of Corporal Punishment

The *Family Violence Surveys* revealed that parents who, as children, were still being physically punished at the relatively late age of 13 were more likely to abuse their children than those who had not been physically punished. Fathers who were still being physically punished at the age of 13 by their fathers were more likely to abuse their own children (13.1 per 100 children versus 8.1 per 100 children for those whose fathers had not physically punished them). The same applied for mothers hit by their fathers (17.6 versus 9.3 per 100 children). Similar rates occurred when the parents had been physically punished by their mothers.

A Legacy of Physical Punishment

Fathers who had seen their own fathers hit their mothers had a slightly higher rate of hitting their own children than those who had not (12.5 versus 10 per 100 children), as did fathers who had seen their mothers strike their fathers (18.5 versus 9.3 per 100 children). Similarly, mothers who had seen their fathers hit their mothers had higher rates than those who had not (20.2 versus 10.1 per 100 children), as did mothers who had seen their mothers hit their fathers (23.1 versus 10.3 per 100 children).

SUPPORT FOR SPANKING

Not all experts are opposed to spanking, however. They point out that most of Straus's work is based on teenagers — an age at which most experts agree parents should no longer be using spanking as a form of discipline — and that he has not adequately proven that the link between corporal punishment and future negative effects was not caused by other factors in the teens' lives. They point to the obvious evidence of millions of successful adults who were spanked as children and who have not been adversely affected.

Robert Larzelere, in *Debating Children's Lives: Current Controversies on Children and Adolescents* (Mary Ann Mason and Eileen Gambrill, eds., SAGE Publications, Thousand Oaks, California, 1994), thought parents should always start with noncorporal methods of discipline and resort to physical punishment only when other methods

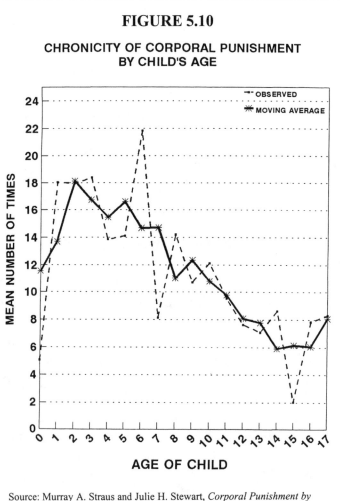

FIGURE 5.10

CHRONICITY OF CORPORAL PUNISHMENT BY CHILD'S AGE

Source: Murray A. Straus and Julie H. Stewart, *Corporal Punishment by American Parents: National Data on Prevalence, Chronicity, Severity, and Duration, in Relation to Child and Family Characteristics*, Family Research Laboratory, University of New Hampshire, Durham, NH, 1998

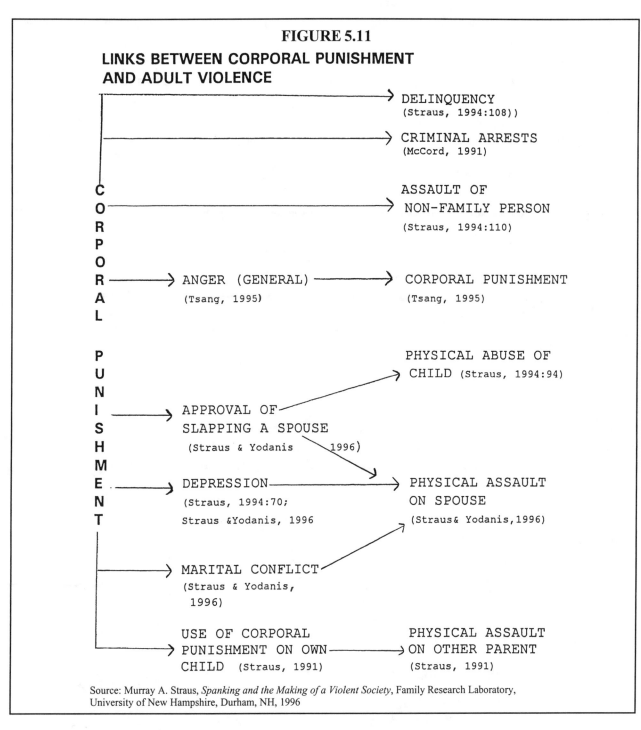

FIGURE 5.11

LINKS BETWEEN CORPORAL PUNISHMENT AND ADULT VIOLENCE

Source: Murray A. Straus, *Spanking and the Making of a Violent Society*, Family Research Laboratory, University of New Hampshire, Durham, NH, 1996

have failed. Spanking, he felt, can play a role in discipline under the following guidelines:

- Spanking is limited to a maximum of two slaps on the bottom with an open hand.

- The child is between ages 2 and 6.

- Spanking is used to supplement positive parenting, not to replace it.

- Spanking is used primarily to back up less aversive discipline responses, such as verbal correction and time-out.

Because the data on moderate spanking is so meager, Larzelere is concerned that

... the antispanking movement is in danger of becoming merely an attempt to impose the values of one segment of society upon others. Well-educated social scientists tend to be highly verbal and thus to favor exclusively verbal solutions to interpersonal conflict of all kinds. To others, however, actions may speak louder than words, a reasonable alternative as long as those actions are not abusive.

STRESS

There arc no "vacations" from being a parent, and parenting stress has been associated with abusive behavior. When a parent who may be predisposed toward maltreating a child must deal with a particularly stressful situation, it is possible that little time, energy, or self-control is left for the children. In times of stress, the slightest action by the child can be "the last straw" and lead to violent abuse.

Often, when the parent is striking out at a child, the parent may be venting anger at his or her own situation rather than reacting to some misbehavior on the part of the child. Children who have been abused indicate that they never knew when their parents' anger would explode and they would be severely beaten for the most minor infractions. Nonetheless, the child may also contribute to the stress. The child may be hostile and aggressive and a behavior problem.

Having Children With Disabilities

Children with disabilities are potentially at risk for maltreatment because they may require a lot of special care and attention, and parents may not have the social support to help ease stressful situations. The degree of stress in parents of disabled children may also be influenced by such factors as socioeconomic status, family structure, and parents' mental health and level of education. With increasing

age, a disabled child may develop some behavior problems that may exacerbate parental stress.

Toilet Training

Toilet training can be one of the most frustrating events in the lives of parents and children. Researchers are now linking it to many of the more serious, even deadly, cases of child abuse in children between the ages of 1 and 4. Some parents have unrealistic expectations, and when their children are unable to live up to these demands, the parents explode in rage. Parental stress and inability to control emotions play a role in child abuse, but they require a trigger to set off the explosion. Soiled clothes and accidents are frequently the triggers for these parents of toddlers.

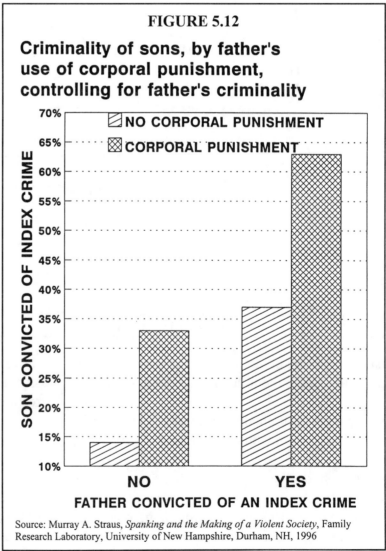

FIGURE 5.12

Criminality of sons, by father's use of corporal punishment, controlling for father's criminality

Source: Murray A. Straus, *Spanking and the Making of a Violent Society*, Family Research Laboratory, University of New Hampshire, Durham, NH, 1996

When children are brought to the emergency room with deep, symmetrical scald burns on their bottoms, it indicates that they were deliberately immersed in hot water and held there (even a one-second contact with 147-degree water can cause third-degree burns), a form of abuse nearly always committed as a result of a toilet accident. Some parents think that immersing the child in hot water will make the child go to the bathroom.

Toileting accidents can be especially dangerous for children because the parent has to place his or her hands on the child to clean up the mess, making it easy for the parent's rage to be taken out on the child's body. This abuse is more common in less-educated, low-income mothers who mistakenly believe that children should be trained by ages 12 to 16 months. More knowledgeable and better-educated parents are more likely to be aware that successful training for girls happens at around 2 years of age and sometimes not until age 3 or later for boys.

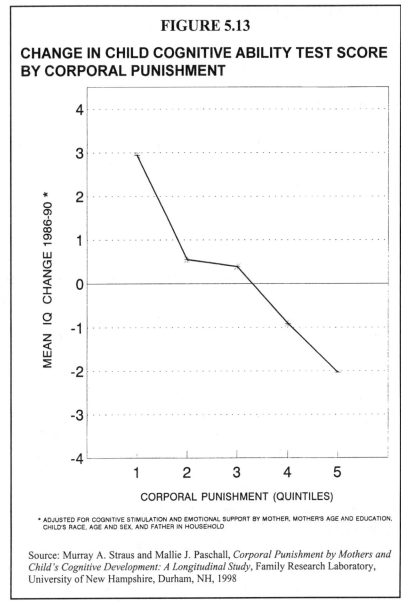

FIGURE 5.13

CHANGE IN CHILD COGNITIVE ABILITY TEST SCORE BY CORPORAL PUNISHMENT

* ADJUSTED FOR COGNITIVE STIMULATION AND EMOTIONAL SUPPORT BY MOTHER, MOTHER'S AGE AND EDUCATION, CHILD'S RACE, AGE AND SEX, AND FATHER IN HOUSEHOLD

Source: Murray A. Straus and Mallie J. Paschall, *Corporal Punishment by Mothers and Child's Cognitive Development: A Longitudinal Study*, Family Research Laboratory, University of New Hampshire, Durham, NH, 1998

IS CHILD NEGLECT A LOST CONCERN?

A simple child,
That lightly draws its breath,
And feels its life in every limb,
What should it know of death?
— William Wordsworth

When most Americans think of child maltreatment, they think of child abuse, not child neglect. Furthermore, research literature and conferences dealing with child maltreatment have generally overlooked child neglect. The congressional hearings that took place before the passage of the landmark Child Abuse Prevention and Treatment Act of 1974 (PL 93-247) focused almost entirely on examples of physical violence. Barely three pages in the hundreds recorded pertained to child neglect.

Nonetheless, every year, national surveys report a very high incidence of child neglect. *Child Maltreatment 1996: Reports From the States to the National Child Abuse and Neglect Data System* (Children's Bureau, U.S. Department of Health and Human Services, Washington, DC, 1998) and *Current Trends in Child Abuse Reporting and Fatalities: The Results of The 1997 Annual Fifty State Survey* (Ching-Tung Wang and Deborah Daro, National Committee to Prevent Child Abuse, Chicago, Illinois, 1998) counted more than twice as many reports of neglect as of physical abuse. (See Chapter IV.) Numerous other surveys confirm these findings.* In addition, around 2 in 5 of the children who die of child maltreatment die of neglect.

Child Neglect — A Major Social Problem

Neglect is an act of omission rather than commission. While the consequences of child neglect can be just as serious as abuse, neglect receives far less attention. Neglect may be evidenced in a child's appearance, such as being unkempt and unbathed or being severely malnourished, but in many cases, neglect leaves no visible marks. Moreover, it usually involves infants and very young children who cannot speak for themselves. (See Chapter II for more information on the different types of neglect.)

Martha Farrell Erickson and Byron Egeland, in "Child Neglect" (*The APSAC Handbook on Child Maltreatment*, SAGE Publications, Thousand Oaks, California, 1996), noted that child neglect is often entangled in patterns of family dysfunctions as well as environmental factors such as poverty. It is, therefore, difficult to assess whether the child's subsequent developmental problems are results of the neglect itself or of other factors in that child's life.

The authors studied neglected children in the *Minnesota Mother-Child Project*, one of the first major studies that focused on the antecedents of child maltreatment and the long-term consequences on children's development. (The antecedents of maltreatment refer to those circumstances that precede the child abuse and/or neglect, often having a causal relationship to the consequences of that maltreatment.) The Project is a longitudinal study (many aspects of the study are still going on) that tracks the development of 267 babies born to first-time mothers who are at risk for parenting problems due to poverty, youth, low level of education, lack of support, and unstable life situations.

Antecedents of Neglect

The *Minnesota Mother-Child Project* has found that "neglectful" parents have a difficult time understanding their relationship with their children. They tend to see situations in black and white and, therefore, cannot respond to the nuances of their children's behavior during their developmental process. This may be due to the parents' own neglected situations as children themselves or to their level of intellectual functioning. In the Minnesota study, among mothers who were neglected as children, 7 of 9 maltreated their children during the first two years of life; most of their children suffered neglect.

The families tracked by the Minnesota study did not have social support in child-raising. Within the same at-risk group of mothers, maltreating families had more stressful life situations than non-maltreating families. Emotional neglect, or "psychologically unavailable parenting," involves a lack of responsiveness to a child's need for attention. The psychologically unavailable mothers tended to be more tense, depressed, angry, and confused. When they did interact with their children, their responses were mechanical, revealing no warmth in their experiences with the children.

Consequences

James M. Gaudin, Jr., in "Child Neglect: Short-Term and Long-Term Outcomes" (*Neglected Children: Research, Practice, and Policy*, SAGE Publications, Thousand Oaks, California, 1999), reported that, compared to non-maltreated and abused children, studies had found neglected chil-

---

* Reports on neglect underestimate the real situation, since many surveys require evidence of serious injury or impairment to the child, which often occurs only in cases of serious neglect. In addition, since child protective services (CPS) agencies are inundated with reports of abuse, many overworked social workers, feeling they must make a choice between child abuse and child neglect, are choosing to file reports on child abuse, which they consider a more immediate danger than child neglect.

dren to have the worst delays in language comprehension and expression. Psychologically neglected children also scored lowest in IQ tests.

Emotional neglect, in its most serious form, can result in the *non-organic failure to thrive syndrome*, a condition in which a child fails to develop physically or even to survive. According to Gaudin, studies found that, even with aggressive intervention, the neglected child continued to deteriorate. The cooperation of the neglectful parents, which was crucial to the intervention, usually declined as the child's condition worsened, indicating that it is sometimes not that easy to change the parental attributes that contributed to the neglect in the first place.

Erickson and Egeland (see above) found that if neglected children manage to survive, the adverse effects of neglect carry over to their future adapting abilities in the school environment and in the outside world. The adverse consequences of neglect include a lack of affection toward the parents, over-dependence on teachers, a lack of enthusiasm and persistence in performing tasks, noncompliance, withdrawal, and, consequently, low peer acceptance. Those who suffer emotional neglect during the first two years of life are the most likely to exhibit these adverse effects. The authors added that the effects of neglect on children's development, contrary to some beliefs, far outweigh the effects of poverty. Erickson and Egeland observed,

Emotionally neglected children expect not to get what they need from others, and so they do not even try to solicit care and warmth. They expect not to be effective and successful in tasks, and so they do not try to succeed…. [T]eachers and peers are often put off by these children's behavior, thus perpetuating their previous relation-

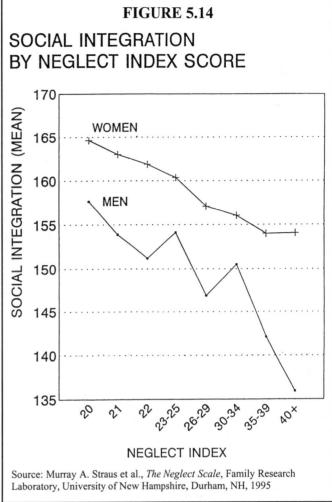

FIGURE 5.14

SOCIAL INTEGRATION BY NEGLECT INDEX SCORE

Source: Murray A. Straus et al., *The Neglect Scale*, Family Research Laboratory, University of New Hampshire, Durham, NH, 1995

ship experience and reinforcing their negative expectations of others and self.

Murray A. Straus, E. Milling Kinard, and Linda Meyer Williams, in *The Neglect Scale* (a paper presented at the Fourth International Conference on Family Violence Research in Durham, New Hampshire, July 23, 1995), found that neglect increases the probability of low social integration, which in turn increases the probability of all types of criminal behavior, including assaults on spouses or partners. In other words, the more neglect suffered in childhood, the lower the degree of social integration, especially as the neglect victim ages. The correlation between neglect and social integration is consistent, especially for men (Figure 5.14).

81

CHAPTER VI

CHILD SEXUAL ABUSE

Then there was the pain. A breaking and entering when even the senses are torn apart. The act of rape on an eight-year-old body is a matter of the needle giving because the camel can't. The child gives, because the body can, and the mind of the violator cannot. — I Know Why the Caged Bird Sings, Maya Angelou, 1970

A BETRAYAL OF TRUST

Many experts believe that sexual abuse is the most underreported type of child maltreatment. A victim, especially a very young child, may not know what he or she is experiencing; in many cases, the child is sworn to secrecy. Adults who may be aware of the abuse sometimes get involved in a conspiracy of silence.

In 1998, a 68-year-old grandfather in Texas was sentenced to prison for the sexual abuse of women in his family for more than 30 years. Trial testimony revealed that many family members knew of the patriarch's pattern of behavior. They not only kept quiet about it but also admonished the victims not to disclose their abuse.

Child sexual abuse is the ultimate misuse of an adult's trust and power over a child. When the abuser is particularly close to the victim, the child feels betrayed, trapped in a situation where an adult who claims to love the child is assaulting him or her. A patient once drew a picture of her father for her therapist, titled "Diagram of a Perpetrator." She drew the face, large hands, heart, and sex organs of her father. Next to the figure she wrote what he told her, including: "Trust me; I'll protect you; I'm not going to hurt you; better me than someone else; I'll make you a woman."

Some victims have described themselves as being nothing more than a sexual receptacle for their abusers. To explain how a victim feels, E. Sue Blume, in *Secret Survivors: Uncovering Incest and Its Aftereffects in Women* (John Wiley and Sons, New York, 1989), wrote,

> Try to imagine the humiliation and violation of a rape. Then imagine it as constant, unpredictable but inevitable. Now place it in the context of imprisonment. And finally, put it at the hands of a beloved caretaker — while he says it's for you that he's doing it. What sense of control over your life would you be able to salvage? Why even use your voice if it is never heard? The child's life becomes like the nightmare that many of us have had: we're in danger, we open our mouths to scream for help, and nothing comes out.

FREUD

The first person to present childhood sexual abuse as a source of psychological problems was Sigmund Freud. Early in his career, Freud proposed that the hysteria he saw in some of his patients was the result of childhood sexual abuse. He thought his patients' symptoms represented symbolic manifestations of their repressed sexual memories.

Freud later changed his mind, however, and denied that he thought abuse had taken place. Instead, he proposed that young children have an unconscious sexual attachment to the parent of the opposite sex and a sense of rivalry with the parent of the same sex. This is called the Oedipus complex in males or the Electra complex in females. Freud theorized that under the normal psychological developmental process, the child starts to identify with the parent of the same sex. If this does not occur, the individual would develop personality disorders in adulthood.

Why Freud lost faith in his patients' memories is unknown. Feminist scholars have proposed that he was pressured by colleagues to recant. Psychoanalyst Alice Miller claims that Freud suppressed the truth so that he, his colleagues, and men in Viennese society would be spared having to examine their own histories. Others believe that he revised his theories to preserve his concept of repression, "the cornerstone on which the whole structure of psychoanalysis rests." When his patients were not cured by revelations of sexual memories, Freud resolved the difficulty by claiming that they were instead repressing the "memories" of their desire for sexual unions they were unable to consummate. Some experts believe that the testimonies Freud originally elicited from his patients were cases of incestuous abuse.

WHAT IS CHILD SEXUAL ABUSE?

In "An Overview of Current Knowledge About Child Sexual Abuse," (a paper prepared for the Surgeon General's Conference on Violence, Leesburg, Virginia, October 1985), Dr. David Finkelhor, co-director of the Family Research Laboratory at the University of New Hampshire, Durham, and a leading researcher on child sexual abuse, defines the abuse as "it is commonly used in North America."

[Child sexual abuse] is sexual activity involving a child that has one of two dimensions: 1) it occurs in a relationship where it is deemed exploitative by virtue of an age difference or caretaking relationship

that exists with the child, or 2) it occurs as a result of force or threat. Thus, in professional and popular terms, there is almost universal agreement that sexual contact between a child and his/her father, stepfather, mother, stepmother, another older relative, teacher, or baby-sitter constitutes sexual abuse. Sexual contact at the hands of any adult or older person, whether known or unknown, is also sexual abuse. And rape and forced sexual contact at the hands of anyone, even a peer, is generally included.

Federal Definition

The first Child Abuse Prevention and Treatment Act of 1974 (PL 93-247) specifically identified parents and caretakers as the perpetrators of sexual abuse (see Chapter II). Sexual molestation by other individuals was considered sexual assault. However, the 1996 amendments to this law include a more comprehensive definition that also includes sexually abusive behavior by individuals other than parents and caretakers.

The Child Abuse Prevention and Treatment Act of 1996 (PL 104-235; Sec. 111 [42 U.S.C. 5106g]) defines child sexual abuse as:

- The employment, use, persuasion, inducement, enticement, or coercion of any child to engage in, or assist any other person to engage in, any sexually explicit conduct or simulation of such conduct for the purpose of producing a visual depiction of such conduct; or

- The rape, and in cases of caretaker or interfamilial relationships, statutory rape, molestation, prostitution, or other form of sexual exploitation of children, or incest with children.

Specific Definition Varies by State

Whereas the federal government has established a broad definition of child sexual abuse, it leaves it up to state child abuse laws to specify detailed provisions. All states have laws prohibiting child sexual molestation and generally consider incest (see below) as illegal. States also specify the age of consent — the age in which a person can consent to sexual activity with an adult, generally the ages between 14 and 18. Sexual activity between an adult and a child below the age of consent is against the law.

TYPES OF CHILD SEXUAL ABUSE

Familial abuse, or incest, involves the use of a child for sexual satisfaction by family members — blood relatives who are too close to marry. Extrafamilial abuse involves a person outside the family. Extrafamilial predators may be strangers, but they may also be persons in a position of trust, such as family friends, teachers, and spiritual advisers.

Some researchers define incest not in terms of blood ties but in terms of the emotional bond between the victim and the offender. Suzanne M. Sgroi, director of the Saint Joseph College's Institute for Child Sexual Abuse Intervention, believes that the presence or absence of blood relationships is far less important than the kinship roles the abusers play. When a live-in help or a parent's lover is the abuser, there may be no blood relationship, but the abuse is still taking place within the context of the family.

FACTORS THAT MAKE
SEXUAL ABUSE POSSIBLE

In *Childhood Sexual Abuse* (ABC-CLIO, Inc., Santa Barbara, California, 1995), Karen Kinnear lists five factors that make the sexual abuse of children possible.

- Force, both physical and psychological, is often used by sexual abusers. This includes bodily harm or killing a pet or other animal in front of the child, or threatening to withhold attention or special favors.

- Secrecy is easily achieved because victims are often convinced that they have done something wrong. Abusers also use psychological force and threats of physical harm to achieve secrecy.

- Lack of consent is a factor, although even if the abuser has consent, sex with a minor is considered abusive and illegal. In cases involving children, the victims are considered incapable of informed consent.

- Exploitation is used when sex offenders select children whom they perceive to be vulnerable to manipulation. Some experts speculate that children who have psychological or cognitive vulnerabilities may be at increased risk for sexual abuse. Exploitation involves a misuse of power, where an older, stronger, and more sophisticated person takes advantage of a younger, smaller, and less sophisticated person in order to satisfy the wishes and feelings of the more powerful person without regard for the less powerful person.

- Ambivalence is necessary on the part of the children, who often enjoy the attention they are receiving — as well as any rewards they may gain because of the abuse — more than they dislike the abuse.

HOW FREQUENT IS ABUSE?

Research on the problem of child sexual abuse is contradictory and the more studies that are done, the more researchers find that the extent of the problem is difficult to measure. Because state definitions vary, the number of cases of abuse may not include acts committed by nonfamily members. Therefore, rates of child sexual abuse reported are generally just estimates. S. K. Weinberg, in *Incest Behavior* (Citadel Press, New York), had calculated the average yearly rate to be only 1.9 cases per million people in 1955.

By 1969, Dr. Vincent De Francis and the American Humane Association had found an annual rate of 40 per 1 million children. In 1996, the *Third National Incidence Study of Child Abuse and Neglect* (NIS-3) reported a rate of 3.2 per 1,000 children under the Harm Standard and 4.5 per 1,000 children under the Endangerment Standard. (See Tables 4.9 and 4.10 in Chapter IV; the chapter also explains the two *NIS-3* standards.)

Some Victims May Not Be Counted

Estimates of the numbers of abuse cases generally do not include the victims of pornographic exploitation and child prostitution. These types of child abuse have only recently become subjects of research, and while they are known to involve multimillion-dollar businesses, little is known about the numbers of child victims involved.

Nor do the estimates include stranger abductions, often for sexual purposes, which result in the death of the child. According to the U.S. Department of Justice, annually, there are about 114,600 attempted abductions of children by nonfamily members and over 354,000 by family members. Another 438,200 children are lost, injured, or otherwise harmed.

In David Finkelhor and Jennifer Dziuba-Leatherman's poll of children ("Children as Victims of Violence: A National Survey," *Pediatrics,* vol. 94, no. 4, October 1994), 6.1 percent of respondents reported ever having been the object of a kidnapping attempt. Of those, 0.2 percent reported that the attempt was completed.

Adults Who Disclose Sexual Abuse

Many individuals who work in the field of sexual abuse believe that, to obtain a more accurate estimate of the rate of abuse, the researcher must ask adults whether they were abused during childhood. In 1995, the Gallup Organization surveyed 1,000 parents nationwide about their sexual abuse experiences as children. When asked if they had been touched in a sexual way or had been asked to touch someone in a sexual way before the age of 18, 22 percent reported that it had happened at least once. Nine percent of the respondents reported that they were forced to have sex before the age of 18. (See Table 6.1.) The questions posed by the Gallup Organization demonstrate one of the problems with studies of sexual abuse. While Gallup pollsters asked questions about touching and having sex, many studies do not ask questions about specific sexual experiences.

David Finkelhor, in the "Current Information on the Scope and Nature of Child Sexual Abuse" (*The Future of Children: Sexual Abuse of Children*, vol. 4, no. 2, Summer/Fall 1994), thought that surveys of adults regarding their childhood experiences (called retrospective studies) "probably provide the most complete estimates of the actual extent of child sexual abuse." He reviewed 19 adult retrospective surveys and found that the proportion of adults who indicated sexual abuse during childhood ranged widely from 2 per-

---

TABLE 6.1

Now I would like to ask you something about your own experiences as a child that may be very sensitive. As you know, sometimes, in spite of efforts to protect them, children get sexually abused, molested, or touched in sexual ways that are wrong. To find out more about how often they occur, we would like to ask you about your own experiences when you were a child....

Before the age of 18, were you personally ever touched in a sexual way, or were you ever forced to touch, an adult or older child in a sexual way – including anyone who was a member of your family, or anyone outside your family? (If "Yes", asked:) Did it happen more than once?

Yes, it happened more than once	14%
Yes, it happened just once	8
No, it did not happen	77
No opinion	1
	100%

Before the age of 18, were you ever forced to have sex by an adult or older child – including anyone who was a member of your family, or anyone outside your family? (If "Yes", asked:) Did it happen more than once?

Yes, it happened more than once	5%
Yes, it happened just once	4
No, it did not happen	90
No opinion	1
	100%

Source: The *Gallup Poll Monthly*, December 1995

cent to 62 percent for females and from 3 percent to 16 percent for males.

Finkelhor observed that the studies that reported higher levels of abuse were those that asked multiple questions about the possibility of abuse. Multiple questions were more effective because they "gave respondents more cues regarding the various kinds of experiences that the study was asking about and because they gave the respondents a longer time and more opportunities to overcome embarrassment and hesitation about making a disclosure." Many experts accept the estimate that 1 in 5 (20 percent) of American women and 1 in 10 (10 percent) of American men have been subjected to some form of sexual abuse as children.

Do some adults exaggerate trivial incidents or fabricate experiences that inflate abuse statistics? Finkelhor believed there is no evidence to suggest that fabrication has distorted the validity of surveys, and yet no study had been done (nor is it likely that it would be possible to do so) that examined the actual circumstances of alleged abuse reported in any large-scale study.

While the actual numbers of sexual abuse can only be roughly estimated, experts do agree that demographic trends suggest that more children are in situations of risk than ever before. More mothers are working outside the home, more children are in day-care centers, and more parents are divorcing and remarrying, bringing stepfamilies together in much greater numbers than ever before.

A Landmark Study of Child Sexual Abuse

One of the early landmark studies of child sexual abuse was conducted by sociologist Diana Russell in 1978. She surveyed 933 adult women in San Francisco about their early sexual experiences (*The Secret Trauma: Incest in the Lives of Girls and Women*, BasicBooks, New York, 1986). Russell found that 38 percent of the women had suffered some type of sexual abuse before their eighteenth birthday. About 16 percent had been abused by a family member.

Russell's study is still frequently cited by experts who believe that much more abuse occurs than is officially reported by government studies. They suggest the high results recorded in her study reflect the thoroughness of her preparation. While other studies have asked one question concerning childhood sexual abuse, she asked 14 different questions, any one of which might have set off a memory of sexual abuse. Some of Russell's colleagues thought her high rate of positive response might be explained by her sample. Perhaps San Francisco attracted more women with a history of abuse than a city in the Midwest.

THE VICTIMS

Start and Duration of Abuse

Kathleen Kendall-Tackett and Roberta Marshall, in "Sexual Victimization of Children" (*Issues in Intimate Violence*, Raquel Kennedy Bergen, ed., SAGE Publications, Thousand Oaks, California, 1998), reported that studies have found that "the mean age of onset is frequently much younger than puberty." The age of victims at the start of the abuse could very likely be anywhere between 7 and 13, although there have been cases of sexual abuse among children 6 years or younger. The sexual abuse may be a one-time occurrence or it may last for several years. The authors found durations of abuse ranging from 2.5 to 8 years.

Race and Ethnicity

In "Sexual Abuse of Children" (*The APSAC Handbook on Child Maltreatment*, SAGE Publications, Thousand Oaks, California, 1996), Lucy Berliner and Diana M. Elliott reported that Black children were more likely to be the youngest victims of sexual abuse, while Asians were more likely to be older at the onset of sexual abuse. Black and Hispanic victims were more likely than White and Asian victims to experience penetration during sexual assault. Asian children tended to be abused by a male relative, while White children were more likely victims of acquaintance assault.

Is Sexual Abuse of Boys Underreported?

Virtually all studies indicate that girls are far more likely than boys to suffer sexual abuse. Under the Harm and Endangerment Standards of *The Third National Incidence Study of Child Abuse and Neglect* (the most comprehensive study of the incidence of child maltreatment in the United States, see Chapter IV), girls were sexually abused about three times more often than boys. (See Tables 4.11 and 4.12 in Chapter IV.)

Dr. William C. Holmes of the University of Pennsylvania School of Medicine claims that "sexual abuse of boys appears to be common, underreported, underrecognized, and undertreated." In "Sexual Abuse of Boys: Definition, Prevalence, Correlates, Sequelae, and Management" (*The Journal of the American Medical Association*, vol. 281, no. 21, December 2, 1998), Holmes reviewed 149 studies of male sexual abuse. These studies, conducted between 1985 and 1997, included face-to-face interviews, telephone surveys, medical chart reviews, and computerized and paper questionnaires. The respondents included adolescents (ninth- through twelfth-graders, runaways, non-sex-offending delinquents, and detainees), college students, psychiatric patients, Native Americans, sex offenders (including serial rapists), substance-abusing patients, and homeless men. Holmes found that, overall, 1 in 5 boys had been sexually abused.

Characteristics of Male Child Victims and Their Families

The studies found that sexual abuse generally began before puberty. Boys younger than 13 years, non-White, of low socioeconomic status, and not living with their fathers were at a higher risk for sexual abuse.

Boys whose parents had divorced, separated, or remarried; had abused alcohol; and had criminal records were more likely to experience sexual abuse. Sexually abused boys were 15 times more likely than boys who had never been sexually abused to live in families in which some members had also been sexually abused.

Sexual Abusers of Boys

Studies of children and young teens revealed that more than 90 percent of sexual abusers of boys were male, while studies of older teens and young adults showed 22 percent to 73 percent of male perpetrators. This older age group also had proportions of female perpetrators ranging from 27 to 78 percent. Adolescent babysitters accounted for up to half of female sexual abusers of younger boys.

More than half of the perpetrators were not family members but were known to the victims. Boys younger than 6 years were more likely to be sexually abused by family and acquaintances, while those older than 12 years were more likely to be victims of strangers.

Duration, Nature, and Consequences of Sexual Abuse of Boys

About 17 to 53 percent of the respondents reported repeated abuse, with victimization continuing from less than 6 months to 18 to 48 months. Anal penetration was more likely to be repeated than other forms of sexual abuse. While male perpetrators used physical force, with threats of physical harm increasing with victim age, female perpetrators used persuasion and promises of special favors. One study found that up to one-third of boys participated in the abuse out of curiosity.

Only 15 to 39 percent of respondents thought that they were adversely affected by the sexual abuse. They stressed that the adverse effects were linked to the use of force, a great difference in victim-perpetrator age, or in cases in which the perpetrator was so much older or the victim was very young. However, Dr. Holmes noted that negative clinical results (in contrast to what the studies subjects reported) included post-traumatic stress disorder, major depression, paranoia, aggressive behavior, poor self-image, poor school performance, and running away from home.

The author also found a connection between sexual abuse and subsequent substance abuse among male victims. Sexually abused males were also more likely to have sex-related problems, including sexual dysfunction, hypersexuality, and the tendency to force sex on others. He surmised that the discrepancy between the respondents' perceptions of the negative consequences of their sexual victimization and those discovered in clinical outcomes may be due to several factors. Holmes explained,

> Perhaps abused males perceive that they have failed to meet a social expectation of self-protection. Rather than accept the failing, they may minimize the event itself. The experience of physical pleasure, as well, may complicate reactions after abuse.

David Finkelhor (*Child Sexual Abuse*, The Free Press, New York, 1984) felt that besides trying to live up to society's expectation of self-protection, boys do not reveal their sexual abuse for fear of being stigmatized as homosexuals, since many of their abusers are male. Boys are generally allowed more freedom than girls are to come and go. Some may fear a loss of this independence if their parents found out about their victimization.

THE PERPETRATORS

While the stereotype of child sexual abuse is often that of a parent abusing a child, studies of victims' retrospective history have found that familial perpetrators make up from one-third to one-half the abusers of girls and only about one-tenth to one-fifth for boys. Children are also abused by neighbors, teachers, coaches, religious leaders, and peers. About one-third of offenders are juvenile perpetrators. This percentage, it should be noted, is based on studies that included date rape and sexual assaults of teenagers by their peers.

Fathers

David Finkelhor, in "The Sexual Abuse of Children: Current Research Reviewed" (*Psychiatric Annals: The Journal of Continuing Psychiatric Education,* April 1987), found that while reports from child welfare systems were dominated by sexual abuse by fathers and stepfathers, they actually made up no more than 7 to 8 percent of all sexual abuse cases. Other family members (usually uncles and older brothers) made up from 16 to 42 percent, while nonrelatives known to the child (neighbors, family friends, child care workers, etc.) accounted for 32 to 60 percent of child sexual abusers.

Linda Meyer Williams and David Finkelhor, in *The Characteristics of Incestuous Fathers* (Family Research Laboratory, University of New Hampshire, Durham, 1992), found that, generally, incestuous fathers had lonely childhoods (82 percent). Almost half (47 percent) had not lived with their own fathers and had changed living arrangements, perhaps as a result of parental divorce or remarriage (43 percent). However, their own parents' alcohol problems were no different from that of the non-abused comparison group. Incestuous fathers were far more likely to have been juvenile delinquents, to have been rejected by their parents, and to have experienced physical and sexual abuse as children. (See Table 6.2.) The researchers also found that the sex education of incestuous fathers while growing up did not come from friends or peers, but from being victims of sexual abuse. See Table 6.3 for the victimization history of incestuous fathers.

Women Who Abuse

Until recently, experts thought female sex abusers were uncommon, and when women were involved, it was thought to be a situation in which a man had forced the woman to commit the abuse. Some experts postulate that women are more maternal and, therefore, less likely to abuse a child. Women are also thought to have different attitudes towards sex — while a man's self-esteem is supposedly related to his sexual experiences, a woman is supposedly less concerned with sexual prowess and more empathetic toward others.

Mothers

Sexual abuse by mothers may remain undetected because it occurs at home and is either denied or never reported. Mothers have more intimate contact with their children, and the lines between maternal love and care and sexual abuse are not as clear-cut as they are for fathers. Furthermore, society is reluctant to see a woman as a perpetrator of incest, portraying the woman as someone likely to turn her pain inward into depression, compared to the man, who acts out his anger in sexually criminal behavior.

Characteristics of Abusing Women

Women in positions of trust have been known to sexually abuse children. In 1997, 35-year-old Mary Kay LeTourneau pleaded guilty to the sexual abuse of her 13-year-old male student. She became sexually involved with the then-sixth grader in 1996, became pregnant, and gave birth to their child in 1997. The court suspended her prison sentence of 7.5 years and sentenced her instead to six months in jail, with credit for time already served. She was also required, among other things, to cease any contact with the boy and undergo a sex-offender treatment program.

In 1998, LeTourneau was re-arrested after having contact with the boy and was sentenced to serve the rest of her 7.5-year prison sentence. She has since given birth to a second child fathered by the student.

Some researchers have proposed that the abusive behavior of women is influenced by severe psychiatric disturbance, mental retardation, brain damage, or male coercion. C. Allen studied female offenders in "A Comparative Analysis of Women Who Sexually Abuse Children" (a final report to NCCAN, Iowa State University, 1990) and found that their lives involved particularly harsh childhoods marked by instability and abuse.

Comparing male and female offenders, Allen found that the females reported more severe incidents of physical and emotional abuse in their pasts, had run away from home more often, were more sexually promiscuous than male offenders, and had more frequent incidents of being paid for sex. Both male and female offenders reported that their victims were most often members of their own families, although female offenders were more likely to admit to abuse with strangers.

Female offenders were less likely to admit guilt because they perceived child sexual abuse as a great social deviance. They were less cooperative than men during the investigations and were angrier with informants and investigators. They also experienced less guilt and sorrow than male offenders following disclosure.

TABLE 6.2

Incestuous and Non-Incestuous Fathers' Childhood Experiences (N = 234)

Childhood Experiences	IF	CN	Sig.	Odds Ratio
Lonely	82%	46%	***	(5.29)
Lived apart from father	47%	36%		
Lived apart from mother	30%	17%	*	(2.02)
Changed living situations	43%	32%		
Resided in an institution	5%	3%		
Father alcohol problem	36%	35%		
Mother alcohol problem	11%	10%		
Problem with stealing	34%	25%		
Problem with bedwetting	30%	22%		
Problem with fire setting	21%	10%	*	(2.33)
Problem with school failure	52%	29%	***	(2.63)
Abuse History				
Severe abuse by father	54%	21%	***	(4.54)
Severe abuse by mother	37%	14%	***	(3.72)
Rejection by mother	67%	30%	***	(4.79)
Rejection by father	31%	6%	***	(6.77)
Child sexual abuse	70%	32%	***	(5.06)

Source: Linda Meyer Williams and David Finkelhor, *The Characteristics of Incestuous Fathers*, Family Research Laboratory, University of New Hampshire, Durham, NH, 1992

Sibling Sexual Abusers

Sibling incest is another form of abuse that has not been well studied. Some experts think, however, that sibling sexual abuse is more common than father-daughter incest. Vernon R. Wiehe, in "Sibling Abuse" (*Understanding Family Violence*, SAGE Publications, Thousand Oaks, California, 1998), believed that the problem of sibling incest has not received much attention because of the parents' attitude towards this type of sexual abuse — the families' reluctance to report to authorities that such abuse is happening in their homes, the parents' downplaying of the fact that "it" is indeed a problem, and the perception that it is normal for brothers and sisters to explore their sexuality.

The author also felt that a very serious factor is that the victim may be living with threats of real harm from the abusive sibling. Indeed, in the author's nationwide survey of survivors of sibling abuse (see also Chapter V), the incest victims reported an interaction of physical abuse and incest, such as threats of physical harm or even death if the parents were told. An interaction of emotional abuse and incest might involve constant humiliation from the sibling perpetrator, such as comments that the victim was no longer a virgin. Wiehe believes that sexual abuse by a sibling should be considered a crime of rape.

In terms of prosecuting the perpetrator, his use of aggression, force, or threats brings his behavior into the realm of rape, regardless of the nature of the activity. For example, fondling a victim's genitals can no longer be labeled less harmful than sexual intercourse because the consequences are the same: The victim's right to privacy has been abused by means of an aggressive act. In other words, the victim has been raped.

TABLE 6.3

Incestuous and Non-Incestuous Fathers' Sexual Victimization History (N = 234)

	IF	CN
Sexually Abused in Childhood	70%	32%
Abused by Multiple Perpetrators	45%	13%
Abused by:		
Mother	12%	0%
Father	9%	0%
Brother	8%	1%
Sister	6%	3%
Male Cousin	8%	1%
Uncle	7%	0%
Female Cousin	5%	3%
Aunt	5%	0%
Grandfather	1%	0%
Non-Family Adult Male	35%	14%
Non-Family Adult Female	24%	14%
Non-Family Male Juvenile	13%	3%
Non-Family Female Juvenile	11%	4%
Stranger	16%	13%

Source: Linda Meyer Williams and David Finkelhor, *The Characteristics of Incestuous Fathers*, Family Research Laboratory, University of New Hampshire, Durham, NH, 1992

Pedophiles

Until recently, a pedophile was stereotyped as a lonely, isolated man who generally sought employment that permitted contact with children. Experts now know that men and women, homosexual and heterosexual, married and single, may be pedophiles. In 1998, employees of a Tulsa, Oklahoma, pediatric dentist notified authorities after discovering pornographic photographs of children in his office. The father of three daughters and youth minister in his church, the dentist had been anesthetizing young patients and photographing them in lewd positions.

This is not to say that the stereotypical pedophile does not exist. For example, a male who delivered vans across the country picked out possible victims in small towns. His victims were girls 2 to 8 years old whom he would follow home, returning late at night to break into the house and molest them either in their homes or in another location. The man told police he had been molested as a child and that it pushed him toward a fascination with pornography. He had fantasies of raping and killing children, but although he claimed to have killed children, the police did not find any evidence to support that claim.

Pedophiles on the Internet

Pedophiles often exploit children they have lured into trusting relationships through attention and gifts. Their victims are often lonely children with low self-esteem who are not well-supervised by adults.

Many pedophiles have found that the Internet gives them easy access to vulnerable children. They target and recruit potential victims through electronic conversations. Pedophiles also contact one another through the Internet and computer online services, transmitting electronic images and sharing experiences.

Under federal law, the possession or transmission of child pornography is illegal. (See Chapter VII.) Since 1993, the Federal Bureau of Investigation (FBI) has been investigating and identifying individuals who originate, upload, or forward child pornography. So far, these efforts have resulted in about 135 arrests nationwide. In 1997, New York State identified over 1,500 people around the world suspected of trafficking in child pornography over the Internet. About 34 people were arrested in New York, and 90 others awaited prosecution in the states and other countries.

The Clergy

The Roman Catholic Church has recently publicly admitted to a number of incidents of sexual abuses committed by priests. In 1998, the Catholic diocese of Lafayette, Louisiana, agreed on a settlement of about $18 million to the 48 young people who had been sexually abused by the priest Gilbert Gauthe and his staff. In 1997, a Dallas, Texas, jury awarded $118 million in damages to 10 men and the family of another man who committed suicide at 20 years of age. Rudoph Kos had sexually abused altar boys, some of them nine-year-olds, when he was a seminary student and later as a priest in three Dallas parishes between 1977 and 1992. Although other priests had complained about his sexual interest in boys, he was ordained in 1988. The jury found that the church not only ignored Kos's actions, but also tried to cover up the abuse.

The Chicago archdiocese has found 37 cases where priests had been guilty of sexual misconduct. In 1993, the Catholic Church settled a case in which 11 friars in a seminary in Santa Barbara had molested dozens of students over the course of more than 20 years. Those making charges against the Church have maintained that priests who are accused of molesting children are simply moved away to another parish, where they are free to molest a new set of children.

Although the Church has settled several claims against priests, not all the claims of abuse are necessarily justified. In 1995, charges of sexual abuse brought against the late Joseph Cardinal Bernadin, Archbishop of Chicago, were dropped when his accuser decided that his recovered memories of abuse were not reliable enough. Catholic priests are not the only representatives of an organized religion to have been exposed for sexually abusing children, but the Catholic Church may get more scrutiny because priests' vows of celibacy might seem to make them more likely offenders.

A PIONEER IN THE STUDY OF DEVIANT SEXUAL BEHAVIOR

A critical step in bringing a scientific focus to the study of sexual deviance was achieved by Kurt Freund, a psychiatrist born in what is now the Czech Republic, when he created a method to test male response to erotic stimuli. With Freund's phallometric device, which some experts have compared to a lie detector, the penis is put into a tube. The tube is sealed, and the man is shown slides or movies of adult men and women and of boys and girls. The air displacement from the tube shows increases in penile volume, which are recorded so the tester can see which images caused the greatest penile reactions. This was the first of many such testing mechanisms since developed. Freund,* who died in October 1996, was among the first to conclude that child molesters were incapable of changing their sexual outlook; today, treatment programs are based on his presumption.

THE EFFECTS OF CHILD SEXUAL ABUSE

Effects on Children and Adolescents

Many studies have been conducted to determine the effects of sexual abuse. Kathleen A. Kendall-Tackett, Linda Meyer Williams, and David Finkelhor ("Impact of Sexual Abuse on Children: A Review and Synthesis of Recent Empirical Studies," *Psychological Bulletin*, vol. 113, no. 1, 1993) reviewed various studies on the impact of child sexual abuse. The most commonly studied behavior was sexualized behavior, often considered the most characteristic symptom of sexual abuse. Case studies revealed 5- and 6-year-old children who sexually attacked playmates, acted out sexually with family pets, compulsively masturbated, and inserted objects into their own bodies.

Other symptoms that were frequently studied included anxiety, depression, withdrawn behavior, aggression, school problems, and regression including enuresis (bed-wetting) and encopresis (passing of feces in unacceptable places after bowel control has been achieved). Post-traumatic stress disorder (PTSD) is a reaction to a traumatic experience, like sexual abuse, that manifests itself by the reliving of the trauma, nightmares, memory impairment, insomnia, and psychological numbness. Poor self-esteem is common among abuse victims, but it is difficult to compare abused children with non-abused children because poor self-esteem can stem from so many different sources. (See Table 6.4.)

However, when sexually abused children were compared to other children receiving psychological help for problems other than abuse, the sexually abused children were actually less symptomatic than the other children except for sexualized behavior and PTSD.

The authors compiled the percentages of children who were reported for different symptoms and found that an average of 20 to 30 percent of victims manifested any particular symptom. Only PTSD was reported by a majority of the victims, although they noted that half of the children included in this calculation were victims of severe ritualistic abuse (see below). (See Table 6.4.) If these children were removed from the data, the percentage dropped to 32 percent, near the level of other symptoms.

When the studies were further divided by children's ages, the researchers found that certain symptoms manifested themselves at different points in the child's life. For children 18 months and younger, the signs of possible sexual abuse included urinary and bowel problems, inappropriate fear of adults, fear of being abandoned, failure to thrive, excessive crying, and sleep disturbances. (See Table 6.5.)

For preschoolers, the most common symptoms were anxiety, nightmares, general PTSD, internalizing, externalizing, and sexual behavior. School-age children were most often affected by fear, neurotic and general mental illness, aggression, nightmares, school problems, hyperactivity, and regres-

---

* Freund and other researchers postulated that homosexuality was not a pathological condition that needed to be treated. In 1973, the American Psychiatric Association took homosexuality off its list of disorders.

TABLE 6.4
Percentage of Sexually Abused Children With Symptoms

Symptom	% with symptom	Range of %s	No. studies	N
Anxiety	28	14–68	8	688
Fear	33	13–45	5	477
Posttraumatic stress disorder				
Nightmares	31	18–68	5	605
General	53	20–77	4	151
Depression				
Depressed	28	19–52	6	753
Withdrawn	22	4–52	5	660
Suicidal	12	0–45	6	606
Poor self-esteem	35	4–76	5	483
Somatic complaints	14	0–60	6	540
Mental illness				
Neurotic	30	20–38	3	113
Other	6	0–19	3	533
Aggression				
Aggressive/antisocial	21	13–50	7	658
Delinquent	8	8	1	25
Sexualized behavior				
Inappropriate sexual behavior	28	7–90	13	1,353
Promiscuity	38	35–48	2	128
School/learning problems	18	4–32	9	652
Behavior problems				
Hyperactivity	17	4–28	2	133
Regression/immaturity	23	14–44	5	626
Illegal acts	11	8–27	4	570
Running away	15	2–63	6	641
General	37	28–62	2	66
Self-destructive behavior				
Substance abuse	11	2–46	5	786
Self-injurious behavior	15	1–71	3	524
Composite symptoms				
Internalizing	30	4–48	3	295
Externalizing	23	6–38	3	295

Source: Kathleen A. Kendall-Tackett, Linda Meyer Williams, and David Finkelhor, "Impact of Sexual Abuse on Children: A Review and Synthesis of Recent Empirical Studies," *Psychological Bulletin*, vol. 113, no. 1, 1993. Copyright © 1993 by the American Psychological Association. Reprinted with permission.

sive behavior. Adolescents' most common behaviors included depression, withdrawal, suicidal or self-injurious behaviors, illegal acts, running away, and substance abuse. (See Table 6.5.) The authors theorized that sexual behavior in preschoolers may be submerged during the school-age period and then resurfaces in adolescence as promiscuity, prostitution, or sexual aggression.

Some Show No Symptoms

A substantial proportion of victims appear to be without any of the symptoms (asymptomatic) measured by the studies. Different studies have found between 21 to 49 percent of the children to be asymptomatic. Experts have offered various explanations for why so many children exhibited no symptoms — the researchers have not used sufficiently sensitive measures or have not looked for the right symptoms; the children have not yet manifested their symptoms and will do so when their "victim status comes to have more meaning or consequences for them;" or asymptomatic children were less affected or not at all affected.

The findings of different studies indicated that abuse characterized by a closely related perpetrator, high frequency of sexual contact, long duration, use of force, penetration, lack of maternal support at the time of disclosure, and a victim's negative outlook or coping style led to increased symptoms. Strong maternal support was the most important factor in reducing symptoms over time.

TABLE 6.5

Percentage of Children With Symptoms by Age Group

Symptom	% of subjects (No. studies/No. subjects)			
	Preschool	School	Adolescent	Mixed
Anxiety	61 (3/149)	23 (2/66)	8 (1/3)	18 (4/470)
Fear	13 (1/30)	45 (1/58)	—	31 (2/389)
Posttraumatic stress disorder				
Nightmares	55 (3/183)	47 (1/17)	0 (1/3)	19 (2/402)
General	77 (1/71)	—	—	32 (3/80)
Depression				
Depressed	33 (3/149)	31 (2/66)	46 (3/129)	18 (2/409)
Withdrawn	10 (1/30)	36 (1/58)	45 (2/126)	15 (3/446)
Suicidal	0 (1/37)	—	41 (3/172)	3 (2/397)
Poor self-esteem	0 (1/25)	6 (1/17)	33 (1/3)	38 (4/438)
Somatic complaints	13 (2/54)	—	34 (1/44)	12 (2/442)
Mental illness				
Neurotic	20 (1/30)	38 (1/58)	24 (1/25)	—
Other	0 (1/37)	19 (1/58)	16 (2/69)	3 (1/369)
Aggression				
Aggressive/antisocial	27 (3/154)	45 (1/58)	—	14 (3/446)
Delinquent	—	—	8 (1/25)	—
Sexualized behavior				
Inappropriate sexual behavior	35 (6/334)	6 (1/17)	0 (1/3)	24 (7/999)
Promiscuity	—	—	38 (2/128)	—
School/learning problems	19 (2/107)	31 (1/58)	23 (2/69)	17 (2/418)
Behavior problems				
Hyperactivity	9 (2/55)	23 (2/75)	0 (1/3)	—
Regression/immaturity	36 (4/159)	39 (2/75)	0 (1/3)	15 (2/389)
Illegal acts	—	—	27 (1/101)	8 (3/469)
Running away	—	—	45 (3/172)	4 (3/469)
General	62 (1/17)	—	—	28 (1/49)
Self-destructive behavior				
Substance abuse	—	—	53 (2/128)	2 (3/658)
Self-injurious behavior	—	—	71 (2/128)	1 (1/369)
Composite symptoms				
Internalizing	48 (1/69)	—	—	24 (2/226)
Externalizing	38 (1/69)	—	—	23 (2/226)

Source: Kathleen A. Kendall-Tackett, Linda Meyer Williams, and David Finkelhor, "Impact of Sexual Abuse on Children: A Review and Synthesis of Recent Empirical Studies," *Psychological Bulletin*, vol. 113, no. 1, 1993. Copyright © 1993 by the American Psychological Association. Reprinted with permission.

Problems Can Be Masked or Even Overcome

In "Treating Abused Adolescents" (*The APSAC Handbook on Child Maltreatment*, SAGE Publications, Thousand Oaks, California, 1996), Mark Chaffin, Barbara L. Bonner, Karen Boyd Worley, and Louanne Lawson noted that little is known about why some children and teenagers are able to overcome the effects of sexual abuse. Nonetheless, this ability to overcome can be explained, in part, by a lack of severe or frequent abuse and, in part, by the "attribution theory," which holds that "abuse effects are mediated not so much by the objective characteristics of the abuse as by how we subjectively explain it to ourselves. Attributions are the internal 'theory' we articulate about what caused and maintained the problem."

Those who use internal attribution (blame themselves) experience depression, greater distress, low self-esteem, and feelings of helplessness because they did not control the situation. On the other hand, those capable of external attribution (blaming someone or something else) manage to come away from sexual abuse with their emotions intact, reasoning that they live in a dangerous world and they were randomly and unavoidably victimized. It is the latter, Chaffin et al. maintain, who can more easily overcome psychological effects of sexual abuse.

High-Risk Behavior by Adolescent Females

Jacqueline L. Stock, Michelle A. Bell, Debra K. Boyer, and Frederick A. Connell, in "Adolescent Pregnancy and Sexual Risk-Taking Among Sexually Abused Girls" (*Family Planning Perspectives*, vol. 29, no. 5, September/October 1997), found that adolescents who had been sexually abused were 3.1 times as likely as those who had not been sexually abused to report that they had ever been pregnant. Moreover, victims of sexual abuse were also more likely to have had intercourse by the time they were 15 years old, to have not used birth control during their last intercourse, and to have had more than one sexual partner.

Effects on Adults

Recently, the issue of the effects of child sexual abuse on adults has become very controversial. Many therapists who specialize in helping adults confront child sexual abuse have developed lists of symptoms so inclusive, critics charge, that based on those criteria, everyone must have been abused. Eating disorders, distorted self-image, depression, low self-esteem, and multiple personality disorder (MPD; now clinically referred to as Dissociative Identity Disorder [DID]) are some of the more commonly cited symptoms.

In "Sexual Abuse of Children" (*The APSAC Handbook on Child Maltreatment*, see above), Lucy Berliner and Diana M. Elliott pointed out that sexual abuse during childhood is a major risk factor for a variety of problems in adulthood. They also noted, however, that the problems are not uniform. Some experience no coping problems or mild coping problems, and others feel overwhelmed and unable to cope. Research on the long-term effects of childhood sexual abuse has focused on women, but the authors explain that adult male victims suffer as well. Men tend to externalize their pain through anger or abuse toward others. Women generally internalize their distress and suffer from depression, self-hatred, and anxiety.

Berliner and Elliott also describe another coping mechanism called dissociation. Often seen in adult survivors of sexual abuse, dissociation is a sort of psychic numbing thought to be a defense against abuse-related memories. Survivors who can dissociate abuse-specific thoughts, effects and memories are able to reduce their importance in their lives. This manner of avoidance, when used to deal with traumatic events, has been associated with amnesia, multiple personalities, and a diminishing ability to appropriately cope with other problems. (See Chapter VIII for a discussion of the controversy about therapists' diagnosis of abuse.)

Diane N. Roche, Marsha G. Runtz, and Michael A. Hunter studied female undergraduate students who had suffered child sexual abuse ("Adult Attachment: A Mediator Between Child Sexual Abuse and Later Psychological Adjustment," *Journal of Interpersonal Violence*, vol. 14, no. 2, February 1999). The researchers found that, overall, the women who were victims of child sexual abuse were less secure and more fearful in their adult relationships, compared to the control group. Moreover, those who suffered family abuse exhibited more negative attachment relationships (see quote below) than those abused by nonfamily.

> [A]buse by a family member violates the child's basic beliefs about safety and trust in important relationships; this likely disrupts the child's developing sense of self. The development of the self continues to be an important task throughout infancy, childhood, adolescence, and early adulthood. Intrafamilial abuse may continue to negatively influence the continuing development of the model-of-self long after the abuse has ended and, therefore, may have a cumulative effect on the abuse survivor's ability to sustain satisfying relationships and secure attachments in adulthood.

The researchers also found that the victim's damaged perceptions of self, others, and relationships may play a role in her resulting psychological problems.

SEXUAL ABUSE IN DAY CARE CENTERS

The changing nature of American society has led to a huge increase in the number of families using child care facilities. Scandals involving sexual abuse of children in day care centers, especially those highly publicized in the 1980s, have caused concern that these facilities may not be safe places to leave children.

David Finkelhor, Linda Meyer Williams, and Nanci Burns of the Family Research Laboratory (*Sexual Abuse in Day Care: A National Study*, Durham, New Hampshire, 1988) studied day care centers from January 1983 through December 1985 in all 50 states. After adjusting for reporting problems, the researchers extrapolated (projected for the whole country) 500 to 550 substantiated cases involving 2,500 young children. Based on their findings, they concluded that the sexual abuse rate for day care centers was 5.5 children sexually abused per 10,000 children enrolled. This was considerably lower than the rate for children under age 6 who were sexually abused in their own homes (8.9 per 10,000 children, based on 1985 data).

Characteristics of Perpetrators in Day Care Centers

Many of the researchers' findings concerning abusers at day care centers did not fit commonly accepted stereotypes. Women made up 40 percent of the abusers, far higher than any other findings on child sexual abuse. However, it must be noted that the overwhelming proportion of workers at day care centers are women. In fact, the researchers noted that "it is actually remarkable that men were still responsible for the majority of abuse in day care when they account for only an estimated 5% of the staff."

Characteristics of Abuse

Two-thirds of the abuse occurred in the bathroom, "a locale where abusers can be alone and unobserved with children who can be tricked into undressing and allowing their genitals to be touched." Touching and fondling of the children's genitals were the most common form of abuse, but penetration (including oral, digital, and object) occurred to at least one child in 93 percent of all cases.

Children were forced to abuse other children in 21 percent of the cases. Pornography production was suspected in 14 percent and drug use in 13 percent of the cases. Ritualistic abuse ("the invocation of religious, magical, or supernatural symbols or activities" — see below) occurred in 13 percent of the cases.

The researchers believed that victims in day care centers were "more threatened, coerced, and terrorized than in many other kinds of sexual abuse" because the abusers probably believed they had to terrorize the children into keeping quiet. In fact, in one-third of the cases, it took more than six months before the children revealed the abuse, and in over half the cases, the children took at least a month to tell of the abuse. On the other hand, in about 20 percent of all cases, the victims disclosed the abuse immediately after its occurrence. Usually, the parents had suspected something wrong with their child and coaxed the story out of him or her, but 37 percent of the cases were simply revealed by the children.

Finkelhor et al. concluded,

Although a disturbing number of children are sexually abused in day care, the large numbers coming to light are not an indication of some special high risk to children in day care. They are simply a reflection of the large number of children in day care and the relatively high risk of sexual abuse to children in all settings.

RITUAL CHILD ABUSE

Adding fuel to the concern about abuses in day care is the link between some day care abuse and alleged satanic rituals so horrible and bizarre they are hard to believe. Nearly all the investigations of these cases are inconclusive because of a lack of evidence and the fact that the tales are so fantastic many people cannot accept them. In June 1984, a case of ritual abuse in Bakersfield, California, started when a 5-year-old girl told her mother that she had been sexually abused by her father and another man. Within a year, the case had grown to include 77 adults, the alleged murders of 27 children, allegations of cannibalism, satanic rituals, and the removal of 21 children from their homes.

According to Richard Wexler (*Wounded Innocents*, Prometheus Books, Buffalo, New York, 1995), the children involved in the case were in-

terviewed by "sheriff's deputies who had not received the specialized training required under state law." He added, "During the interviews, the deputies would tell the children what happened and get upset if the children didn't confirm it." The case was dropped after one of the children said that the social worker covering the case was herself part of the satanic cult and was molesting children. Furthermore, no bodies were ever found.

Are children all over the country lying when they tell remarkably similar, bizarre stories? Wexler is not alone in claiming the stories are similar because they are implanted into the minds of the children through the poor investigative techniques of therapists and other professionals. (See Chapters VII and VIII.)

This is not to say that ritual sex abuse does not exist, but despite the myriad of allegations involving ritual sacrifice of young children, no actual victims have ever been found. Therapists who accept ritual abuse cases claim to be treating an increasing number of patients exhibiting symptoms of multiple personality disorder (MPD; see also above), a disorder thought to be a coping mechanism by the children to deal with the extreme trauma they are forced to endure in satanic abuse. These therapists claim personalities, or "alters," are created to take the pain, or to handle anger, or any other part of life that the child cannot deal with. (See Chapter VIII.)

Occasionally, some evidence of ritual abuse does surface. A case in Manchester, England, uncovered limestone tunnels in a cemetery where children claimed to have been abused, as well as a small altar and traces of wax. On the other hand, similar claims were also made in the McMartin Preschool case in California (see Chapter VII).

A Study of Ritual Abuse

David W. Lloyd (*Ritual Child Abuse: Understanding the Controversies*, National Resource Center on Child Sexual Abuse, Huntsville, Alabama, 1990), in exploring the controversies surrounding ritual child abuse, found no specific symptoms in a child that definitively pointed to ritual abuse. Neither could he find accuracy in adult reports of being victimized as children by satanic cults. However, he felt the public should not be too quick to either reject or believe the occurrence of ritual child abuse, presenting instead the arguments of doubter and believers.

Those with doubts argue that if these cults were in existence 20 and 30 years ago, at the time these adults were children, we should have heard the same rumors of child maltreatment that we hear today. Instead, there is little or no evidence of their existence — no corpses, satanic paraphernalia, or diaries by participants — and there have been few identified survivors that could independently corroborate each other's accounts or experiences in the same location. Further, these individuals frequently suffer from multiple personality disorder or from post-traumatic stress disorder as a result of some traumatic childhood experience, but state that they had no conscious memories of these events until they had undergone hypnosis. A number of forensic experiments with hypnotic suggestion raises doubts about the accuracy of recall of events after hypnotic trances.

On the other hand, since the effects of psychological intimidation can be long-lasting, survivors of ritual child abuse may not have felt safe in coming forward until recently, when the public has been more able to accept the reality of child sexual abuse. In addition, the public has only learned about post-traumatic stress disorder and multiple personality disorder within the last few years. It is possible that those children and adults in previous decades who dared to report their childhood victimization were not believed and sent to mental health professionals where they were misdiagnosed as psychotic, without any meaningful investigation by law enforcement officials.

A Study of Ritual Abuse Reports and Evidence

Gail S. Goodman et al., in *Characteristics and Sources of Allegations of Ritualistic Child Abuse*, a report to the National Center on Child Abuse and Neglect (Washington, DC, 1994), discussed four studies that dealt with the evidence or lack of evidence in ritual abuse cases. For comparison, the investigators also looked into allegations of religion-related abuse (for example, withholding of medical care, or abuse by religious officials, such as priests).

In the first study, the objective was to survey clinicians who might work with ritual and religion-related abuse cases. A total of 720 clinical psychologists, psychiatrists, and social workers provided information on 1,548 such cases. These cases had been reported to them by victims who were either adult survivors or children. Claims of the adult ritual cases were the most extreme and involved more severe types of abuse, such as murder, cannibalism, and baby breeding for ritual sacrifice. Victims in adult ritual cases were most likely to be diagnosed with multiple personality disorders. The only evidence reported in ritual abuse cases was the patient's disclosure during hypnotherapy and, in a few cases, scars. "Even when there were scars," Goodman wrote, "it was not determined whether the victims themselves had caused them."

Child cases involved more evidence than adult cases. Child religion-related cases were more likely to involve solid evidence of harm than other categories. Child religion-related cases also led to more affirmative legal outcomes, while adult ritual cases led to the fewest outcomes.

In the second study, Goodman et al. surveyed different agencies that were involved with just child abuse allegations — offices of district attorneys, departments of social services, and law enforcement agencies. Generally, this group described reports of ritual abuse as involving multiple perpetrators and victims and relatively high numbers of female perpetrators and male victims. In both studies, adult and child religion-related cases were alleged to have been committed by people in positions of trust, such as parents or religious leaders. However, allegations against strangers or acquaintances were the more common norm in ritual abuse.

The third study examined repression and recovery of memories of early abuse. Repressed memory (RM) cases were characterized by more types of abuse and a larger number of perpetrators than those not based on RM. The alleged abuse started earlier and lasted longer and was more likely to involve ritual abuse than non-RM cases. According to Goodman, "None of the evidence indicated the existence of the bizarre and horrible satanic ritual abuse scenarios which allegedly occurred in many RM cases." (See Chapter VIII for more on repressed memory.) The investigators noted that the clinicians believed their patients' allegations of abuse, whether ritual or religion-related.

The fourth study examined whether a child's suggestibility promotes false reports of ritual child abuse. In other words, the study examined if children have the knowledge base to create details of ritual abuse. Of the children surveyed, those ages 3 to 12 had little knowledge of satanic child abuse. Generally, the older the child, the more knowledge of satanic as well as religious activities he had. The fact that younger children had little knowledge of ritual abuse does not mean their reports of satanic abuse were true. Goodman felt it means that children were unlikely to have made up such reports.

She also warned that the results of the fourth study must be interpreted cautiously. For ethical reasons, the children were not asked about satanic ritual abuse. Instead, they were asked about God, the devil, heaven, hell, symbols, and pictures.

Kenneth V. Lanning, a Supervisory Special Agent with the Federal Bureau of Investigation (FBI) and one of the foremost national experts on child molestation, claims that satanic or ritual abuse is rare and that the FBI has never found evidence or credible witnesses indicating the existence of satanists who ritually abuse children sexually. In "Investigator's Guide to Allegations of Ritual Child Abuse" (FBI, Washington, DC, 1992), Lanning wrote,

Any professional evaluating victims' allegations of "ritual abuse" cannot ignore or routinely dismiss the lack of physical evidence (no bodies or physical evidence left by violent murders); the difficulty in successfully committing a large-scale conspiracy crime (the more people involved in any crime conspiracy, the harder it is to get away with it); and human nature (intragroup conflicts resulting in individual self-serving disclosures are likely to occur in any group involved in organized kidnapping, baby-breeding, and human sacrifice). If and when members of a destructive cult commit murders, they are bound to make mistakes, leave evidence, and eventually make admissions in order to brag about their crimes or to reduce their legal liability.

CHAPTER VII

CHILD ABUSE AND THE LAW

JUVENILE COURTS

As early as the mid-seventeenth century in colonial America, adults accused of child abandonment, excessive physical abuse, and of depriving their children of basic necessities faced criminal trials. It was not until 1899 that a statewide (Illinois) juvenile court system was created to prosecute abusive adults in civil trials. Today, all 50 states have authorized juvenile family courts* to intervene in child abuse cases, and all 50 states consider child abuse of any kind a felony and a civil crime. A felony could result in a prison term; a loss of a civil suit could result in the payment of a fine or in losing custody of children.

In civil child protection cases, the accused has the right to a closed trial (a hearing with no jury and closed to the public), in which court records are kept confidential, although a few states permit jury trials. On the other hand, in criminal child protection cases, the person charged with abuse is entitled to the Sixth Amendment right to an open trial (a jury trial opened to the public), which can be waived only by the defendant.

In 1967, *In re Gault* (387 U.S.1) substantially changed the nature of juvenile courts. Initially, children were not subject to constitutional due process rights or legal representation, and judges presiding over these courts were given unlimited power to protect children from criminal harm.

Gault established that children — whether they have committed a crime or are the victims of a crime — are entitled to due process and legal representation. These rights, however, are interpreted differently among the states.

Court-Appointed Special Advocate (CASA)

As a judge, I had to make tough decisions. I had to decide whether to take a child from the only home he's ever known, or leave him someplace where he might possibly be abused. I needed someone who could tell me what was best for that child — from the child's viewpoint. That's what CASA does.
— Judge David W. Soukup, founder of CASA

In the past, for many abused and neglected children who could not be reunited with their families, foster care became a permanent placement. In the 1970s, David W. Soukup, presiding judge of the King County Superior Court in Seattle, Washington, realized that judges did not always have enough information to make the right decision to serve the best interests of the child.

Traditionally, the child's advocate in court had been the guardian *ad litem*, an attorney appointed by the court. The lawyers, however, usually did not have the time or training to conduct a thorough review of each child's case. Judge Soukup

---

* While many states have distinct and separate juvenile courts, some states try juvenile or family cases in courts of general jurisdiction, where child protection cases are given priority over other cases on the court's docket.

recruited and trained community volunteers to serve as the children's long-term guardians *ad litem*. The role of the Court-Appointed Special Advocate (CASA) was born on January 1, 1977, and Seattle's program has since been adopted nationwide.

The role of CASA volunteers varies in different states. They either act as or work with the guardians *ad litem*. Each trained volunteer works only with one or two children at a time, thereby enabling him or her to research and monitor each case thoroughly.

DISCLOSURE

The relationship between child abuse and the law is often controversial when it deals with sexual abuse. Physical abuse and neglect usually leave unmistakable marks, and the physical abuser is less likely than a sexual abuser to deny responsibility when confronted.

What should parents do when their children claim to have been abused? It may come as an off-hand remark, as if the child is testing to see what a parent's reaction will be. Perhaps the child is engaged in sexualized behavior (a common symptom of sexual abuse) and then adds that this is what a parent, stepparent, relative, or a teacher at school has done.

A major preschool sexual abuse case against Margaret Kelly Michaels, a teacher at the Wee Care Nursery School in Maplewood, New Jersey, began when a boy at the pediatrician's office who was having his temperature taken rectally looked up and remarked, "That's what my teacher does to me at school." The statement ultimately led to Michaels' being charged with various forms of sexual abuse and a nine-month trial at which several children testified. (See below for outcome of trial.)

Sometimes a parent realizes that something is wrong when the child's behavior changes. Some young children have an especially hard time expressing themselves verbally and may instead begin having sleep difficulties, such as nightmares and night terrors; eating problems; a fear of going to school (if that is the site of the abuse); regression; acting out, such as biting, masturbating, or sexually attacking other family members; and withdrawing. However, these behavior changes do not necessarily mean that the child is being sexually abused. Children may also express themselves in their drawings.

The abuse may have occurred for a long time before children tell. Why do children keep the abuse a secret? Children who reveal their abuse through the nonverbal ways listed above may be afraid to speak out because they believe the threats of death or punishment made by their abusers. Child Abuse Listening Mediation (CALM), a California counseling organization, lists some of the reasons children do not tell:

- Children feel responsible for what happened to them.

- Children fear adults will not believe them.

- Children believe threats from the offender.

- Children do not know how to describe what has happened to them.

- Children are taught to be respectful of adults.

- Children fear getting an adult in trouble or disobeying an adult who has requested secrecy.

According to CALM, children tell

- When they come in contact with someone who appears to already know.

- When they come in contact with someone who does not appear to be judgmental, critical, or threatening.

- When they believe a continuation of the abuse will be unbearable.

- When physical injury occurs.

- When they receive sexual abuse prevention information.

- If pregnancy is a threat.

- When they come into contact with someone who may protect them.

If parents believe their child, particularly if the abuser is not a family member, their first reaction may be to file charges against the alleged perpetrator. Parents rarely realize how difficult and painful the process can be. Some experts claim that children psychologically need to see their abuser punished, while others feel the court process victimizes the children again, only this time by the very people who are supposed to protect them.

THE CHILD'S STORY

Some experts believe children do not lie about abuse. They point out that children cannot describe events unfamiliar to them. For example, the average six-year-old has no concept of how forced penetration feels or how semen tastes. Experts also note that children lie to get themselves out of trouble, not into trouble, and reporting sexual abuse is definitely trouble. The child who accuses her father of abuse does not necessarily get any support at home. In "The Child Sexual Abuse Accommodation Syndrome" (*Child Abuse and Neglect*, No. 7, 1983), Dr. Roland Summit, an advocate for sexually abused children, described the all too common result of accusation.

In the chaotic aftermath of disclosure, the child discovers that the bedrock fears and threats underlying the secrecy are true. Her father abandons her and calls her a liar. Her mother does not believe her or decompensates into hysteria and rage. The girl is blamed for causing the whole mess, and everyone seems to treat her like a freak. Unless there is special support for the child and immediate intervention to force respon-

sibility on the father, the girl will follow the "normal" course and retract her complaint. The children learn not to complain. The adults learn not to listen.

Children sometimes recant, or deny that any abuse has happened, after they have disclosed it. Perhaps the reaction to the disclosure was unfavorable or the pain and fear of talking about the experience was too great. If the child recants under interrogation in a court of law, it is extremely damaging to the case and encourages claims that children make false accusations.

Not A Lie But Not The Truth Either

Kenneth V. Lanning of the Federal Bureau of Investigation (FBI; see Chapter VI), in "Criminal Investigation of Suspected Child Abuse — Criminal Investigation of Sexual Victimization of Children" (*The APSAC Handbook on Child Maltreatment*, SAGE Publications, Thousand Oaks, California, 1996), claimed that "children rarely lie about sexual abuse." However, some children may recount what they believe in their mind to be the truth, although their accounts may turn out to be inaccurate. Lanning gave the following explanations for these inaccuracies (in author's own words):

- The child may be exhibiting distortions in traumatic memory.

- The child's account might reflect normal childhood fears and fantasy.

- The child's account might reflect misperception and confusion caused by the deliberate trickery or drugs used by perpetrators.

- The child's account might be affected by suggestions, assumptions, and misinterpretations of overzealous interveners.

- The child's account might reflect urban legends and shared cultural mythology.

The Pressure of the Judicial System

Once the child becomes enmeshed in the courts, his or her testimony may become muddled. Children, by definition, are immature in their physical, reasoning, and emotional development. In "Early and Long-Term Effects of Child Sexual Abuse" (*Professional Psychology*, no. 21, 1990), David Finkelhor, co-director of the Family Research Laboratory at the University of New Hampshire, Durham, pointed out that "the validity of reports declines with distance from the event." Therapists who believe children do not invent abuse feel that if a child's story changes, then psychological progress is being made because the child is dealing with the emotional trauma. For the courts, however, changing stories raises doubts.

Often, the goals of the therapist and the judicial system are at odds. The therapist's goal is to protect the best interests of the child. If, to encourage the child to speak out, a therapist asks leading questions (questions that suggest a specific answer — "Did daddy take his clothes off?" — rather than "What did daddy look like? What was he wearing?"), the purpose is to help the child remember painful events that need to be expressed. The courts, however, look at such questions as leading the witness. Cases have fallen apart when it appeared that therapists put words in the children's mouths. Critics charge that an alleged abuse may go to trial because an overzealous therapist or investigator has implanted the occurrence of abuse into the child's impressionable mind.

By the time a case makes it to the courtroom, most children are under a great deal of stress. Many will have undergone a thorough genital/rectal examination by a physician and relentless interrogations by innumerable strangers. A child may have been interviewed over 30 times by therapists, lawyers, the police, child protective services workers, and the parents. Some of these people may have experience with sexual abuse cases; many may not, and their goals will be very different. How can a child possibly be able to handle this? Nonetheless, our legal system demands this process in order to give every accused person a fair trial and a chance to be cleared of the charges.

Sexual abuse cases are different from most trials in that the question is not just who did it, but did it actually happen? In cases where there is frequently no physical evidence of the crime, it is crucial for the jury to hear the children testify. Many people, however, feel that children are not able to present credible evidence to a jury. Testimony by others, such as the parents, is often excluded by hearsay rules (rules that prevent a witness from repeating in court those statements someone else has made about the case).

THE CHILD AS A COMPETENT WITNESS

Traditionally, judges protected juries from incompetent witnesses, which originally included women, slaves, and children. Children were believed to live in a fantasy world, and their inability to understand terms like "oath," "testify," and "solemnly swear" denied them the right to appear in court. In 1895, the U.S. Supreme Court, in *Wheeler v. United States* (159 U.S. 523), established the rights of child witnesses. The Court explained,

> There is no precise age which determines the question of competency. This depends on the capacity and intelligence of the child, his appreciation of the difference between truth and falsehood, as well as of his duty to tell the former. The decision of this question rests primarily with the trial judge, who sees the proposed witness, notices his manner, his apparent possession or lack of intelligence, and may resort to any examination which will tend to disclose his capacity and intelligence as well as his understanding of the obligation of an oath. To exclude [a child] from the witness stand would sometimes result in staying the hand of justice.

As a result of this ruling, the courts formalized the *Wheeler* decision, requiring judges to interview all children to determine their competency. It was not until 1974 that the revised Federal Rules of Evidence abolished the competency rule so that children may testify at trial in federal courts regardless of competence.

In state courts, judges sometimes still apply the competency rule regardless of state laws that may have banned it. In the 1987 Margaret Kelly Michaels case (see below), the judge chatted with each child witness before he or she testified, holding a red crayon and asking questions like, "If I said this was a green crayon, would I be telling the truth?"

THE CONFRONTATION CLAUSE

It is difficult for children to deal with the fear and intimidation of testifying in open court. The person who has allegedly abused and threatened them may be sitting before them, while the serious nature of the court can be intimidating to them. The use of videotape and closed-circuit television has become common methods to relieve the pressure on the child who must testify. Currently, 35 states and the federal government recognize the right to use videotaped testimony taken at depositions or preliminary hearings for children under age 18. In addition, 34 states and the federal government recognize the right to use closed-circuit television testimony.

Using closed-circuit television testimony has been challenged on the grounds that the defendant's Sixth Amendment constitutional right permits him or her to confront an accuser face to face. The Confrontation Clause of the Sixth Amendment states, "In all criminal prosecutions, the accused shall enjoy the right … to be confronted with the witnesses against him…."

Several court rulings in the last decade (see below) had generally, but not always, upheld the introduction of closed-circuit television, but only when it had been used carefully and with full recognition of the rights of the accused. Those who disagree with these rulings claim that this method unfairly influences the jury to think the accused is guilty simply because this procedure was permitted, and, worse, it deprives the defendant of his or her constitutional right to confront the accuser face to face.

State Rulings

State v. Lomprey

In 1992, Mark Lomprey appealed a conviction for sexually abusing his niece (*State of Wisconsin v. Lomprey*, 496 N.W.2d 172 [Wis.App. 1992]). The defendant maintained that his right to cross-examine the child in a videotaped interview that was shown to the court was denied because when he entered the room, she curled herself up into a ball ("withdrew into her shell") and refused to speak. The trial court made two more efforts to provide both sides with opportunities to interrogate the child, but she would not respond. She was so withdrawn that the defendant's attorney did not even attempt to question her. The appeals court found that the child's behavior was "in fact, a statement." A statement includes "nonverbal conduct of a person if it is intended by him as an assertion." The court found that the child asserted through her conduct that she feared the defendant.

Commonwealth v. Willis

Leslie Willis, who was indicted for the sexual abuse of a five-year-old child, claimed that the child was an incompetent witness and should, therefore, not be allowed to testify in his trial. The trial judge conducted a private hearing to determine the child's competency, but the child was unresponsive.

The prosecution proposed that, pursuant to the Kentucky statute allowing the testimony of a child abuse victim age 12 or younger to testify by videotape or closed-circuit television, the trial should proceed using such method. The state statute permits such testimony if there is "substantial probability that the child would be unable to reasonably communicate because of serious emotional distress produced by the defendant's presence." The trial judge ruled to exclude the child's testimony because he was of the opinion that the provisions of the Kentucky statute allowing such testimony were unconstitutional. He held the statute not only violated the Sixth Amendment Confrontation Clause (see above) and Section Eleven of the Kentucky Constitution "to meet the witnesses face to face," but also the separation of powers doctrine of the state Constitution.

Without the testimony of the child witness to the alleged crime, the case could not go to trial. Therefore, the prosecution appealed the case. The Kentucky Supreme Court, in *Commonwealth v. Willis* (Ky., 716 S.W.2d 224 [1986]), upheld the state law permitting the child to testify by videotape or closed-circuit television. It ruled that the law did not violate the defendant's state and federal rights of confronting his witness. The Court pointed out that the defendant's right to hear and see the witness testify remained intact. He could "object to and seek exclusion of all portions of a tape which he consider[ed] unfair or unduly prejudicial." He also had the right of cross-examination through consultation with his lawyer. Moreover, the jury could assess the credibility of the witness.

The Court also ruled that the state law did not violate the separation of powers doctrine of the Kentucky Constitution, because the law left it up to the judge to use his discretion in applying the law. The Court concluded,

> The strength of the State and Federal Constitutions lies in the fact that they are flexible documents which are able to grow and develop as our society progresses. The purpose of any criminal or civil proceeding is to determine the truth. [The law] provides such a statutory plan while protecting the fundamental interests of the accused as well as the victim.

Federal Rulings

Coy v. Iowa

In June 1988, the U.S. Supreme Court ruled on a similar case — an Iowa trial court, pursuant to a state law enacted to protect child victims of sexual abuse, allowed a screen to be placed between the two child witnesses and the alleged abuser. The lighting in the courtroom was adjusted so that the children could not see the defendant, Coy, through the screen. However, Coy was able to dimly see the children and hear them testify. The trial judge cautioned the jury that the presence of the screen was not an indication of guilt. Coy was convicted.

In *Coy v. Iowa* (397 N.W.2d 730, 1986), Coy appealed to the Iowa Supreme Court, arguing that the screen denied him the right to confront his accusers face to face as provided by the Sixth Amendment. In addition, he claimed that due process was denied because the presence of the screen implied guilt. The Iowa Supreme Court, however, upheld the conviction of the trial court, ruling that the screen had not hurt Coy's right to cross-examine the child witnesses, nor did its presence necessarily imply guilt.

The U.S. Supreme Court, however, in a 6-2 decision, reversed the ruling of the Iowa Supreme Court and remanded (sent back) the case to the trial court for further proceedings. In *Coy v. Iowa* (487 U.S. 1012, 1988), the High Court maintained that the right to face-to-face confrontation was the essential element of the Sixth Amendment's Confrontation Clause. It held that any exceptions to that guarantee would be allowed only if needed to further an important public policy. The Court found no specific evidence in this case that these witnesses needed special protection that would require a screen.

The two dissenters, Justice Harry A. Blackmun and Chief Justice William Rehnquist, argued that the use of the screen is only a limited departure from the face-to-face confrontation, justified by a substantially important state interest that does not require a case-by-case scrutiny.

Maryland v. Craig

In June 1990, in a 5-4 decision, the U.S. Supreme Court upheld the use of one-way closed-circuit television. In *Maryland v. Craig* (497 U.S. 836), a six-year-old child alleged that Sandra Craig had committed perverted sexual practices and assault and battery on her in the pre-kindergarten run by Craig. In support of its motion to permit the child to testify through closed-circuit television, the state presented expert testimony that the child "wouldn't be able to communicate effectively, would probably stop talking and would withdraw, and would become extremely timid and unwilling to talk."

The High Court decision, written by Justice Sandra O'Connor, noted that, although "it is always more difficult to tell a lie about a person 'to his face' than 'behind his back,'" the Sixth Amendment Confrontation Clause does not guarantee *absolute* right to a face-to-face meeting with the witness. The closed-circuit television does permit cross-examination and observation of the witness's demeanor. "We are therefore confident," Justice O'Connor declared, "that use of the one-way closed-circuit television procedure, where necessary to further an important state interest, does not impinge upon the truth-seeking or symbolic purposes of the Confrontation Clause."

Justice Joseph Scalia, dissenting, felt that the Constitution had been juggled to fit a perceived need when the Constitution explicitly forbade it. He stated, "We are not free to conduct a cost-benefit analysis [comparison of the benefits] of clear and explicit constitutional guarantees and then to adjust their meaning to comport [agree] with our findings."

HEARSAY EVIDENCE

Hearsay rules give special exemptions to the basic law, which prohibits admitting statements into testimony that are said by individuals who are not witnesses to the case. Together with the Sixth Amendment Confrontation Clause, hearsay rules were intended to prevent the conviction of defendants by reports of evidence offered by someone they would be unable to challenge.

Certain exceptions to the ban on hearsay have always been allowed. A dying person's last words are permitted in court because it is thought that dying people no longer have anything to gain (or lose) by lying and will speak the truth on their deathbeds. Whether or not to accept the hearsay evidence from a child's reports of abuse to a parent has been frequently debated.

In *Ohio v. Roberts* (448 U.S. 56, 1979), the U.S. Supreme Court established the basis for permitting hearsay — the actual witness has to be unavailable and his or her statement has to be reliable enough to permit another person to repeat it to the jury. Many judges have chosen to interpret unavailability on physical standards rather than the emotional unavailability that children who are afraid to testify may exhibit. Furthermore, legal experts insist that the reliability of a statement does not refer to whether the statement appears to be truthful, but only that it has sufficient reliability for the jury to decide if it is true or not.

Spontaneous declarations (unprompted statements made in a nonlegal situation) and statements made to medical practitioners are two exceptions that have also been permitted in some states. For example, in *State v. Nelson* (110 S.Ct. 835, 1990), a psychologist was allowed to repeat in a Wisconsin courtroom the statements of a child about abuse because the child believed she was visiting the psychologist as part of her treatment.

However, Josephine A. Bulkley, J.D., a consulting attorney with the American Bar Association's Center on Children and the Law, pointed out, in "Child Abuse and Neglect Laws and Legal Proceedings" (*The APSAC Handbook on Child Maltreatment*, SAGE Publications, Thousand Oaks, California, 1996), that some states have concluded that children, especially younger children, do not understand "that psychological treatment will make them better, and so the motive of being truthful does not exist. Therefore the child's statements do not qualify as statements for the purposes of medical diagnosis or treatment."

Hearsay evidence is especially important in cases of child sexual abuse. Cases often take years to come to trial, by which time a child may have forgotten the details of the abuse or may have made psychological progress in dealing with the trauma, and the parents may be reluctant to plunge the child back into the anxious situation suffered earlier. Hearsay evidence can also be crucial in determining the validity of sexual abuse charges in custody cases. In these cases, juries need to know when the child first alleged abuse, to whom, under what circumstances, and whether the child ever recanted.

The Greenbrook Preschool case (reported in *On Trial: America's Courts and Their Treatment of Sexually Abused Children* by Billie Dziech and Charles Schudson, Beacon Press Books, Boston, Massachusetts, 1989, with all identifying details changed to protect the families) was lost largely because of the judge's strict interpretation of hearsay. The parents of the children were not permitted to tell the jury anything the children had revealed in conversations during the year between the discovery of the abuse and the trial. Illogical court testimony ensued.

At one point, the defense asked one of the parents to relate a conversation she had had with the school's teacher and director. "I asked if they [the teacher and director] had any explanation for the sexual detail that Laurie had gone into." (The jury had no knowledge of the sexual detail because the court had not permitted Laurie's mother to talk about it.) The defense objected, and the judge sustained the objection, saying, "The jury will not assume that she went into sexual detail because that would be hearsay."

The Validity of Hearsay Evidence

In *United States v. Inadi* (475 U.S. 387, 1986), the U.S. Supreme Court clarified its intentions on hearsay evidence that did not concern child sexual abuse. The Court explained that "unavailability" was not a required criterion for the admission of hearsay. In fact, the Court wrote that some statements "derive much of their value from the fact

they are made in a context very different from trial and, therefore, are usually irreplaceable as substantive evidence." The Arizona Supreme Court in *State v. Robinson* (735 P.2d 801, 1987) permitted hearsay evidence from a ten-year-old girl to her psychologist.

An additional factor of great weight in this case is the unlikelihood that more trustworthy or probative evidence could have been produced by [the child's] in-court testimony. A young child's spontaneous statements about so unusual a *personal* experience, made soon after the event, are at least as reliable as the child's in-court testimony, given months later, after innumerable interviews and interrogations may have distorted the child's memory. Indeed, [her] statements are valuable and trustworthy in part because they were made in circumstances very different from interrogation or a criminal trial.

White v. Illinois

In *White v. Illinois* (502 U.S. 346, 1992), the U.S. Supreme Court dealt with both the hearsay rules and the Confrontation Clause of the Sixth Amendment. Randall White was charged with sexually assaulting a four-year-old girl, S.G., in the course of a residential burglary. The child's screams attracted the attention of her babysitter, who witnessed White leaving the house. S.G. related essentially the same version of her experience to her babysitter, her mother (who returned home shortly after the attack), a policeman, an emergency room nurse, and a doctor. All of these adults testified at the trial. S. G. did not testify, being too emotional each time she was brought to the courtroom.

White was found guilty and appealed on the grounds that, because the defendant had not been able to face the witness who had made the charges of sexual assault, her hearsay testimony was invalid under the Confrontation Clause. The High Court, in a unanimous decision, rejected linking the Confrontation Clause and the admissibility of hearsay testimony.

S. G.'s statements fulfilled the hearsay requirements in that they were either spontaneous declarations or made for medical treatment and, therefore, in the eyes of the Court, "may justifiably carry more weight with a [court] than a similar statement offered in the relative calm of the courtroom." The Court concluded that whether the witness appeared to testify had no bearing on the validity of the hearsay evidence. Furthermore, because the hearsay statements in this case fit the "medical evidence" and "spontaneous declaration" exceptions, the Court decision upheld hearsay evidence as valid.

This decision, coupled with the *Inadi* decision (see above), has affected hundreds of child abuse cases. More prosecutors can now risk taking on abuse cases without having to rely on a frightened child's testimony to reveal the full story.

EXPERT WITNESSES

Videotaping and closed-circuit television permit juries to see and hear child witnesses, but it does not mean that the juries will understand or believe them. Prosecutors often request permission to bring in an expert witness to clarify an abused child's behavior, particularly to explain why a child might have waited so long to make an accusation or why the child might withdraw an accusation made earlier.

The danger of bringing in an expert witness is that the expert often conveys to the jury a stamp of authenticity to the child's truthfulness. If an expert states that children rarely lie about sex abuse, that expert might be understood by the jury to be saying that the defendant is guilty. In some highly contested cases, expert witnesses swayed the jury in their decision. In the Margaret Kelly Michaels case (see below), an expert witness explained how the children's problems were symptomatic of their abuse. In the Eileen Franklin case (see Chapter VIII), the expert witness convinced the jury of the

validity of repressed memory and explained that inconsistencies in Franklin's story were symptoms of her trauma.

Expert Witnesses Differ

M. A. Mason, in "A Judicial Dilemma: Expert Witness Testimony in Child Sex Abuse Cases" (*Psychiatry and Law,* vol. 42, 1991), analyzed 122 appellate court cases of child sexual abuse. She found that experts cited both consistent and inconsistent accounts by children at the trials as evidence of abuse. In addition, other researchers have found that in some cases "expert testimony" has been offered by a child protective services employee with as little as "six months on the job and knowledge of three or four pertinent articles." It would appear that in some trials, neither the jury nor the "experts" are aware that sexualized behavior, inappropriate knowledge of sex, and inconsistent accounts are frequently found in non-abused children who have been exposed to suggestive sexual influences.

For expert testimony to be acceptable in the court, the statements made must be very general and explain only psychological tendencies, never referring specifically to the child witness. For example, a Wisconsin court permitted testimony on why a victim does not always report sexual abuse right away, while a Kentucky court reversed a decision when a social worker testified that the child's behavior was consistent with "sexual abuse accommodation syndrome" (accepting the abuse and not reporting it) and that few children invent such allegations.

The Federal Court of Appeals, in *U.S. v. Azure* (801 F.2d 336, 1986), reversed the conviction of the defendant. An expert witness had testified that the alleged victim was believable. According to the court, "by putting his stamp of believability on [the young girl's] entire story, [the expert] essentially told the jury that [the child] was truthful in saying that [the defendant] was the person who sexually abused her. No reliable test for truthfulness exists and [the expert witness] was not qualified to judge the truthfulness of that part of [the child's] story."

In *State v. Milbradt* (756 P.2d 1372, 1988), the Oregon Supreme Court strongly condemned expert testimony on the truthfulness of children. The court wrote,

> We have said before, and we will say it again, but this time with emphasis — we really mean it — no psychotherapist may render an opinion on whether a witness is credible in any trial conducted in this state. The assessment of credibility is for the [court] and not for psychotherapists.

Expert witness testimony is acceptable if:

- The expert testimony remains general.

- It is necessary in order to answer charges from the defense.

- The child is young.

- The alleged perpetrator is a family member, making it more likely to need an explanation of delayed reporting and recantation.

"Relevance Analysis" Rule

Until recently, the courts used the "general acceptance" rule in deciding whether to use expert testimony. This rule held that expert testimony based on new scientific principles was not admissible if it had not gained the "general acceptance in the field in which it belongs."

In 1993, the U.S. Supreme Court adopted the "relevance analysis" rule (*Daubert v. Merrell Dow Pharmaceuticals, Inc.*, 509 U.S. 579). With relevance analysis, the judge conducts an inquiry to determine the reliability and validity of new scientific principles. While this rule was adopted as the result of a lawsuit involving expert testimony from chemists, physicians, and biologists, it may be used for all types of expert witnesses, including psychologists in child abuse cases. Under this rule, expert witnesses are not limited to testimony based on established principles, but can testify about new theories and scientific principles as long as they have been scrutinized.

PROBLEMS FOR THE PROSECUTOR

For the prosecutor's office, child sexual abuse can present many problems. The foremost is that the victim is a child. This becomes an even greater problem when the victim is very young (from birth to age six) since the question of competency arises. In "What Young Children Recall: Issues of Content, Consistency, and Coherence" (*Memory and Testimony in the Child Witness*, SAGE Publications, Thousand Oaks, California, 1995), R. Fivush and J. Shukar found that children under the age of six, who often face multiple interviews, can be inconsistent in recalling and retelling past events. Different settings and interview techniques can result in children remembering different details at different times.

The prosecutor may also worry about the possible harm the child may suffer, having to relive the abuse and being interrogated by adversarial defense attorneys. If the child is an adolescent, the defendant's attorney may accuse the teenage victim of seducing the defendant or willingly taking part in the acts.

Other factors prosecutors must consider include the slowness of the court process and the possibility that the case may be delayed, not just once, but several times. This is hard enough for adults to tolerate, but it is particularly difficult for children. The delay prolongs the child's pain. Children may become more reluctant to testify or may even no longer be able to accurately retell their stories. There is a far greater difference between a 31-year-old testifying about something that happened when he or she was 26 and an 11-year-old retelling an event that happened at six years of age. Prosecutors are also obliged to keep the child's best interests in mind and to try to preserve the family.

INNOVATIONS IN THE COURT

Anatomically Detailed Dolls

Many professionals use dolls with sexual organs made to represent the human anatomy to help children explain what happened. Advocates of the use of dolls report that they make it easier to get a child to talk about things that can be very difficult to discuss. Even when children know the words, they may be too embarrassed to say them out loud to strangers. The dolls allow these children to point out and show things difficult or even impossible for them to say. Some experts claim dolls work because children find it easier to use something that is age-appropriate and familiar to them.

There are, however, potential problems in using dolls. Critics of this method believe that dolls suggest fantasy to children, and the exaggerated sexual organs on a doll (they are proportionately larger than lifesize) may suggest improper sexual activity. Since most children's dolls do not have such sexual parts, the appearance of such parts on a doll might bring to a child's mind things he or she might not have thought of otherwise. According to the "affordance phenomenon," children will experiment with any opportunities provided by a new experience. Some experts believe that what might appear to be sexual behavior, like putting a finger in a hole in the doll, may have no more significance than a child putting a finger through the hole in a doughnut. Such exploratory play can have disastrous effects when it is misinterpreted as the re-creation of sexual acts.

In *Professionals' Standards of "Normal" Behavior with Ana-* *tomical Dolls and Factors that Influence These Standards* (Family Research Laboratory, University of New Hampshire, Durham, New Hampshire, 1991), Kathleen Kendall-Tackett studied how professionals interpreted a child's play with anatomical dolls. She found that most professionals interpreted overtly sexual behaviors, such as demonstrating intercourse or oral-genital contact, as abnormal for non-abused children. More ambiguous behaviors, such as touching, however, were not as easy to define. For example, about one-third of the professionals thought that a child's showing of dolls kissing was, at least, questionable. (See Table 7.1.)

TABLE 7.1

Ratings of Behaviors with Anatomical Dolls for Nonabused Children Ages 2-5.9 years.

Child Behavior	Rating		
	Normal	Questionable	Abnormal
		(% of professionals)	
AMBIGUOUS BEHAVIOR			
Undressing the Dolls	97.4	2.6	0
Looking at Dolls' Genitals	77.1	20.3	2.6
Touching Dolls' Genitals	77.6	21.9	.5
Touching Dolls' Anal Area	60.4	31.8	7.8
Touching Dolls' Breasts	75.5	21.4	3.1
Avoiding Dolls	15.7	56.5	27.7
Placing Dolls on Top of Each Other Lying Down	6.8	54.7	38.5
Showing Dolls Kissing	64.6	30.2	5.2
HIGHLY SEXUALIZED BEHAVIOR			
Showing Vaginal Penetration	.5	11.5	88.0
Showing Anal Penetration	0	9.9	90.1
Showing Oral-genital Contact	0	7.8	92.2
Showing Genital-Genital Contact	1.0	16.1	82.8
Showing Fondling/Digital Penetration	3.6	16.7	79.7

Source: Kathleen A. Kendall-Tackett, *Professionals' Standards of "Normal" Behavior with Anatomical Dolls and Factors That Influence These Standards*, Family Research Laboratory, University of New Hampshire, Durham, NH, 1991

Law enforcement professionals and women were more likely to view ambiguous behaviors as abnormal. Kendall-Tackett warned that the lack of standards for interpreting the children's use of the dolls shows the need for better professional training. The emphasis, so far, has been on presenting the dolls in a way that is not suggestive to the child, and little time has been spent on how to interpret the child's response.

Children Interact With Dolls Differently

Over the past ten years, most research of children's interaction with anatomically detailed dolls has concentrated on White, middle-class children. Lane Geddie, Brenda Dawson, and Karl Weunsch, in "Socioeconomic Status and Ethnic Differences in Preschoolers' Interactions With Anatomically Detailed Dolls" (*Child Maltreatment*, vol. 3, no. 1, February 1998), found that cultural differences may influence the manner in which children interact with dolls.

A study of a sample of non-abused preschoolers confirmed the findings of previous studies that non-abused children are not likely to exhibit sexualized behavior with dolls. However, the researchers found that the Black children who were of low socioeconomic status were more likely to demonstrate sexualized behavior with the dolls.

Black families are more likely than White families to have older siblings and other family members supervising the children. This means the children are exposed to a variety of experiences, such as watching an explicit movie with an older sibling. Children in low-income families are also more likely to share their parents' bedroom, which may account for inadvertent exposure to parental relations and nudity. This study shows that professionals have to be cautious in their interpretations of children's interaction with anatomically detailed dolls.

Videotaped Interviews

Videotaping, like closed-circuit television, is another technical innovation that some experts have hoped will increase a child's opportunity to present the truth. A videotape of the pre-trial interviews shows the jury how the child behaved and whether the interviewer prompted the child. Often prepared soon after the abuse, videotaped interviews preserve the child's memory and emotions when they are still fresh. Because a videotaped interview presents an out-of-court statement, which the alleged abuser cannot refute face to face, it can only be admitted as a hearsay exception.

Many states have enacted laws that permit videotapes under certain circumstances. In Kentucky, Texas, and Louisiana, a videotape is permitted if it is of the child's first statement, the questioning was by someone other than an attorney, and both the interviewer and the child are available for cross-examination at the trial. Videotaping can cut down on the number of interviews the child must undergo, and prosecutors indicate that this method encourages guilty pleas. (See above court cases involving the use of videotaped interviews and hearsay evidence.)

Videotapes can be powerful tools to deal with the problem of the child who recants his or her testimony when put on the witness stand. The district attorney of Tarrant County, Texas, Steve Chaney, explained at a National Policy Conference on Legal Reforms,

Recanting is a major problem for the legal system. Recanting is an expected reaction of an abused child who has reported the abuse, although this is not well understood or accepted by the legal community. Most prosecutors believe that the videotape has a major benefit in this area. If the child later recants, even at the time of trial, the case can still be prosecuted by using a good tape and psychological experts to explain the recanting symptoms. The [jury] is confronted with two opposing statements from the child and often the tape statement containing sufficient detail elicited by non-leading questions is the more compelling evidence.

Many state laws permit the use of videotaped testimony taken at a deposition or preliminary hearing instead of live testimony at a trial. Depositions, however, can be as demanding and difficult as a trial. They often take place in small rooms, forcing the child and defendant closer together than they might have been in a courtroom. The judge might not be there to control the behavior of the defendant or his attorney. Individuals who might offer the child support, such as victim advocates, may not be permitted to attend.

Furthermore, if the prosecutor claims the child is unable to handle the emotional trauma of the witness stand, the child may have to undergo medical or psychiatric tests by the state or defense attorney in order to permit videotaped testimony. This could be as traumatic as going through with a personal appearance at the trial. Some states permit the child to sit behind a one-way mirror so that the defendant can see the child and communicate with the defense attorney, but the child is shielded from direct confrontation.

Critics of videotaping have suggested other possible problems:

- It is not inconceivable, they say, that people "perform" for the camera instead of communicating.

- Victims are placed under subjective scrutiny by juries when every gesture, change in voice or speech pattern, and eye movement are judged.

- There is no accountability for the videotapes. Multiple copies of tapes are sometimes made and given to various attorneys and witnesses. Some tapes are used at training sessions, often without concealing the victims' names.

JUDICIAL REFORMS

As of 1998, 25 states and the federal law require that a child victim be granted a speedy trial, although these laws are rarely put into practice.

Defendants usually ask for additional time to prepare an effective defense, and every case generally involves at least one continuance due to too many cases on the court docket.

Concerned about how long it takes to resolve child abuse cases, many communities are taking things in their own hands. For example, in St. Paul, Minnesota, the police department has assigned a special investigator to review abuse reports at the child protective services agency. This investigator determines which cases will need criminal justice intervention and which will not. The National Council of Juvenile and Family Court Judges (Reno, Nevada) has also issued guidelines for courts to help facilitate the resolution of civil child protection cases.

FALSE ACCUSATIONS OF CHILD SEXUAL ABUSE

The responses to accusations of child sexual abuse have gone from disbelief to almost total acceptance by experts who claim children do not lie about these things. The responses have now swung back to doubt, especially when the accusations are made as part of a divorce/custody battle between parents. (See Chapter VIII for doubts on adult repressed memories of childhood sexual abuse.) Edwin Mikkelsen et al. examined studies of false abuse allegations and found rates that ranged from 2 to 8 percent of abuse cases referred to child abuse clinics, 6 percent of emergency room referrals, and much higher rates (36.4 percent to 55.5 percent) in cases arising out of custody disputes ("False Sexual Abuse Allegations by Children and Adolescents: Contextual Factors and Clinical Subtypes," *American Journal of Psychotherapy,* vol. XLVI, no. 4, 1992).

Mikkelsen et al. defined four types of false allegations, although many cases involve a combination of the four types.

Subtype I is the most common and appears in the context of a custody dispute. This is the conscious manipulation on the part of one parent or caregiver to obtain custody of children from another parent or caregiver. The parent may coerce the child into alleging abuse. In these cases, the description of the abuse may be on a more sophisticated level than a child would be expected to know at that age. In one case, an 11-year-old boy related sexual activity but could not explain the meaning of the sophisticated language he used to describe it.

Subtype II is an allegation that results from the accuser's psychological disturbance. The accuser may be a child or a parent/caregiver. When it comes from a child, the child is unable to differentiate fantasy from reality; in a parent, it is a delusional (a strong belief maintained despite evidence to the contrary) process in an individual who otherwise appears to be functioning adequately. For example, a mother who had been sexually abused by her 14-year-old brother when she was 12 became convinced her daughter was being abused by her brother when the children reached the ages of 12 and 14, respectively.

Subtype III is an allegation that is a conscious manipulation by the child. In these cases, the child makes an allegation as a means to obtain a specific goal out of vindictiveness or desire for revenge or rage. Children who are in a living situation they dislike are the most common accusers. An example is a child who lives with a parent and stepparent and would rather live with the other natural parent.

Subtype IV is iatrogenic (induced in a client/patient by a professional, such as a therapist or social worker). Iatrogenic cases include those in which a therapist claims he or she can tell from the way a person enters a room if that person was abused. A pediatrician in England insisted she could detect sexual abuse based on subtle physical symptoms she could see but which the person would not reveal. Based on this, charges were made against several parents in one English village.

NEWLY ENACTED STATE LAWS

The rise in public awareness about child abuse and the need to protect children from repeat abusers and various forms of abuse have led to the continuing enactment of state laws to protect children and families. The National Conference of State Legislatures, in the *1997 Domestic Violence Legislative Summary* (Denver, Colorado, 1998), reported that states enacted more than 200 domestic violence laws in 1997, about one-quarter of them dealing with children and violence at home.

Twelve states enacted laws requiring courts to consider evidence of domestic violence or child abuse in custody decisions. At least nine states passed laws to fund programs that will look into the link between domestic violence and child abuse. Utah now allows courts to issue a warrant giving a peace officer the right to search a home for a child believed to be maltreated. Connecticut makes it unlawful for a parent, guardian, or any individual responsible for a child to knowingly leave that child unsupervised in a motor vehicle or any place of public accommodation. Delaware insurers cannot limit the medical coverage of any child referred by the child protective services agency for suspected abuse or neglect. Several states also require operators of child care facilities to conduct a child abuse registry check of potential employees.

THE REGISTRATION
OF SEX OFFENDERS

The Jacob Wetterling Act

The Jacob Wetterling Crimes Against Children and Sexually Violent Offender Registration Act (PL 103-322; also known as the Jacob Wetterling Act), was signed into law on September 13, 1994, as part of the Violent Crime Control and Law Enforcement Act of 1994 (PL 103-322). The Act provides funding to states to establish registration systems for sex offenders. States must require abusers who have committed a criminal offense against a minor to register every year for 10 years after release from prison, parole, or probation. Sexually violent predators* must report their addresses to the state every 90 days until it is determined they are no longer threats to public safety.

Jacob Wetterling was an 11-year-old boy kidnapped near his home in St. Joseph, Minnesota, by an armed, masked man on October 22, 1989. His abduction was similar to a case involving a boy from a nearby town who was kidnapped and sexually assaulted earlier that year. Jacob has never been found, but police believed the cases were linked and encouraged the creation of a database so that police departments could share information.

Megan's Law

Megan's Law (PL 104-145), signed May 17, 1996, amended the Jacob Wetterling Act by requiring states to release information on registered sex offenders if needed to protect the public. In 1994, the nation's first notification law was enacted in New Jersey after seven-year-old Megan Kanka was raped and murdered by a convicted sex offender who lived across the street from her family. Since then, every state has enacted legislation (Ashley's Law in Texas and Polly Klass's Law in California, for instance) that requires the registration and tracking of sex offenders.

The Pam Lychner Act

The Pam Lychner Sexual Offender Tracking and Identification Act (PL 104-236), signed on October 3, 1996, also amended the Jacob Wetterling Act by requiring the Federal Bureau of Investigation (FBI) to establish a National Sex Offender Registry (NSOR) to help state-to-state tracking and management of released sex offend-ers. It further allows the FBI to conduct sex offender registration and community notification in states that have not established "minimally sufficient" systems in place for such purposes. The Pam Lychner Act was named after a victim's right activist who was killed in an airplane crash in 1988.

CHILD PORNOGRAPHY

Pornography on the Internet

Congressional debate continues on how the government should enforce obscenity standards in cyberspace. Some policy makers believe any obscenity standards could interfere with free speech and would be difficult to enforce, while others believe this is an issue relating to child protection, not to the First Amendment.

In October 1998, Congress enacted the Child Online Protection Act (PL 105-277), which amends the Communications Act of 1934 (47 U.S.C. 201) "to require persons who are engaged in the business of distributing, by means of the World Wide Web, material that is harmful to minors to restrict access to such material by minors, and for other purposes." The Child Online Protection Act (COPA) requires all commercial sites in the Internet to obtain from users credit card numbers or adult identification numbers. Violation of COPA entails heavy fines and up to six months in jail.

COPA was set to be enforced on November 20, 1998, but that same day, commercial World Wide Web (the "Web") providers and Web site users who use the materials described by COPA filed a complaint with the U.S. District Court for the Western District of Pennsylvania, challenging the constitutionality of the law. The plaintiffs argued that they would be forced to either establish age-verification barriers or delete from their Web sites materials that may be perceived to violate

---

* Sexually violent predators include those who have committed sexually violent crimes and those who may not have committed sexual crimes, but suffer from mental abnormalities or personality disorders that may predispose them to commit predatory and violent sex offenses.

COPA. The plaintiffs asked the court to issue a temporary restraining order prohibiting the U.S. Attorney General from enforcing COPA.

In *American Civil Liberties Union et al. v. Janet Reno, Attorney General of the United States* (Civil Action No. 98-5591, 1998), Federal District Judge Lowell A. Reed, Jr., issued a preliminary injunction against the enforcement of COPA. Judge Lowell ruled,

> The Supreme Court has repeatedly stated that the free speech rights of adults may not be reduced to allow them to read only what is acceptable for children....

> While the public certainly has an interest in protecting its minors, the public interest is not served by the enforcement of an unconstitutional law. Indeed, to the extent that other members of the public who are not parties to this lawsuit may be affected by the statute, the interest of the public is served by the preservation of the status quo until such time that this Court ... may more closely examine the constitutionality of this statute.

In October 1998, Congress, in an effort to further protect children from sexual predators who target minors through the Internet, enacted the Child Protection and Sexual Predator Punishment Act (PL 105-314). The bill provides punishment for any individual who knowingly contacts, or tries to contact, children under 18 in order to engage in criminal sexual activity, or who knowingly transfers obscene material to children.

PROSECUTION FOR DRUG USE DURING PREGNANCY

In November 1997, the South Carolina Supreme Court, in *Whitner v. South Carolina* (SC SupCt, No. 24468), ruled that a viable fetus is legally a "child" and, therefore, a pregnant woman who uses drugs can be criminally prosecuted for child abuse. Under an expanded state definition of child abuse, Cornelia Whitner was sentenced to eight years in prison for using crack cocaine while pregnant and endangering a fetus. This was the first time the highest court of any state upheld the criminal conviction of a woman charged with such offense.

Currently, South Carolina is the only state that allows such criminal prosecution. The Supreme Courts of Florida, Kentucky, Nevada, and Ohio had considered this issue but found it to be unconstitutional and without legal basis. In March 1998, Malissa Ann Crawley, charged with the same criminal offense, began serving a five-year prison sentence in South Carolina. In June 1998, the U.S. Supreme Court refused to hear an appeal by Whitner and Crawley.

Whitner's lawyer had argued that if a woman could be prosecuted for child abuse for having used drugs while pregnant, what was to keep the law from prosecuting her for smoking or drinking or even for failing to obtain prenatal care? Other critics claim that women who are substance abusers, fearing prosecution, might not seek prenatal care and counseling for their drug problem.

SECRECY LAWS

In some states, programs and laws designed to protect children from abuse have inadvertently protected abusers. New York State had previously strictly forbidden the release of information about previous allegations of child abuse, even if the allegations were substantiated. The state also required that records of unsubstantiated allegations be destroyed. Without the ability to review case histories, it was impossible to establish patterns of abuse.

New York's strict confidentiality provisions were loosened in February 1996, dramatically changing the way the state's child protective services (CPS) system worked. Elisa's Law forbids the destruction of any abuse records for 10 years after the child has turned 18. It also enables officials to inquire into previous allegations involving child abuse, whether they have been substantiated or not.

"Elisa's Law" was named for six-year-old Elisa Izquierdo who died after years of abuse from her mother and stepfather. It was prompted by public outcry after Elisa's neighbors and teachers protested that authorities ignored their repeated warnings that the girl was in danger. The New York Civil Liberties Union argues that the law violates individuals' privacy rights and harms those who are falsely accused.

MAJOR PRESCHOOL ABUSE CASES

Reports of mass child molestation receive a lot of media attention and can lead to hysteria not only among the parents of children who are involved in the case but also among the public. Several 1980s cases of alleged sexual abuse of children in day care facilities have dragged on into the 1990s.

The Fells Acres Case

In June 1998, a judge in Massachusetts ordered a new trial for one of the defendants in an alleged mass child molestation case that started in 1985. Cheryl Amirault LeFave, her mother Violet, and her brother Gerald were convicted of sexually abusing about 40 children at the Fells Acres day care center. The accusers, now teenagers, have never recanted their allegations of abuse, but the judge found that the investigators had asked the children leading and suggestive questions. LeFave's mother has since died, but her brother, tried and convicted in a separate trial, remains in jail. The judge ruled that the children cannot testify in the coming trial for Cheryl LeFave because of the children's prior tainted testimony.

The McMartin Case

The McMartin Preschool trial is a good example of how a case can be mishandled by everyone involved and eventually fall apart regardless of the strength or weakness of the evidence of abuse. In 1983, a parent of a child enrolled at the

McMartin Preschool was told by the UCLA hospital that her son had signs of rectal trauma, including evidence of sodomy (anal penetration). She went to the police, who then arrested Raymond Buckey, the preschool director's adult grandson. Soon after, other parents claimed to remember strange happenings, such as their children sometimes coming home in underwear and clothes that were not their own. There were also behavior changes for which the parents could find no explanation.

The children began to tell stories about being drugged, sodomized, penetrated with sharp objects, and used in games like "the naked movie star game." When they were asked why they had kept it a secret, sometimes for years, they said that every once in a while one of the gerbils or rabbits that the school kept as pets was killed in front of them as a warning of what would happen to them. In addition, they were coached on how to deal with the nightmares they might have. "You sit up in bed and say, 'I promise I'll never tell anybody what happened to me.' And the monsters will go away."

When the case finally came to trial, the children were 8 to 12 years old and were recounting events that occurred when they were 3 to 5 years old. Prosecutors claimed that defense attorneys used delaying tactics, because they knew that the longer it had been since the abuse, the easier it was to confuse the children.

The McMartin pretrial hearings included videotaped interviews with the children conducted by a child sex abuse expert. Defense attorneys, however, used the tape as proof of how interrogators had misled the children with their questions. The district attorney himself admitted that his predecessors had made serious mistakes.

As the trial wore on, the allegations grew more fantastic (drinking blood in a church, riding in a van with a half-dead baby). The children turned out to be unreliable witnesses and many recanted their earlier statements. By the end of the pretrial hearing (four years and $6 million later), charges (originally 354 counts and 41 child witnesses) were dropped against all but two of the defendants, Ray Buckey and his mother, Peggy McMartin Buckey. In January 1990, they were acquitted of all charges.

The Margaret Kelly Michaels Case

In 1988, Margaret Kelly Michaels was found guilty of 115 charges out of 131 counts of sexual abuse against 19 children at the Wee Care day care center in New Jersey and sentenced to 730 years in prison. She was charged with inserting objects, including serrated eating utensils, into the children's genital organs, forcing them to eat a cake made of feces, and playing the piano naked. The parents of the preschool children were advised by a child sexual abuse expert to look for changes in their children's behavior as evidence of abuse. In 1993, an appeals court, after reviewing Michaels' trial, reported,

Certain questions [by investigators] planted sexual information in the children's minds and supplied the children with knowledge and vocabulary, which might be considered inappropriate for their age. Children were encouraged to help the police "bust this case wide open." Peer pressure and even threats of disclosing to the other children that the child being questioned was uncooperative were used.

Upon appeal, the New Jersey Supreme Court ruled that the investigators in Michaels' case had conducted "coercive and highly suggestive" interviews. A hearing was ordered to determine if the children's testimony was tainted, but the prosecution decided to drop the case.

CHAPTER VIII

FALSE MEMORIES?

It isn't so astonishing, the number of things that I can remember, as the number of things I can remember that aren't so. — Mark Twain

Memory is life. — Saul Bellow

Throughout the 1980s, the numbers of children reported to have been sexually abused steadily increased. Many experts claim that 1 in 5 (20 percent) of American women and 1 in 10 (10 percent) of American men have been subjected to some form of sexual abuse as children. (See Chapter VI.) Just as accusations of alleged ritual abuse in day care centers have come under scrutiny, a major controversy has developed over the validity of repressed memories of childhood sexual abuse that are recovered in adulthood through therapy.

Some mental health professionals believe that the mind can reject unpleasant ideas, desires, and memories by banishing them into the unconscious. This theory of repression explains why a victim of a traumatic experience, such as childhood sexual abuse, may not remember the incident. It is also referred to as the mind's defense mechanism against horrible experiences. The memory of the unpleasant occurrence supposedly remains repressed until it is triggered by some event.

Revelations of abuse have been made primarily by White, well-educated, middle-class women (there are some men, but women predominate). Often, the individual experiencing some distress or anxiety in her life turns to a psychotherapist, who then suggests that the patient's problems stem from childhood sexual abuse that has been repressed. Critics charge that the numbers of women having allegedly suffered childhood sexual abuse is vastly exaggerated and that the issue of sexual abuse has become a politicized, feminist cause.

DO PHYSICAL SYMPTOMS INDICATE CHILDHOOD SEXUAL ABUSE?

Because the accepted symptoms of childhood abuse vary widely (see Chapters V and VI), nearly everyone is liable to find clues to suggest he or she was abused in the past. Ellen Bass and Laura Davis, in *The Courage to Heal: A Guide for Women Survivors of Child Sexual Abuse* (HarperCollins, New York, 1988), claim that Sigmund Freud was right about his first theory (see Chapter VI) that the physical symptoms of hysteria in his patients were indicative of childhood sexual abuse.

The Courage to Heal has often been described as the "bible" of the recovered-memory movement, a survivor's guide for adult victims of child sexual abuse. The authors state, "If you think you were abused and your life shows the symptoms, then you were." They ask women readers how often they suffer the following physical symptoms of childhood sexual abuse:

- You feel that you are bad, dirty, or ashamed.

- You feel powerless, like a victim.

- You feel that there is something wrong with you deep down inside or that if people really knew you, they would leave.

- You feel unable to protect yourself in dangerous situations.

- You have no sense of your own interest, talents, or goals.

- You have trouble feeling motivated.

- You feel you have to be perfect.

On one side of the repressed-memory controversy are clinical therapists who believe that repressed sexual trauma can be determined from a checklist of symptoms such as stated above and that treatment is required to uncover the abuse. They believe that memories rediscovered through hypnosis and other recovery techniques are true and that they must be acknowledged for treatment to be successful. They are concerned that questioning the validity of these memories provides offenders with an easy way to avoid responsibility for their actions.

On the other hand, more skeptical experimental psychologists wonder how therapists can be so sure of their diagnosis from a list of symptoms that could be the result of many different conditions. They cite one therapist who claimed that sexual abuse is "so common that I'll tell you that within 10 minutes; I can spot it as a person walks in the door often before they even realize it. There's a certain body language that says I'm afraid to expose myself, I'm afraid to be hurt."

Many mental health professionals point out that the public should be wary not only of unscrupulous therapists but also of those who have no training in mental health. For example, the authors Bass and Davis (see above) are not licensed therapists — Bass was a creative-writing teacher and Davis was a student in one of her writing workshops.

Looking for Answers to Symptoms

When an anxious, unhappy patient seeks help, she (most patients are female) is looking for an explanation for what are often vague symptoms that do not appear to have a source. According to accounts from patients, the therapist may ask, "Your symptoms sound like you were sexually abused as a child. What can you tell me about this?"

Some therapists feel it is imperative to ask about sexual abuse in the first meeting with every new patient.

If the patient repeatedly reports no memories, however, she may feel she is letting down the therapist, and that she does not have a valid reason to be in therapy. On the other hand, when the patient does recover repressed memories, she gains a comprehensive reason for all her problems that originate outside of herself, absolving her of responsibility. In addition, she earns approval and sympathy from her therapist.

Therapists who believe in repressed memory may encourage a patient to "remember" that she had been sexually abused in childhood. They usually recommend that a patient cut off all ties with the families to speed recovery. The patient may end up depending on the therapist for a long period of time, sometimes for many years.

Carolyn Zerbe Enns ("Counselors and the Backlash: 'Rape Hype' and 'False Memory Syndrome,' " *Journal of Counseling and Development*, vol. 74, March/April 1996) warns against condemning all therapists just because some are unscrupulous. "Although the targets of criticism have been incompetent therapists or inappropriate institutional policies, the real victims of these criticisms are most likely to be survivors of violence who may feel silenced, isolated, and fearful that no one will believe them." On the other hand, Enns notes, "Any attempt to force memory is an abuse of power or a shortcut that may result in overwhelming the client."

Michael Yapko, a clinical psychologist and a memory expert, is critical of therapists who "treat their clients on the basis of personal beliefs and philosophy, rather than according to an objective consideration of the facts. Too many therapists seem ignorant about the suggestibility inherent in the therapy process, and ignorant about the workings of human memory...." (*Suggestions of Abuse: True and False Memories of Childhood Sexual Abuse*, Simon and Schuster, New York, 1994)

Dissociative Identity Disorder (DID)

Some recovered-memory therapists believe sexual abuse can be so psychologically destructive that the victim, in order to save herself (or himself) from total insanity, splits her personality into separate parts, each one of which is assigned a particular aspect of life to control. This condition was originally labeled multiple personality disorder (MPD), but it has now been clinically replaced with the term Dissociative Identity Disorder (DID).

Daniel L. Schacter (*Searching for Memory: The Brain, the Mind, and the Past*, HarperCollins, New York, 1996) questions whether a patient can have dissociated so much of her past without it being obvious in her behavior long before she came to a therapist. "If they [the patients] have engaged in extensive dissociation, then patients who recover previously forgotten memories involving years of horrific abuse should also have a documented history of severe pathology that indicates a long-standing dissociative disorder."

In a case cited by Schacter, the therapist of a DID patient brushed off questions as to the lack of evidence from his patient's childhood. "I don't care if it's true. What's important to me is that I hear the child's truth, the patient's truth.... What actually happened is irrelevant to me."

Does Multiple Personality Disorder, or DID, Really Exist?

In the 1970s, the publication and the making into a movie of the book *Sybil* helped popularize multiple personality disorder (MPD). Considered a rare mental condition, the incidence of MPD increased from fewer than 50 cases prior to the publication of the book to over 40,000 cases by 1995. In 1998, recovered tapes of interviews by the author, Flora Rheta Schreiber, of Sybil's psychoanalyst, Dr. Cornelia Wilbur, revealed the doctor describing her use of hypnosis and sodium pentathol to "help develop" Sybil's other personalities.

RECOVERED-MEMORY THERAPY

Recovered-memory therapists are convinced their patients cannot heal until they face their memories. They often suggest that the patient sue the offending parent in court. Critics charge that such therapy does not heal and often destroys.

In 1996, psychologist Elizabeth F. Loftus (a memory expert and leading opponent of the recovered-memory movement; see below) presented a study of the Washington State Crime Victims Compensation Program to the Southwestern Psychological Association. Loftus found that all 30 claimants in the study were still in therapy three years after their first recovered memory; 18 were still in therapy after five years. While only three thought about suicide or attempted suicide before recovering their first memory, 20 killed themselves after therapy. Two had been hospitalized prior to their first recovered memory, compared to 11 after they retrieved memories. Before therapy, 25 had been employed; after therapy, only three still had jobs. Of the 23 who had been married, 11 divorced. Seven lost custody of their children.

SATANIC ABUSE

In addition to repressed memories of incest, the recovered-memory movement has found increasingly frequent reports of ritual, or satanic, abuse. Satanic rituals allegedly include ritual rape and impregnation, murdering of babies, and drinking of blood. During the mid-1980s, recovered-memory therapists linked DID (see above) with satanic abuse and started finding more and more patients who, through hypnosis, revealed remarkably similar horrific tales of satanic cult abuse.

Kenneth V. Lanning of the Federal Bureau of Investigation (FBI; see also Chapter VI) has studied the sexual victimization of children since 1981. Lanning is concerned that society has created an environment where victims are rewarded and comforted in direct proportion to the severity of their claims of abuse. The FBI has never found evidence of a national or international conspiracy of satanists. Those who believe these reports of satanism respond that the FBI is part of the conspiracy to cover up the evidence. Satanic cults have been blamed for between 50,000 and 60,000 people killed every year, although the annual total of homicides averages fewer than 25,000. Law enforcement has not found any evidence of satanic abuse — no bones, no fetuses, no reliable eyewitnesses.

The False Memory Syndrome Foundation (an association that questions the validity of repressed memory, see below) reported the experiences of a DID patient who recanted.

> Eventually, I said I had taken part in Satanic Rituals, been buried alive, drank blood, and helped to kill a baby. With every new memory, my therapist was intrigued and building a case to prove he was right about me all along. I was rewarded with his attention to me and was his "best" patient. But, I started to have feelings of death and became suicidal.

> I truly exhibited all the MPD symptoms even though I had learned them. Control of my mind, emotion, and will was given to the personalities the therapist had empowered.

In her report to the Southwestern Psychological Association on a study of the Washington State Crime Victims Compensation Program (see above), Elizabeth F. Loftus stated that of the 30 claimants, nearly all (29) reported memories of satanic abuse, with seven months being the average age of the onset of abuse. The claimants reported 150 murders, and 29 remembered physical torture and mutilation. However, none of the medical records of these patients corroborated these claims.

Tales of satanic abuse are so improbable that many supporters of recovered memory fear these claims may harm the image of the movement. Richard Ofshe and Ethan Watters, in *Making Monsters: False Memories, Psychotherapy, and Sexual Hysteria* (Scribners, New York, 1994), described

allegations of satanic abuse as a pure product of suggestion and predicted it will become the Achilles heel (the weak spot that will lead to the downfall) of the recovered-memory movement.

MEMORY

How memory works and its reliability play a major part in the controversy of recovered memory. Historically, the workings of the mind and memory have been described according to contemporary technology. Thus, during the Industrial Revolution, the brain was likened to a machine; after the invention of the telephone, to a switchboard; after the invention of the movies, to a camera; after Univac, the first computer, to a computer.

In 1897, Sigmund Freud wrote to his colleague about his memory of an event that occurred at 11 months old, "and [I could] hear again the words that were exchanged between two adults at that time! It is as though it comes from a phonograph." Today, the brain is often described as a video camera, and when the right tape is inserted, the memories will be played back.

Elizabeth F. Loftus (see above), author of *The Myth of Repressed Memory: False Memories and Allegations of Sexual Abuse* (St. Martin's Press, New York, 1994), wrote,

> If repression is the avoidance in your conscious awareness of unpleasant experiences that come back to you, yes, I believe in repression. But if it is a blocking out of an endless stream of traumas that occur over and over that leave a person with absolutely no awareness and re-emerge decades later in some reliable form, I don't see any evidence for it. It flies in the face of everything we know about memory.

Generally, research has found that children who have suffered serious psychological trauma do not repress the memory; rather, they can never forget it. Survivors of concentration camps or children who have witnessed the murder of a parent never forget. In fact, they may seek therapy to help suppress the horrible memories so they can go on with their lives.

Evidence in the Brain

Recent research has tried to find evidence of memory in the brain. Daniel L. Schacter et al. (*Neuron*, August 1996) showed volunteers an initial list of words and then a second list incorporating words that were similar but had not appeared in the original list. More than half the words the volunteers "remembered" were not on the first list. Using positron emission tomography scans (PET scans measure changes in blood flow, and blood flow indicates neural activity), Schacter found that parts of the brain involved in memory (the hippocampus) became active regardless of whether the memories were true or false.

In the cases of true memories, however, an area that processes information about sounds of recently heard words also lit up. False memories, on the other hand, showed more activity in portions of the brain that had been found to struggle to recall the context of an event. Schacter warned, however, "This is only a first step in specifying brain processes involved in false memories. These PET results don't generalize to memories about one's past, and this technique can't be used as a lie detector test."

Implanting Memories

Many scientific studies have shown that false memories can be implanted into a person's mind, leading the subject to "remember" events that never happened. Hypnosis has especially been cited for producing "memories" that may or may not be true. Once these memories have been introduced, they become as real to that person as what happened the previous week.

A major split has occurred between researchers and clinicians over the role of memory. Memory researchers have shown that false memories can be implanted fairly easily in the laboratory. Elizabeth F. Loftus has experimented with implanting the traumatic memory of being lost in a shopping mall. She had the older brother of a 14-year-old boy tell his brother that at age five the boy had gotten lost at the mall. Two days later, the boy remembered his feelings; on the third day he recalled a conversation with his mother; on the fourth day he described the older man who found him; on the fifth day he remembered the mall and a conversation with the stranger. Within two weeks he had a complete, detailed memory of being lost when he was five and, when questioned, was convinced that it was a true memory.

Recovered-memory advocates insist that while it may be easy to implant memories of common emotions (being lost), it is not possible to implant memories of something unusual like sexual abuse. Researchers cannot experiment with implanting sexual abuse memories because of the obvious ethical considerations and possible repercussions.

In an unusual situation, Richard Ofshe, social psychologist and expert on cults, successfully implanted a memory of abuse in Paul Ingram's mind. Paul Ingram, a conservative, religious family man, was charged by his children with extensive sexual and satanic abuse. After months of interrogations and pressure from a psychologist and police detectives, Ingram began to confess to all kinds of horrific behavior. As his children brought up new charges, he would search his memory until he finally remembered and could even supply details of the events.

Richard Ofshe, who had been hired by the prosecution, did not believe Ingram's memories were genuine. Ofshe told Ingram he had spoken to one of Ingram's sons and one of his daughters, and they related the time Ingram forced them to have sex in front of him. This was one of the few charges that had not been brought against Ingram, and never was, but within a day, Ingram submitted a written confession with details of the memory of the event. When Ofshe informed Ingram he was mistaken, Ingram protested, "It's just as real to me as anything else."

The Case of Eileen Franklin

In 1990, George Franklin was convicted of murdering his daughter Eileen's friend twenty years earlier. Eileen initially claimed to have recovered memories of her father's murderous act after they came to her in hypnosis while in therapy. Later on, she changed her story, reporting that, one day in 1989, the play of sunlight and shadow on her six-year-old daughter's face brought back the image of her playmate on the day she was murdered. Eileen suddenly remembered herself as a nine-year-old watching her father kill her friend.

Lenore Terr, a clinical professor of psychiatry, was an influential expert witness at this first criminal trial in the United States involving recovered memory. Terr who supports the idea of repressed memory later wrote about Eileen's story in the book *Unchained Memories: True Stories of Traumatic Memories, Lost and Found* (BasicBooks, New York, 1994).

Harry MacLean, who reported on the case in his book, *Once Upon a Time: A True Story of Memory, Murder, and The Law* (HarperCollins, New York, 1993), claimed that Terr had repeatedly distorted the facts to suit her purpose. Terr claimed to offer a dramatic proof of Eileen's truthful testimony when she described the "body memory" (a physical manifestation of trauma that the conscious mind has forgotten) of Eileen's repressed trauma. According to Terr, Eileen had a habit of pulling her hair out, resulting in a "big, bleeding bald spot near the crown." Eileen had allegedly seen her father murder her friend with a blow to the head using a large rock.

According to MacLean, in his interviews with Eileen's mother, sisters, school friends, and teachers, none could remember Eileen's pulling out her hair or having a bleeding spot on her scalp. Ofshe and Watters (*Making Monsters*, see above) found more than 40 photos taken of Eileen during the relevant period that were wrongly withheld from the defense and which showed no trace of a bald spot.

On November 20, 1995, a federal appeals court overturned George Franklin's murder conviction. By this time, Franklin had served almost seven years of a life sentence. The court found that the trial had been tainted by the improper allegation that Franklin had confessed and by the exclusion of crucial evidence — Eileen had been hypnotized by her therapist Kirk Barrett prior to the first trial, making her testimony unreliable. The court ordered a retrial. On July 2, 1996, the prosecution dropped the charges, citing the problem of Eileen's hypnosis, which, by California law, would probably prevent her from testifying. In addition, new DNA evidence showed that it was impossible for Franklin to have committed a second murder his daughter had accused him of, which she claimed happened when she was 15.

In June 1997, George Franklin filed a civil suit in federal court against his daughter, her therapist Barrett, Lenore Terr, and county officials, claiming violation of his civil rights. The suit alleged, among other things, that Eileen, Barrett, and county officials conspired to deny Franklin the due process of law and violated his Fifth, Sixth, and Fourteenth Amendment rights to confront witnesses against him. Lenore Terr and the district attorney were also being sued because they "knowingly presented false testimony regarding recovered memories without any basis in social science research."

Scientific Proof of Repressed Memory?

While memory experts such as Lenore Terr dismiss all laboratory experiments on memory as invalid, others have tried to scientifically prove that memories can be forgotten. Linda Meyer Williams, of the Family Research Laboratory of the University of New Hampshire, Durham, studied the recall of women who had been abused in childhood for whom there were medical records proving the abuse ("Recall of Childhood Trauma: A Prospective Study of Women's Memories of Child Sexual Abuse," *Journal of Consulting and Clinical Psychology*, vol. 62, no. 6, 1994). Other studies attempting to prove memory repression have relied on the subjects' own assertions that they had suffered past traumas and then had forgotten them.

Williams used data gathered between 1973 and 1975 on 206 girls (ages 10 months to 12 years) who had been examined for sexual abuse in a city hospital emergency room. In 1990 and 1991, 129 of these women were included in a study that was, they were told, a follow-up on the lives and health of women who had received health care as children at the hospital. The women, now between the ages of 18 and 31, were not told of their history of child sexual abuse, although some women suspected the reason for their hospital visit.

Of the 129 women, 38 percent failed to report the sexual abuse that had been documented by the hospital; however, of this group, 68 percent reported other childhood sexual abuses. Williams doubted that the women were simply unwilling to discuss the abuse because other personal subjects, such as abortions, prostitution, or having sexually transmitted diseases, were not withheld.

Twelve percent (15 respondents) of the total sample reported that they were never abused in childhood. Williams suggested that this was an undercount of the likely number of women who had forgotten childhood abuse. Because the abuse these women suffered was known to at least one other person (the person who brought the child to the hospital), it was less likely to have been repressed than abuse that was always kept a secret.

"If, as these findings suggest," Williams concluded, " having no recall of sexual abuse is a fairly common event, we should not be surprised by later recovery of memories of child sexual abuse by some women." In fact, 16 percent of the women who recalled the sexual victimization that brought them to the hospital, reported there were periods of time when they "forgot" the abuse. In a second paper on her research ("Recovered Memories of Abuse in Women with Documented Child Sexual Victimization Histories," *Journal of Traumatic Stress*, October 1995), Williams described the in-terviews with some of the women who had forgotten. It is not clear whether the women were truly amnesiac or whether the abuse was simply not a part of their conscious lives for a period of time.

One woman said, "I don't know how old I was, I used to think about it for the first two years, then I just blocked it out. I may not have completely forgot, I just didn't think about it." Most reported that they recalled the abuse when a television movie or some other event jogged their memory. None had turned to the help of a therapist to uncover repressed memories. Williams suggested that these women (inner-city, mainly Black women) did not have the financial resources or knowledge to turn to professional help.

A Rebuttal

Critics of Williams' conclusions pointed out that one of the reasons she found women who had forgotten their abuse was that the trauma had occurred in infancy. (Experts contend that events that happen before the acquisition of language at 2 to 3 years of age are forgotten because there is no way to express the event.) Williams disagreed, noting that, while 55 percent of those who had been abused at 3 years or younger had no memory of the occurrence, 62 percent of those who were 4 to 6 years old also did not remember.

In addition, critics questioned how Williams could be certain that those who claimed not to remember were actually telling the truth. The researchers never confronted the women who did not report abuse by showing them their hospital records.

The American Psychological Association Report

The American Psychological Association (APA) assembled a group of clinicians and researchers to produce "The Final Report of the APA Working Group on the Investigation of Memories of Childhood Abuse" (1996). The group was split between practitioners who supported the concept of recovered memories and scientists who studied memory. The report included a list of final conclusions, which stated that most abused children remember all or part of their abuse; however, "it is possible for memories of abuse that have been forgotten for a long time to be remembered."

In addition, the group reported that it is also possible to construct convincing false memories, but there are gaps in understanding the processes that lead to accurate and inaccurate memories of childhood abuse. The bulk of the 293-page report, however, was a battle between the clinicians and scientists, each citing research and evidence to support their group's position.

HYPNOSIS

Most experts skeptical of repressed memory do not claim that it is impossible to forget traumatic events, but they are suspicious of how frequently repressed memory appears to occur, especially when it is brought out in therapy, hypnosis, or through self-help books and recovery groups. Michael Yapko (*Suggestions of Abuse: True and False Memories of Childhood Sexual Trauma*, Simon and Schuster, New York, 1994), concerned about the possible disastrous repercussions of misdiagnosing sexual abuse, conducted a study of therapists' attitudes.

Approximately one-third of respondents agreed and 12 percent agreed strongly with the statement, "The mind is like a computer, accurately recording events as they actually occurred." About one in 10 therapists believed that "memory is not significantly influenced by suggestion." Forty-one percent believed that "early memories, even from the first year of life, are accurately stored and retrievable," and 43 percent agreed that "if someone doesn't remember much about his or her childhood, it is most likely because it was somehow traumatic."

More than half the therapists (57 percent) admitted that they did nothing to differentiate true memories from false memories in their patients' accounts. Yapko was concerned that if a therapist is blinded to the true problems, he cannot help his client with the real issues in the client's life. (Yapko's book opens with the account of a patient who suffered such severe post-traumatic stress from his experiences in Vietnam that he committed suicide. Only after his death did his wife search the records to discover that her husband had never served in Vietnam.)

Researchers on hypnosis do not agree on whether it is a reliable method of memory retrieval or whether it increases the tendency to accept suggested memories or create false ones that are accepted by the patient as real. Three-quarters of Yapko's respondents thought of hypnosis as a tool for facilitating accurate recall, while 83 percent thought it helped to lift repressed memory into conscious awareness. Nearly half (47 percent) agreed with the statement, "Therapists can have greater faith in details of a traumatic event when obtained hypnotically than otherwise." Nearly two-thirds (64 percent) agreed that hypnosis could be used to create false memories, but more than a quarter (27 percent) did not think false memories could be generated by hypnosis.

Yapko did not deny the possibility of repressed memory, but he was wary of therapists who accept controversial theories of memory without a clear understanding of the complexities and ambiguities. There is no definite way to determine if memories are true, but there are circumstances that make stories of abuse more likely to be genuine — "1) They arise on the basis of a free narrative, 2) unprompted by leading or suggestive questions, 3) in an atmosphere free of coercion, 4) with a therapist who manifests a neutral position, and 5) allows both him or herself and the client the freedom to plead ignorance about what really happened."

The Opinion of the
American Medical Association

Memory experts generally agree that memories are fragments and that they are easily influenced and distorted. They claim that memory is a reconstructive process in which the brain can take a story and embellish it, creating a memory from something that never actually occurred. In 1985, *The Journal of the American Medical Association* published an article on memory recovered through hypnosis (Council on Scientific Affairs of the American Medical Association [AMA], "Scientific Status of Refreshing Recollection by the Use of Hypnosis," vol. 253), which focused on the use of hypnosis to help remember crime scenes.

Hypnosis, they concluded from the research, produces one of the following outcomes: 1) the recollections under hypnosis are not substantially different from those without hypnosis; 2) it yields more inaccurate recollections; or 3) most frequently, it produces memories that are both inaccurate and accurate. In this third condition, however, the subject is unable to distinguish between the accurate and inaccurate memories. The panel found no data to support the idea that hypnosis increases remembering only accurate information. "Consequently, hypnosis may increase the appearance of certitude without a concurrent increase of veracity."

In 1994, the AMA's Report of the Council on Scientific Affairs on child abuse (5-A-94) included a policy (515.978) on recovered memories stating that, "The AMA considers recovered memories of childhood sexual abuse to be of uncertain authenticity, which should be subject to external verification. The use of recovered memories is fraught with problems of potential misapplication."

Verification

Many professionals consider the acceptance of child abuse reports without some external verification as malpractice. Paul McHugh, Chief of Psychiatry at the Johns Hopkins University, believes that "to treat for repressed memories without any effort at external validation is malpractice pure and simple; malpractice on the basis of standards of care that have developed out of the history of psychiatric service and malpractice because the misdirection of therapy injures the patient and his or her significant others."

David Spiegel, in the *Harvard Mental Health Letter* (September 1998), observed that "no memory, whether it is evoked with or without hypnosis, can be shown to be true without corroboration by external evidence." The False Memory Syndrome Foundation claims that, in not a single case that has come to their attention, has the therapist sought the patient's pediatrician's records, and in only a few of the 2,800 cases was there any attempt to consult school records, other family members, or any independent sources.

Some Professionals Fail to
Verify Patient's Account

Psychiatrist Judith Herman explained on the Public Television program "Divided Memories" (April 4, 1995),

As a therapist, your job is not to be a fact finder. Your job is not to be a judge or a jury and your job is also not to make the family feel better. Your job is to help the patient make sense out of her life, make sense out of her symptoms, cope better with her symptoms and make meaning out of her experience. That's your job.

Judith Alpert, therapist and chair of the Working Group on the Investigation of Memories of Childhood Abuse of the American Psychological Association, in "Analytic Reconstruction in the Treatment of an Incest Survivor" (*Psychoanalytic Review*, vol. 81, no. 2, 1994), described the case of a woman who was so sure she had been sexually abused by her father, although she had no memory of her father having indeed committed the abusive act. Alpert did not question the veracity of her patient's account; rather, she concluded,

All of these repetitive representations and fragments of memory pointed to the accuracy of the narrative.... While the abuse may not have taken place exactly as it has been woven in the analytic situation, the network of convergence from many lines convinces me that it is a reconstruction in the arena

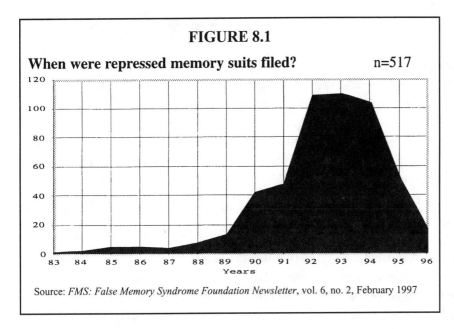

FIGURE 8.1

When were repressed memory suits filed?   n=517

Years

Source: *FMS: False Memory Syndrome Foundation Newsletter*, vol. 6, no. 2, February 1997

tion of their therapists. Between 1983 and 1996, a total of 517 civil (85 percent) and criminal (15 percent) suits based on "repressed memory" were filed. After a sharp rise in 1992, the year the False Memory Syndrome Foundation (FMSF) was created, there has been a steep drop since 1994. (See Figure 8.1.) An informal tally of cases by the FMSF has found that two-thirds of the civil suits had been dropped, dismissed, or concluded in favor of the alleged abusers.

of historical truth, capturing the core of reality.

Informed Consent

As of 1998, only Indiana had an informed consent law that requires therapists to tell their patients of the possible risks of hypnosis. However, Indiana's informed consent law does not warn the patient that he or she may come away from hypnosis believing he/she was sexually abused as a child even if it did not happen.

GOING TO COURT

Suing Alleged Abusers

While the courts (see Chapter VII) readily accepted some early cases of child sexual abuse, courts in more and more states are becoming increasingly suspicious of accounts of outrageous abuse. Therapists are being held liable for malpractice not only by their patients, but also often by third parties (usually the accused parents of someone who has allegedly recovered memories of sexual abuse).

Starting in 1983, individuals who "recovered" memories of childhood sexual abuse filed suits against their alleged abusers, many at the instiga-

Suing the Therapist

In what was one of the longest (13 weeks) malpractice trials in the American justice system, the jury awarded Elizabeth Carlson of Minnesota over $2.5 million. Carlson had accused Dr. Diane Bay Humenansky of "negligent psychotherapy by using hypnosis, misinformation, coercion, threats, and suggestions to implant false memories of childhood abuse" (*Carlson v. Humenansky*, District Ct., Ramsey Co., Minnesota, Case No. CX 93-7260). The patient claimed that under Dr. Humenansky's treatment, she became convinced she had developed "alters" or multiple personalities to help her cope with sexual abuses by her parents, relatives, and neighbors.

Carlson reported that during her more than two years of therapy, she felt worse and worse. Humenansky gave her books to read on incest, multiple personality disorder, and satanic abuse. Carlson also started believing that she was part of an intergenerational satanic cult. When Carlson and other patients of the psychiatrist met without the doctor, they were shocked to discover that they shared remarkably similar memories of abuse and had alternate personalities with the same names and traits. Since then, eight other former patients have sued Humenansky.

Third-Party Suits

The courts now often hold therapists liable to a third party, usually the patient's accused parent, when they implant or reinforce false memories in their patients. *The False Memory Syndrome Foundation (FMSF) Legal Survey* found that, as of December 1998, 158 malpractice suits had been brought by a third party against a negligent mental health provider. The FMSF believes that the total number of lawsuits is probably larger.

Social worker Susan L. Jones, while treating Joel Hungerford's daughter Laura, convinced her that her anxiety attacks were the results of sexual abuse by her father. Jones not only advised Laura to cease contact with her father, but also convinced the patient to file a complaint of aggravated felonious sexual assault against Hungerford. In addition, Jones contacted the police regarding the alleged assault and aided the prosecution in indicting Hungerford.

When Hungerford sued Jones for the misdiagnosis and negligent treatment of his daughter's condition, the therapist claimed that she owed Hungerford no duty of care. On December 18, 1998, in *Joel Hungerford v. Susan L. Jones* (No. 97-657, 1998 N.H. LEXIS 94), the New Hampshire Supreme Court, in this case of "first impression" (with no existing precedent), ruled,

> [W]e hold that a therapist owes an accused parent a duty of care in the diagnosis and treatment of an adult patient for sexual abuse where the therapist or the patient, acting on the encouragement, recommendation, or instruction of the therapist, takes public action concerning the accusation. In such instances, the social utility of detecting and punishing sexual abusers and maintaining the breadth of treatment choices for patients is outweighed by the substantial risk of severe harm to falsely accused parents, the family unit, and society.

The Statute of Limitations

One of the legal issues contested in cases of repressed memory is how long the statute of limitations should run since, typically, the victim has allegedly repressed the memories for many years. The NOW (National Organization for Women) Legal Defense and Education Fund supports an incest survivor's right to bring a civil suit against a perpetrator at any time based on an assumption that

> Psychological research has demonstrated conclusively that most victims of childhood sexual abuse are so powerless and so traumatized by the experience that they do not fully recognize what has happened to them until many years into adulthood.

> Allowing incest survivors their "day in court" will empower them and prove to society at large that violent male tyranny over female family members will not be tolerated. Granting access to the courts does not guarantee that the victim will win, of course. She still bears the burden of proving her claims — a powerful deterrent to frivolous suits.

Elizabeth F. Loftus, writing on this question in the September 1994 *American Bar Association Journal*, disagreed.

> What decades of memory research have shown, however, is that [repressed-memory therapy] can seriously contaminate memories, and even create false memories in vulnerable minds.

> What should the legal system do when claims are based on "de-repressed memories" decades after some alleged acts? In some rare cases, the legal system might want to allow victims to use the justice system to bring their suits, regardless of the limits placed upon their action by traditional statutes of limitations. But the cases

should not go forward without full recognition of the rights of the mothers, fathers, teachers, neighbors and others who are being accused.

A recent trend in court actions has been to question the validity of repressed memories and, therefore, the necessity for an extended statute of limitations. In 1996, the U.S. Supreme Court declined to review a Wisconsin Supreme Court case (*Pritzlaff v. Archdiocese of Milwaukee* 194 Wis.2d 303, 533 N.W.2d 780, 1995), thereby letting the state court's decision stand. The Wisconsin court had pointed out that when cases of environmental injury or malpractice are brought after a delay, there is a specific physical injury which can be objectively traced back to a particular cause. In this case, the plaintiff could only claim "emotional" and "psychological" damage that had allegedly happened 27 years in the past. The court did not think it would be able to accurately reveal the truth.

WHY MAKE THE ACCUSATIONS?

Why would someone make such terrible accusations? In fact, one of the arguments in support of repressed memories is exactly that — "No one would make up something so horrible and painful." If one accepts that premise, however, there is no way for an alleged abuser to prove his or her innocence.

Dr. Harold Lief, professor of psychiatry, emeritus, at the University of Pennsylvania, proposes a number of possible explanations for why someone might make accusations of abuse, including to attract attention, to place the responsibility for problems on someone else, to have one simple answer for all of life's problems, and to punish oneself or someone else.

Critics worry that women are drawn to the recovered-memory movement because of its cult-like atmosphere and the concern and attention the women receive from making their revelations. Investigators who have attended self-discovery weekends report that the person who can tell the most horrifying tale of abuse (satanic rituals are especially effective) gets the most love and attention.

Carol Tavris, Ph.D., author of *The Mismeasure of Woman*, suggested some of the motivations behind accusations of abuse in *The New York Times Book Review* ("Beware the Incest-Survivor Machine," January 3, 1993). In her opinion,

The sexual abuse-victim story crystallizes many of society's anxieties about the vulnerability of children, the changing roles of women and the norms of sexuality. It draws like a magnet those who wish to invoke a measure of sympathy in these unsympathetic times. It is no wonder that publishers and talk shows have a thriving business exploiting stories of abuse for commercial reasons, for these are stories that sell.

Critics of recovered-memory therapy charge that therapists create total dependence in their patients, thereby ensuring payment for treatment for years. Much of this has been covered by insurance. However, with the recent changes to managed care plans, there may be much less money available for therapy. Some predict that the combination of managed care and the increasing number of law suits and retractors (patients who have withdrawn claims of sexual abuse) will accomplish what professional conflict has not — put an end to the issue of recovered memory.

THE PARENTS

When a child accuses her parent/parents of sexual abuse, she is likely ruining their lives. A daughter who decides to confront her abuser has usually been prepared by her therapist or by her readings to expect that her parents will disavow any knowledge of abuse, a symptom, according to her therapist, that her parents are "in denial."

Very often, families are split as family members are forced to take sides. Nineteen-year-old Beth Rutherford of Springfield consulted a church counselor due to job stress. By the end of her two-

and-a-half-year therapy with Donna Strand, she had recovered "memories" of being impregnated twice by her minister father and of his performing a coat-hanger abortion on her. Fearful of their father, Beth and her middle sister fled to another state, while her youngest sister went into hiding. Beth had since been reunited with her parents. Court findings revealed that Beth was still a virgin and her father had had a vasectomy. In 1996, the Missouri church where Strand practiced paid the Rutherford family $1 million as a court settlement (*Rutherford v. Strand et al.*, Circuit Ct., Green Co., MO, No. 1960C2745).

Nothing short of murder is considered so heinous as child sexual abuse and once someone has been accused, it is extremely difficult for that person to clear himself/herself. The television show *Dateline* polled 502 adults, "If someone has been charged and acquitted in a child abuse case, would you still be suspicious of them [sic]?" Twelve percent were not sure and 11 percent said no. An overwhelming majority, 77 percent, said they would still be suspicious, even if the subject was cleared.

THE FALSE MEMORY SYNDROME FOUNDATION

As part of the backlash against the growing number of cases of repressed memory, an organization of parents claiming to have been falsely accused of child sexual abuse was formed in 1992. The False Memory Syndrome Foundation (FMSF) was founded by Pamela Freyd, whose daughter had accused her father of childhood abuse. (The daughter, Jennifer Freyd, is a psychologist at the University of Oregon who specializes in memory.) The FMSF publishes a monthly newsletter and organizes conferences to support falsely accused parents. The Foundation distributes information on what it sees as a dangerous movement in psychotherapy to encourage and accept all claims of childhood abuse without verification.

The FMSF and other experts who question the validity of repressed memory do not question whether sexual abuse occurs — it questions how often. Furthermore, they are concerned that false accusations will throw doubt on genuine cases of abuse.

Ironically, just as their children have often recounted remarkably similar stories of abuse, parents have amazingly similar stories of how their children have remembered the abuse, disclosed it to the family, demanded acceptance of the alleged abuse, and then cut off all communication with the family, turning instead to the therapist and support groups. In cases in which the child has retracted her accusations, some families have seen the renewed contact with their children as a gift. Others cannot forgive the pain their children have caused them and have been reluctant to welcome the accuser back into the family.

Some mental health professionals have dismissed the FMSF as an extreme organization. The Foundation has been accused of protecting child abusers and attempting to discredit the psychiatric profession. "I think they overplayed their hand by taking an adversarial and hostile stance from the outset," law professor Alan Scheflin explained. Rather than work toward improving therapy, the FMSF sided with "extremist elements" on its scientific board. (The board includes acknowledged experts such as Elizabeth F. Loftus, Richard Ofshe, and Paul McHugh.) In Schelflin's view, recovered-memory therapy is "just the practice of a very small group of therapists." On the other hand, for the families torn apart by what they insist are false memories, the FMSF has been a lifeline to others suffering the same accusations.

Since its creation in March 1992, the FMSF has received thousands of telephone calls from families who have been falsely accused of child sexual abuse. The Foundation stopped counting when the number of cases reached 10,000. However, as the judicial system started holding therapists accountable for their patients' well-being and liable to an accused third party, the number of repressed-memory cases has declined. In January 1999, the Foundation reported that "the number of families newly accused on the basis of recovered memory is now no more than a trickle."

IMPORTANT NAMES AND ADDRESSES

American Bar Association
Center on Children and the Law
740 15th St. NW
Washington, DC 20005
(202) 662-1720
FAX (202) 662-1755

American Humane Association
Children's Division
63 Inverness Dr. East
Englewood, CO 80112-5117
(303) 792-9900
FAX (303) 792-5333

Center for the Future of Children
The David and Lucile Packard
Foundation
300 Second St., #200
Los Altos, CA 94022
(650) 948-7658
FAX (650) 948-6498

Child Welfare League of America
440 First St. NW, 3rd Floor
Washington, DC 20001-2085
(202) 638-2952
FAX (202) 638-4004

Children's Defense Fund
25 E St. NW
Washington, DC 20001
(202) 628-8787
FAX (202) 662-3510

Children's Healthcare Is a Legal
Duty, Inc. (CHILD, Inc.)
P.O. Box 2604
Sioux City, IA 51106
(712) 948-3500

False Memory Syndrome
Foundation
3401 Market St., #130
Philadelphia, PA 19104-3315
(800) 568-8882
(215) 387-1865
FAX (215) 387-1917

Family Research Laboratory
126 Horton Social Service Center
University of New Hampshire
Durham, NH 03824
(603) 862-1888
FAX (603) 862-1122

Family Violence and Sexual
Assault Institute
1200 Fuller Wiser Rd., #2518
Euless, TX 76039
(817) 540-4496
FAX (817) 540-4393

Juvenile Justice Clearinghouse
P.O. Box 6000
Rockville, MD 20849-6000
(800) 638-8736
FAX (301) 519-5212

Kempe's Children Center
1825 Marion St.
Denver, CO 80218
(303) 864-5252
FAX (303) 864-5179

National Center for Missing and
Exploited Children
2101 Wilson Blvd., #550
Arlington, VA 22201-3052
Hotline (800) 843-5678
(703) 235-3900
FAX (703) 235-4067

National Center for Prosecution of
Child Abuse
99 Canal Center Plaza, #510
Alexandria, VA 22314
(703) 739-0321
FAX (703) 549-6259

National Child Abuse Hotline
(800) 422-4453

National Children's Advocacy
Center
200 Westside Square, #700
Huntsville, AL 35801
(256) 534-0531
FAX (256) 534-6883

National Clearinghouse on Child
Abuse and Neglect Information
330 C St. SW
Washington, DC 20447
(800) 394-3366
(703) 385-7565
FAX (703) 385-3206

National Committee to Prevent
Child Abuse
200 S. Michigan Ave., #200
Chicago, IL 60604
(312) 663-3520
FAX (312) 939-8962

National Council of Juvenile and
Family Court Judges
Family Violence Project Resource
Center
University of Nevada
P.O. Box 8970
Reno, NV 89507
(800) 527-3223
(702) 784-6012
FAX (702) 784-6628

National Council on Child Abuse
and Family Violence
1155 Connecticut Ave. NW, #400
Washington, DC 20036
(202) 429-6695
FAX (202) 467-4924

National Resource Center on
Child Sexual Abuse
107 Lincoln St.
Huntsville, AL 35801
(800) 543-7006
(205) 534-6868
FAX (205) 534-6883

Office on Child Abuse and Neglect
Children's Bureau
U.S. Department of Health and
Human Services
200 Independence Ave. SW
Washington, DC 20201
(202) 619-0257

RESOURCES

The National Child Abuse and Neglect Data System (NCANDS) of the U.S. Department of Health and Human Services (HHS) is the primary source of national information on child maltreatment known to state child protective services (CPS) agencies. The latest findings from the NCANDS are published in *Child Maltreatment 1996: Reports from the States to the National Child Abuse and Neglect Data System* (1998). *The National Incidence Study of Child Abuse and Neglect* (NIS-3; 1996) is the single most comprehensive source of information about the incidence of child maltreatment in the United States. The NIS-3 findings are based on data collected not only from CPS but also from "sentinels" in various community agencies, such as law enforcement, schools, hospitals, day care, voluntary social services, etc. Three NIS studies have been congressionally mandated — NIS-1 (1981), NIS-2 (1988), and the latest, NIS-3 (1993). The National Clearinghouse on Child Abuse and Neglect Information of the HHS provided an assortment of helpful publications used in the preparation of this book.

Other federal government publications used for this book include "In the Wake of Childhood Maltreatment" (*Juvenile Justice Bulletin*, 1997); *Child Protective Services: Complex Challenges Require New Strategies* (U.S. Government Accounting Office, 1997); "Family Violence Education in Medical School-Based Residency Programs — Virginia, 1995" (*Morbidity and Mortality Weekly Report*, 1996); and "The Cycle of Violence" (National Institute of Justice, 1992). The U.S. Advisory Board on Child Abuse and Neglect published *A Nation's Shame: Fatal Child Abuse and Neglect in the United States* (HHS, 1995). Gail S. Goodman et al. researched the *Characteristics and Sources of Allegations of Ritualistic Child Abuse* (1994) for the National Center on Child Abuse and Neglect, an agency recently replaced by the Office on Child Abuse and Neglect.

The National Committee to Prevent Child Abuse (NCPCA) published the annual survey, *Current Trends in Child Abuse Reporting and Fatalities: The Results of the 1997 Annual Fifty State Survey* (1998) and *Public Opinion and Behaviors Regarding Child Abuse Prevention: 1998 Survey* (1998). Information Plus thanks the NCPCA for permission to use graphics from both publications. The National Conference of State Legislatures listed the state domestic violence laws enacted in 1997 in the *1997 Domestic Violence Legislative Summary* (1998).

The Family Research Laboratory (FRL) at the University of New Hampshire, Durham, New Hampshire, is a major source of studies on domestic violence. Murray A. Straus, Richard J. Gelles, Linda Meyer Williams, David Finkelhor, Kathleen Kendall-Tackett, Glenda Kaufman Kantor, and many others associated with the laboratory have done some of the most scientifically rigorous researches in the field of abuse. Studies released by the FRL investigate all forms of domestic violence, many based on its two major surveys — *National Family Violence Survey* (1975) and *National Family Violence Resurvey* (1985). Much of the research from these two surveys has been gathered into *Physical Violence in American Families: Risk Factors and Adaptions to Violence in 8,145 Families* (Straus, Gelles, and Christine Smith, ed., Transaction Publishers, New Brunswick, New Jersey, 1990). Straus and Gelles have also published some of their research in *Intimate Violence: The Definitive Study of the Causes and Consequences of Abuse in the American Family* (Simon and Schuster, New York, 1988).

Murray A. Straus and Glenda Kaufman Kantor compared the 1975 and 1985 *National Family Violence Surveys* to the *1992 National Alcohol and Family Violence Surveys* and reported their findings in *Trends in Physical Abuse by Parents from*

1975 to 1992: A Comparison of Three Surveys (1995). Straus, E. Milling Kinard, and Linda Meyer Williams studied the correlation of childhood neglect and social integration in *The Neglect Scale* (1995).

Kathleen Kendall-Tackett and Roberta Marshall reported on the "Sexual Victimization of Children" (*Issues in Intimate Violence*, Sage Publications, Thousand Oaks, California, 1998). Additional sexual abuse research can be found in *Characteristics of Incestuous Fathers* (David Finkelhor and Williams, 1992) and in the "Current Information on the Scope and Nature of Child Sexual Abuse" (Finkelhor, *The Future of Children: Sexual Abuse of Children*, vol. 4, no. 2, 1994).

Murray A. Straus and Julie H. Stewart reported on a national survey of American parents regarding their use of corporal punishment in *Corporal Punishment by American Parents: National Data on Prevalence, Chronicity, Severity, and Duration, in Relation to Child and Family Characteristics* (1998). Straus and Mallie J. Paschall prepared the *Corporal Punishment by Mothers and Child's Cognitive Development: A Longitudinal Study* (1998). Straus, David B. Sugarman, and Jean Giles-Sims studied the link between corporal punishment and increased antisocial behavior among children in "Spanking by Parents and Subsequent Antisocial Behavior of Children" (*Archives of Pediatrics and Adolescent Medicine*, vol. 151, no. 8, 1997). Straus further studied the connection between corporal punishment and criminal violence in *Spanking and the Making of a Violent Society* (1996). Dr. Murray A. Straus and the Family Research Laboratory have kindly granted permission to use graphics from their publications.

Many journals published useful articles on child maltreatment that were used in the preparation of this book. Diane N. Roche et al. studied female victims of child abuse in "Adult Attachment: A Mediator Between Child Sexual Abuse and Later Psychological Adjustment" (*Journal of Interpersonal Violence*, vol. 14, no. 2, 1999). Azmaira Hamid Maker et al. researched the "Long-Term Psychological Consequences in Women of Witnessing Parental Physical Conflict and Experiencing Abuse in Childhood" (*Journal of Interpersonal Violence*, vol. 13, no. 5, 1998). Jeffrey L. Edleson reported on "The Overlap Between Child Maltreatment and Woman Battering" (*Violence Against Women*, vol. 5, no. 2, 1999). William C. Holmes provided current data on "Sexual Abuse of Boys: Definition, Prevalence, Correlates, Sequelae, and Management" (*The Journal of the American Medical Association*, vol. 281, no. 21, 1998). Brett Drake and Susan Zuravin discussed "Bias in Child Maltreatment Reporting: Revisiting the Myth of Classlessness" (*American Journal of Orthopsychiatry*, 68 (2), 1998).

In "Child Fatalities From Religion-motivated Medical Neglect" (*Pediatrics*, vol. 101, no. 4, 1998), Seth M. Asser and Rita Swan reviewed the deaths of children in faith-healing religious sects. Jacqueline L. Stock et al. provided information on "Adolescent Pregnancy and Sexual Risk-Taking Among Sexually Abused Girls" (*Family Planning Perspectives*, The Alan Guttmacher Institute, vol. 29, no. 5, 1997). Frances A. Althaus discussed "Female Circumcision: Rite of Passage or Violation of Rights" (*International Family Planning Perspectives*, The Alan Guttmacher Institute, vol. 23, no. 3, 1997). Other helpful journals include the *American Journal of Psychotherapy, Child Abuse and Neglect, Psychological Bulletin, Journal of Counseling and Development, Social Problems, Journal of Consulting and Clinical Psychology, Psychiatry and Law, Professional Psychology,* and the *Journal of Traumatic Stress.*

The American Professional Society on the Abuse of Children (APSAC), in *The APSAC Handbook on Child Maltreatment* (1996), brought together a variety of child abuse experts to discuss

RESOURCES (Continued)

ongoing controversies in their fields, as well as to challenge long-held assumptions and conclusions. APSAC's interdisciplinary journal *Child Maltreatment* reports on current scientific information and technical innovations in child maltreatment research. The Center for the Future of Children of the David and Lucile Packard Foundation publishes information on major issues related to children's well-being. *The Future of Children: Protecting Children from Abuse and Neglect* (1998) provided invaluable data on the role of child protective services agencies in child protection. *The Future of Children: Sexual Abuse of Children* (1994) also furnished helpful information. The Center for the Future of Children graciously granted permission to use graphics from its publications.

Helpful books used for this publication include *Neglected Children: Research, Practice, and Policy*, Howard Dubowitz, editor (SAGE Publications, Thousand Oaks, California, 1999); *Understanding Family Violence: Treating and Preventing Partner, Child, Sibling, and Elder Abuse* by Vernon R. Wiehe (SAGE Publications, 1998); *Debating Children's Lives: Current Controversies on Children and Adolescents*, Mary Ann Mason and Eileen Gambrill, editors (SAGE Publications, 1994); *Current Controversies on Family Violence*, Richard J. Gelles and Donileen Loseke, editors (SAGE Publications, 1993); *Wasted: The Plight of America's Unwanted Children* by Patrick T. Murphy (Ivan R. Dee, Inc., Chicago, Illinois, 1997); *The Book of David: How Preserving Families Can Cost Children's Lives* by Richard J. Gelles (BasicBooks, New York, 1996); *Childhood Sexual Abuse* by Karen Kinnear (ABC-CLIO, Inc., Santa Barbara, California, 1995); *Wounded Innocents: The Real Victims of the War Against Child Abuse* by Richard Wexler (Prometheus Books, Buffalo, New York, 1995); *Secret Survivors: Uncovering Incest and Its Aftereffects in Women* by E. Sue Blume (John Wiley and Sons, New York, 1989); *On Trial: America's Courts and Their Treatment of Sexually Abused Children* by B.W. Dziech and Judge C. Schudson (Beacon Press, Boston, 1989); *The Secret Trauma: Incest in the Lives of Girls and Women* by Diana Russell (BasicBooks, New York, 1986); and *Child Sexual Abuse: New Theory and Research* by David Finkelhor (The Free Press, New York, 1984).

Books used for information on recovered memory include *Searching for Memory: the Brain, the Mind, and the Past* by Daniel Schacter (BasicBooks, New York, 1996); *The Myth of Repressed Memory: False Memories and Allegations of Sexual Abuse* by Elizabeth F. Loftus (St. Martin's Press, New York, 1994); *Suggestions of Abuse: True and False Memories of Childhood Sexual Abuse* by Michael Yapko (Simon and Schuster, New York, 1994); *Making Monsters: False Memories, Psychotherapy, and Sexual Hysteria* by Richard Ofshe and Ethan Watters (Scribners, New York, 1994); *Unchained Memories: The Stories of Traumatic Memories, Lost and Found* by Lenore Terr (BasicBooks, New York, 1994); *Once Upon a Time: A Story of Memory, Murder, and the Law* (HarperCollins, New York, 1993); and *The Courage to Heal: A Guide for Women Survivors of Child Sexual Abuse* by Ellen Bass and Laura Davis (HarperCollins, New York, 1988).

Information Plus thanks the False Memory Syndrome Foundation for granting permission to reproduce graphics from its monthly *False Memory Syndrome Foundation Newsletter*. *Child Newsline* of the UNICEF graciously provided us with articles and graphics relating to child abuse worldwide. As always, we are grateful to the Gallup Organization for continued permission to use its surveys.

134

INDEX